Janet Reno

UNIVERSITY PRESS OF FLORIDA

Florida A&M University, Tallahassee

Florida Atlantic University, Boca Raton

Florida Gulf Coast University, Ft. Myers

Florida International University, Miami

Florida State University, Tallahassee

New College of Florida, Sarasota

University of Central Florida, Orlando

University of Florida, Gainesville

University of North Florida, Jacksonville

University of South Florida, Tampa

University of West Florida, Pensacola

JANET RENO
A LIFE

JUDITH HICKS STIEHM

UNIVERSITY PRESS OF FLORIDA

Gainesville / Tallahassee / Tampa / Boca Raton

Pensacola / Orlando / Miami / Jacksonville / Ft. Myers / Sarasota

28 27 26 25 24 23   6 5 4 3 2 1

Library of Congress Cataloging-in-Publication Data
Names: Stiehm, Judith Hicks, 1935– author.
Title: Janet Reno : a life / Judith Hicks Stiehm.
Description: 1. | Gainesville : University Press of Florida, 2023. |
Includes bibliographical references and index.
Identifiers: LCCN 2022045031 (print) | LCCN 2022045032 (ebook) | ISBN
9780813069685 (hardback) | ISBN 9780813072821 (ebook)
Subjects: LCSH: Reno, Janet, 1938–2016. | Attorneys general—United
States—Biography. | Women politicians—United States—Biography. |
BISAC: BIOGRAPHY & AUTOBIOGRAPHY / Political | BIOGRAPHY & AUTOBIOGRAPHY
/ Lawyers & Judges
Classification: LCC KF373.R45 S75 2023 (print) | LCC KF373.R45 (ebook) |
DDC 353.4092 [B]—dc23/eng/20221025
LC record available at https://lccn.loc.gov/2022045031
LC ebook record available at https://lccn.loc.gov/2022045032

The University Press of Florida is the scholarly publishing agency for the State University System
of Florida, comprising Florida A&M University, Florida Atlantic University, Florida Gulf Coast
University, Florida International University, Florida State University, New College of Florida,
University of Central Florida, University of Florida, University of North Florida, University of South
Florida, and University of West Florida.

University Press of Florida
2046 NE Waldo Road
Suite 2100
Gainesville, FL 32609
http://upress.ufl.edu

CONTENTS

PROLOGUE

Miami Roots

Janet Reno is deeply rooted in Miami. Thus, it is important to introduce Miami/Dade with, perhaps, more detail than the reader would prefer.[1] Currently Miami is called "The Magic City." It is also described as vibrant, international, and lawless. It has never been called boring.

Many Americans don't realize that St. Augustine, Florida, founded in 1565, was the first permanent European settlement in what is now the United States. Nor do many know that the first Europeans to settle in what would become Miami were stranded Spanish mutineers, or that the first group to come on purpose was led by a Jesuit priest who in 1567 founded a mission on the north shore of what is now known as the Miami River. It was named Tequesta after the local chief. The mission was short lived, though, and the next effort to build there did not occur until 1743, close to two hundred years later. The second settlement was named Puebla de Santa Maria de Loreto. The local Native Americans, however, were resistant, and there was little profit to be made. The Spanish king soon ordered the settlement closed.

In the 1763 Treaty of Paris, Spain gave Florida to the English; in exchange, Spain recovered Cuba. A scant twenty years later England gave Florida back to the Spanish and was given the Bahamas in return. Spain made several generous land grants in the Miami area, which was by then called Cape Florida, but few settlers arrived, and in 1821 Spain had had enough. Florida was turned over to the United States, even though many Americans shared the view of Virginia Representative John Randolph that "Florida, sir, is not worth buying. It is a land of swamps, of quagmires, of frogs, alligators and mosquitoes! A man, sir, would not immigrate into Florida—no, not from Hell itself."[2]

Randolph had it about right. At that time Miami's population included a handful of Europeans, escaped African slaves, and Native Americans who resisted settler encroachment in three Seminole Wars between 1814 and 1858. When Florida became the twenty-seventh state in 1845, Miami had less than one hundred residents. By the time the U.S. Civil War broke out in 1860, most Seminoles had been forcibly dispatched west of the Mississippi—thanks to General and later President Andrew Jackson. Miami's sparse population, though, did include a number of Blacks.

After the Civil War, speculators enthusiastically launched a variety of enterprises in the Miami area. Most failed. Basically, the mosquitoes, sand flies, poor soil, and heat won. In 1876 all of what is now Dade County had only seventy-three registered voters. Its mail came once a week by schooner from Key West 160 miles to the south. It had not yet made a mark.

The remaining Native Americans lived apart, and may have outnumbered the city residents. In the 1880s, however, the first tourist hotel was established in what is now the Coconut Grove section of Miami; a community of Black Bahamians put down roots there as well. The seeds for a tourist Miami with a substantial population of Caribbean Blacks had been planted.

The Great Freeze of 1894 destroyed most of Florida's tropical produce. Only Miami's crops survived, and interest in Miami was revived. Enter Julia Tuttle, a dynamic widow from Cleveland, who persuaded Henry Flagler to extend his railroad some seventy miles from Palm Beach to Miami and also to build the elegant Royal Palm Hotel there.[3] In 1896 the brand new the *Metropolis*[4] newspaper reported that Miami had been incorporated as a city by a vote of 343 registered voters, a majority of whom were Black.[5] Three-fourths of the merchants were Jewish. Seminoles were a part of the community, too. Unlike most of the rest of the United States, Miami was multicultural from the start.

Miami Beach was incorporated in 1915, but Dade County's boom didn't occur until after World War I when developments like Coral Gables and Hialeah were created.[6] In 1910 Miami's population was 5,500; in 1920 it was 30,000; by 1930 it had risen to 110,000.

Among those who came to seek their fortune were Janet Reno's grandparents—both maternal and paternal. In 1925 the Chamber of Commerce reported 300,000 winter visitors. Some like J. P. Morgan and Andrew Carnegie arrived by yacht with uniformed crews. The boom, which allegedly included the sale of nonexistent land, ended shortly thereafter when the Miami real estate bubble burst.[7] Nineteen of twenty-one local banks collapsed. Land that had sold for $50,000 in 1925 went for $600 in 1926.

That same year, 1926, a category four hurricane struck taking 242 lives and destroying much of the city.[8] Miami's Great Depression had arrived, preceding by several years the depression that would engulf the rest of the country. Its effects would last more than a decade. Still, some parts of Miami's economy did prosper. Those included tourism, but also prostitution, legal and illegal gambling, and bootlegging. Indeed, Biscayne Bay was said to be dangerous once night fell. Then rum-runners might be chased by hijackers who were in turn chased by the Coast Guard—all with guns blazing. Moonshine was produced in the Everglades, and alcohol of all sorts moved north in cars with reinforced springs so that a car's sagging rear would not betray its cargo.[9]

New arrivals included Al Capone, "The King of the Underworld," and other assorted criminals. They would be among the subjects of a *Miami Herald* police reporter, Henry Reno, Janet's father. During his long career, Reno wrote many a dramatic story. Perhaps the most sensational dealt with the 1933 attempted assassination of President-elect Franklin Delano Roosevelt in Miami's Bayfront Park.

Like other cities, Miami benefitted from a variety of government programs during the Depression. One was the building of the Orange Bowl. Also, as in many other cities, it was World War II that finally lifted Miami's economy. While World War II was "over there" for most Americans, Miamians could see a flaming tanker that had been torpedoed by German submarines just off shore. Emptied of tourists, Miami Beach hotels became the site of an Army Air Force training center and an officer candidate school as well. German POWs were incarcerated in an old Civilian Conservation Corps camp. Hotels became hospitals. In fact, the landmark Biltmore Hotel remained a government hospital until 1968 and was not restored to four-star status until 1987.

Good times were had by many, but Black troops had to find theirs separate from Whites. Only in 1945 did Blacks get access to a beach—one which could only be reached by boat.

By mid-century Miami had become a city, with big-city problems. Still, nature played a role in changing Miami's landscape as well. A series of hurricanes created enough damage, principally from flooding, that the federal government constructed an Everglades drainage system, creating more land for more homes. The program shrank the Everglades, and the remainder was simultaneously declared a national park. Still, Miami's was a frontier culture. Crime flourished, some forty private clubs were stocked with slot machines, and hundreds of bookies gave citizens and tourists additional opportunities to throw their money away.

In 1948, the year Janet Reno would turn ten, a committee of six business leaders decided that it was time for Miami to address public corruption. Their strategy was exposure: in newspapers and on the airways. Among those targeted were the Dade County Sheriff and Florida's governor. Further, in 1950 Senator Estes Kefauver brought his organized crime hearings to Florida. The brand new Miami television station, WJTV, promptly sent those hearings across the country. Many were soon indicted. None were ever jailed.

In 1950 Miami's population was 172,000; by 1960 it had reached 291,000. Many of the new inhabitants were veterans with government money to spend on houses and on education. Developers prospered, and so did the University of Miami.

Television connected Miami to the rest of the country, but there was another technological advance that was of crucial importance: air-conditioning. Air-conditioning made Miami a full- rather than a half-year city, and by 1950 the county's population was almost a half million, and the resort hotels on Miami Beach were featuring shows with the likes of Elvis Presley, Groucho Marx, Rosemary Clooney, and Lucille Ball and her Cuban husband, Desi Arnaz.

Cubans were no strangers to Miami. There was regular travel in both directions, but that was about to change. In January 1959, Castro's revolutionaries succeeded in throwing out Cuban dictator Fulgencio Batista. Exiles living in Miami rushed to Cuba, and a new set of exiles—many successful and highly educated—rushed to Miami.

By mid-1960 an estimated 100,000 Cubans had arrived in a county with a population under one million. From 1965 to 1973, twice-a-day Freedom Flights brought more than 250,000 Cubans to Miami. The 1966 Cuban Adjustment Act provided the newcomers with medical care, free lessons in English, loans and scholarships for college, and permanent residency after one year. The 1980 Mariel boatlift brought another 125,000, many from lower classes than earlier arrivals and some recently released from prisons and mental institutions. In the 1994 Cuban Rafter Crisis in which Cubans were trying to reach the United States in primitive, homemade rafts, a new policy was formulated. It was "wet foot," return to Cuba, "dry foot," remain.

The Miami to which Janet Reno would return after law school to begin her career in 1963, then, had changed significantly from her youth, but it was neither affluent nor sophisticated. It did have a host of tourist attractions: a wax museum, alligator wrestling, Parrot Jungle, Monkey Jungle, Fairchild Tropical Botanic Garden, and Hialeah Park Race Track famous for its flamingos. The next wave of developments would be equally transformative. Miami Dade Community College, which was launched in 1960, currently boasts 125,000 students. Opened in 1972, Florida International University would be graced by PhD programs and a medical and a law school. More recently, the Adrienne Arsht Center for the Performing Arts, the second largest such center in the United States, began as the Carnival Center only in 2006. Miami's Art Basel brings more than 250 galleries and 75,000 visitors to town, but it was launched only in 2002, and even the famed, eight-day Miami Book Fair with more than three hundred authors and exhibitors dates only to 1984. The 2020 U.S. Census has estimated the county's population as some 2.7 million with Black/African-Americans as 17 percent of that total, White non-Hispanic 14 percent, and Hispanic/Latino 69 percent.[10] Further, in the period 2007–2011, the Census reported that over half of the Miami-Dade County population was foreign born, that median family income was $44,000, and that 18 percent of the population lived below the poverty line, even though mansions were frequently sold for cash and ocean view condos were purchased as vacation homes—and as safe havens in the event of a revolution in a home country. Janet Reno's hometown is today a cosmopolitan, international city, but it remains a cultural frontier with a fluid social structure and certainly no enduring "establishment."

INTRODUCTION

"Screeeeeeck!" The Georgetown dinner party fell silent. Waiters froze. Forks were suspended. Attorney General Janet Reno had imitated a gecko for her dinner partner. She smiled and shrugged her shoulders. For her it was natural to provide the uninitiated with a sample of life in the Everglades. After the nominations of two talented women failed because of issues related to the legal status of their nannies, the William Jefferson Clinton team nominated Miami's plain, unmarried, 6'3" state attorney for the job. Reno breezed through the confirmation hearings, but Washington would soon find that there was some getting used to to do.

Reno had a Harvard law degree, but she was by no means part of the East Coast elite who participate in federal level politics while rotating in and out of administrations, law schools, and foundations. Reno grew up in a rural setting and attended segregated, public schools in a small southern city. Hers was in many ways an uncomplicated, White middle-class life. Yes, a host of New Yorkers had found their way to Miami Beach; and, yes, illegal alcohol built local fortunes; and, yes, gambling did net $100 million a year according to reporter Jane Reno, Janet's mother. Nevertheless, Reno's daily routine as a girl was prosaic, although, perhaps by some standards eccentric.

This was because mother Jane was a stirrer. After bearing four children in four years, Jane Reno proceeded to personally build the family home. Life there was mostly conducted on a fifty-foot screened porch. In addition there was, originally, a kitchen and two bedrooms (for a family of six), no interior doors, no locks on the exterior doors, and no air-conditioning. There were, though, peacocks and chickens, donkeys and horses, snakes and dogs. The Reno homestead was literally located where paved roads ended.

There were only two rules for the Reno children, but they were strictly, even physically, enforced: 1) tell the truth and 2) be kind. It would have been easy to be parochial, even narrow, living off the grid as the family did, but Janet's father, Henry, was a crime reporter for the *Miami Herald,* and the variety of people who congregated on the Reno porch on Sunday afternoons conducted energetic and knowledgeable conversations, much of it political.

Janet Reno ventured north for college—to Cornell and then to Harvard Law School. After finishing law school, she turned down opportunities in Washington, DC, to return to her Miami roots. No major Miami firm was interested in hiring a woman, even one with a Harvard degree, but Reno was hired by a firm specializing in real estate law where she developed an effective courtroom style. Prepared, often overprepared, she learned to use her height to intimidate witnesses. A few years later, she set up a practice with a fellow Harvard graduate. It was 1967, an era of political turbulence. Lyndon Johnson had twisted enough arms to win the Civil Rights Bill in 1964; in 1967 Thurgood Marshall was confirmed to the Supreme Court; and in *Loving v. Virginia* that court declared a ban on interracial marriage unconstitutional. In the next year both Robert Kennedy and Martin Luther King Jr. were assassinated. Soon thereafter Silent Generation Reno began a most unquiet public life.

Reno went to work for the Miami-Dade state attorney and later became the Miami-Dade state attorney herself, a position she would hold for fifteen turbulent years. These years included killings of Blacks by police officers and riots like that in Liberty City in which eighteen died, hundreds were injured, and thousands arrested.

The call to Washington came in 1993. Attorney generals are often the president's attorney rather than the nation's. Examples would include Jack Kennedy's brother, Robert, and Ronald Reagan's buddy Edwin Meese III. Reno, though, saw her job as the country's law enforcement officer. This would make for an awkward relationship with her president, Bill Clinton, who would soon be besieged by legal problems and by Republicans who hoped to impeach and then remove him from office.

In the first weeks of her tenure, Reno was faced with the siege of the Branch Davidians in Waco, Texas. The next year featured Kenneth Starr's

Whitewater investigation of Clinton investments in a failed real estate venture and other items including his scandalous relationship with Monica Lewinsky. Then there was the horrific Oklahoma City bombing. But perhaps the most agonizing decision came in 1998, which involved Elián González, a Cuban child who survived an attempt to cross from Cuba to Miami, but whose mother did not. Miami's Cuban community insisted that Elián must stay in Miami. Acting against the views of virtually all she consulted, Reno decided that Elián belonged with his father, even if that father was in Cuba. Her decision was not popular.

Returning to Miami after eight years in Washington, DC, Reno found that the Elián decision had made it impossible for Donna Shalala, a fellow Clinton Cabinet member and the new president of the University of Miami, to give her an appointment at the law school. The Elián decision also contributed to Reno's loss in a run for governor. Still, there were numerous "kind" things to do, and lessons to be learned. Her life demonstrated that it is possible for a woman to serve in high office, both elected and appointed, and to do so while scrupulously adhering to a mother's code to "tell the truth and be kind." Both Reno's shattering of glass ceilings and her consistent, ethical conduct reinforce what a good civics class teaches students: that one can successfully engage in the political while remaining both human and honest.

1

FAMILY

In the early twentieth century, Janet Reno's grandfather, Robert Marius Rasmussen, left his family in Odense, Denmark, to see if there truly was a pot of gold to be found in the United States. He went to work in a tire factory in Ohio, saved his wages, and in 1913 returned to Denmark to collect his wife, Louise, and sons Henry Olaf, then eleven, and Paul, seven.[1] Because he had been harassed about his Scandinavian name in Ohio, he changed the family's surname to Reno, selected, family lore has it, by looking at a U.S. map and choosing the shortest, easiest name to pronounce that he could find.

Traveling through the Great Lakes, the family landed first in Withee, a small Danish community in central Wisconsin. Soon they moved to the Milwaukee area where Robert tried his hand as a photographer, while his sons, Henry and Paul, attended school and scrambled to learn English.[2] Four years later, young Henry began his journalism career by serving as editor of his high school newspaper. He was also active in student politics, and mock high school presidential ballots show that there were five choices: Democrat, Republican, Independent Republican, Prohibition, and Socialist.[3]

Henry Reno entered the University of Wisconsin to study animal husbandry in 1921, but when the family moved to Knoxville, Tennessee, seeking better prospects, Henry transferred to the state university there. However, his college education came to an end when the Reno family moved again. This time, like thousands of others, they headed to magic Miami. Henry's father became a photographer for the *Miami Herald,* and in 1924 Henry, Janet Reno's father, became a police reporter for the *Herald,* a job he would hold for more than four decades.

In 1951 the *Miami Herald* and the *Brooklyn Eagle* would share a Pulitzer Prize for Public Service for their crime reporting. Henry Reno, who was known for his fabulous contacts, was central to that reportage.[4]

Janet Reno's mother, Jane, was a Wood, a family well established in Sunnyside, Georgia.[5] Janet's maternal grandfather, George W. Wood Jr., was a lawyer in Macon, Georgia.[6] When his practice collapsed along with the town's cotton economy, the Woods—George, his wife, Daisy Sloan Hunter Wood, and their five children including Jane—packed up and headed for Miami Beach. They arrived in 1925—just in time for the real estate bust and for the devastating 1926 hurricane.[7]

Jane was the oldest of the Wood children and exceptional. In 1924 at age eleven, she was given an intelligence test. As she later told the story, the results were announced in a headline in the local newspaper: "Jane Wood Declared Genius." Again, as Jane told the story, it was necessary to demonstrate that she was "still me" with fisticuffs. It seemed, she often said, that there was nothing like being declared a genius to make other people hate you. Jane's obvious ability led her to skip three grades and to graduate from Miami High at age fifteen. During high school, she worked for the student newspaper and wrote about high school sports for the *Miami News.* Jane was especially thrilled to have an interview with Marjory Stoneman Douglas, whose journalism already had a large following and who was an ardent proponent of women's suffrage and other progressive causes. Among Jane's high school classmates were Bebe Rebozo, who would become a close friend of Richard Nixon, and Dante Fascell, who would serve in the House of Representatives for almost forty years.

Jane's next stop, at age fifteen, was the University of Miami, where she claimed to have majored in drink and carousing—during Prohibition. In the spirit inspired by others' swallowing of goldfish, she once downed five home brews before noon. During her sophomore year, she joined three older girls in an adventure that involved hitchhiking to Ocala, Florida. A Miami newspaper headline reported "Four Miami U Girls Missing, Foul Play Feared." On the second day of the adventure, two of the girls wired home "Am married going north." Jane wired "back tomorrow, don't worry." Her father drove to Ocala and retrieved all four girls. Jane's college years were soon interrupted when she flunked journalism and physical education, two subjects in which she was, perhaps, too talented to take seriously.

Jane then decamped to Greece where she was hosted by her mother's sister, Margaret, and her husband, Dr. Marshall Balfour, an international expert on malaria working for the Rockefeller Foundation. (Later Balfour would work and travel through India and the Far East, and the Balfours were actually in China when the Japanese invaded.) Jane spent some time in Greece teaching English and more time traveling through the Greek Isles.

When she returned to Miami and the University of Miami, she switched her major to physics and graduated at age twenty-one in 1934. By then the Great Depression dominated everything, and Jane went to work as a social worker for fifteen dollars a week. In an essay, "The Best We Could," Jane recounted community efforts to ameliorate the suffering caused by the economic calamity. This included a commissary, but also a "Hobo Express" that involved police rounding up homeless people and sending them North—by freight car. In another essay, Jane described her fellow caseworkers as some were sadists, some were sentimentalists, but the worst were the bureaucrats. "The dead, total lack of emotion that infects a bureaucrat . . . is with us always and it is one of the great threats of our lifetime." "Triple vomits" were her response to the day-by-day workings of the welfare bureaucracy. On the other hand, those social workers who assumed the responsibility of trying to change the system were seen as "but little lower than the angels."[8]

Always restless, Jane soon moved on to the *Miami Herald* where she got a job as a writer of obituaries. She also had the food and fashion beat.[9] Most importantly, she met crime reporter Henry Reno. The family story is that she invited herself to go crawfishing with him, and he reluctantly agreed if she met him at Coral Gables City Hall at 4:30 a.m. She did. Another story has her responding to him "Yes, I will marry you!," although it wasn't quite clear that that was in fact the question he had asked. In any event, Henry Reno and Jane Wood were married within a year. They built a small house at 3600 Avocado in Coconut Grove and promptly began a family.[10] Janet was born on July 21, 1938, at Jackson Memorial Hospital. Within eighteen months the family expanded to include Robert Marius Reno, and within two additional years, Margaret Sloan Reno and Mark Wood Reno as well. As adults, all continued to be referred to by their childhood nicknames: Janny, Bobby, Maggy, and Marky.

Grandparents Robert and Louise Reno (who was said to have the best lap for sitting ever), were known as Bestafar and Bestamor and lived on 36th Street north of the airport in Allapattah, not far from their adult sons, Henry and Paul. The senior Renos' two-bedroom house had a manicured garden with a tree planted for each grandchild. After his wife died, Robert moved in with Paul and his wife, Doris, in Coconut Grove. Paul was an artist. After the move to Miami, he first worked in a framing store. Later he became a professor of art at the University of Miami. Doris followed the family practice of writing for the *Miami Herald;* her charge there was music and art criticism. Paul Reno's two daughters, Lisa and Susie, straddled the ages of Henry's four children, so a good time was had by all during holidays and other family gatherings.

The families regularly visited each other because Miami, although spread out, was, in fact, a small town. In the summer the Paul Reno children would spend a week with the Henry Renos in South Miami where the six children slept in a single room. A favorite activity was riding Tony, Janet's beloved pinto pony, who ran away at every opportunity. A Christmas present to Janet, he had even run away in the interval between the time he had been tied up on Christmas Eve and the time Janet was supposed to discover him on Christmas morning; all she found then were some telltale droppings.

On another occasion Janet and Lisa, who was afraid to ride alone, rode Tony in circles for a half hour when suddenly the saddle slipped and the girls fell off. Janet was hurt, and Lisa had a rapidly swelling eye that Jane quickly smothered in steak. The worst had happened; the next day, Lisa proudly rode by herself for the first time.

Cousin Susie was younger than the Henry Reno children. Lisa was two years older, but three years ahead of Janet in school, so they were never at Coral Gables High at the same time. They were close, though, and Lisa did coach Janet: "Don't worry about high school—in the long run being tall will be all right, and the acne will go away."

In 1943, while Miami bristled with military activity, the Henry Reno family moved to what was then 11th Street in Larkin.[11] Close to what is now Red Road and Highway One, the area was distinctly rural. The household continued its expansion to include Felix and Pedro (two donkeys), a cow, goats, ducks, bees, turkeys, and chickens: enough of a farming operation to make a profit from the sale of chickens and eggs as well as cream and butter.

Guinea fowl noisily announced any visitors, while Tom Turkey was likely to attack anyone who invaded his turf. Tony, Janet's pony, was beloved for providing pony rides at the annual South Miami Carnival. He could be useful, for example, during the war when the family was out of gas rationing tickets, they all (six) would crowd into Tony's buggy to do their errands or to go visiting.[12] Tony could also be a nuisance snacking on other people's gardens. Indeed, Janet was famously remembered for punching him soundly on the nose after a particularly annoying transgression.

While the family was living a country life on the edge of town, Henry continued in his comparatively urban career as a police reporter. As part of his routine, Henry regularly made a pilgrimage from the offices of the Florida Highway Patrol to those of the Dade County Sheriff, to those of the Miami Police Department, and, finally, to those of the Medical Examiner. Henry was an Honorary Deputy Sheriff of Dade County and also an Honorary Member of the Miami Police Benevolent Association. He was said to speak with a perfect southern police accent in contrast to his artist brother, Paul, who was said to speak with a perfect English accent.

Henry was reputed to be a master fixer of traffic tickets, although apparently he fixed them by simply paying them. He was a favorite among the secretaries, who regularly received roses and gardenias from Henry. Further, seeing himself as a "fellow working stiff," he was likely to turn up with donuts for anyone required to work on the Sabbath. He was quiet, a listener, a man fascinated by the varieties of his fellow man, and a man who loved to tell stories. He was also a reader, famed for taking Dostoevsky's *The Brothers Karamazov* to a friend in jail. Sunday afternoons were devoted to listening to opera on 78 records and conversing with friends on the screened porch of his home.

Mother Jane had a business that consisted of providing plucked chickens to her neighbors. Janet and Lisa had the assignment of delivering them to customers; for this they received one dollar, and on the way home it was usually spent on ice cream at OK Food Store on Dixie Highway. Another time the six children decided to camp out. After eating dinner, they took a path into the Everglades and found a promising flat and dry place to pitch a tent. Some three hours later they began to hear eerie sounds of animal and bird nightlife and headed for home as fast as they could go.

While there were a limited number of playmates nearby, the four Renos led a vigorous and adventurous life: riding, climbing trees, and exploring the undeveloped neighborhood. They set up a stand to sell apples harvested from a nearby rose apple tree. When no one came by, they used the apples to throw at each other. They put socks over their hands to slide down a rope hung from a tree. Mark claims that if the children fought, Jane simply spanked all of them. Clever Bob claimed to wear two pairs of pants minimizing the pain, and Maggy and Mark, who sometimes resisted, got double spankings. One neighbor left her daughter to play with the Renos while she ran errands. She returned to find the five children merrily playing together—in the nude.[13]

The Reno children had chores and participated in farm tasks such as plucking chickens, butchering pigs, and making homemade soap.[14] Only Janny was allowed to milk; she also raised a calf, meticulously keeping track of every expense. In summer the children swam in the fresh spring water of Coral Gables's Venetian Pool or in salt water at Matheson Hammock, where one could wade into the Atlantic for one hundred yards. In Miami's steaming summers, minimal clothing was quite sensible, and the girls were often barefoot and topless—until they approached puberty. Then Jane ordered T shirts. Mark remembers Janny, at age eleven, as stamping her foot in anger at the new clothing regime. Until then she had happily swum topless in a public pool.

Jane had quit working as the demands of motherhood became clear, but she was not tamed. She continued to drink like a fish. She was also opinionated, outspoken, and sometimes outrageous. Propriety and fashion were of no interest to her, even though, as a young woman, she had written about fashion for the *Herald*. Her typical public attire included tennis shoes, a flowered cotton dress, and sometimes a large straw hat. She reveled in her children, playing baseball with them, taking them on expeditions, and reciting poetry for them. She read to them regularly; Grahame's *The Wind in the Willows* may have been the children's favorite—and was certainly Janet's— who later would give copies not only to children but also to any adult who confessed to never having read it. Jane gave her children far more freedom than most mothers, but she could be a stern disciplinarian who did not hesitate to hit them with a bridle on the few occasions she detected dishonesty or just mean behavior. Independence, confidence, and "doing the right thing" were the goals of Jane's parenting.[15]

In 1947, when Janet was nine, the family moved again, this time to SW 88th Street (Kendall Drive) and 112th Avenue where paved roads ended.[16] The area was subject to regular fires, and its meager foliage meant one could see for a mile. The Reno menagerie continued to expand to include a macaw named Simon Legree who had a threatening laugh, a one-winged egret, and a boa constrictor. There was also a horse for Janet, named Hoodlum or Hoodie, a Tennessee Walker named Big Red for Maggy, and a mean mare named Dotty for Bob. Mark had no horse, but he cherished his Red Ryder BB gun. BB guns were not entirely safe; indeed, Mark was shot in the rear by brother Bob, and Henry was accidentally shot in the stomach while cleaning a gun. Close in age and living far from the madding crowd, the four children composed a closely knit troop, or as Maggy has described it "an undisciplined pack."

That year, 1947, Miami experienced 108" of rain. The Renos' home was entirely surrounded by water, and they were forced to move in with their Wood grandparents at 901 Castillo in Coral Gables. Still, the children enjoyed great freedom to explore their surroundings and discovered an abandoned house and some abandoned gas pumps hidden within walking distance. The parents took turns reading to the children each night. Mark claims it was the same book over and over, *The Wind in the Willows,* although he also remembers Uncle Wiggly stories and poetry such as John Masefield's "Spanish Waters." Radio programs such as *Tom Mix, Our Miss Brooks,* and *Sam Spade* were regular evening entertainment. Brother Bob was the leader and devised games and theatricals for his brother and sisters. Except for a fall from her horse that resulted in a concussion and five days in bed at her grandmother's, neither Janet nor the other children endured anything beyond the routine hazards of childhood.

The Renos' twenty-one acres were purchased for $500 an acre. In later years portions would be sold at a healthy profit to finance the children's college educations. The first residence on Kendall was "the little yellow house" already located on the property. Water was obtained from a 20' well; hot water was obtained by heating it on the stove. That house would be sold off after the family home, occupied by Janet Reno until her death, was built. Accessed by a rutted, dirt driveway, the home is well hidden by foliage, but when the Renos first moved there, the landscape included only some palmetto palms and "Florida holly," which Jane soon dispatched with a chain saw. An avocado grove was planted, and Jane put peacock eggs she had purchased for a dollar each under a duck. They hatched, and their descendants still roam the neighborhood! The Reno home is now behind a funeral home and across the street from a Walgreens, but gumbo-limbo trees, pines, wild oak, palmettos, and sea grape still provide a cool shade and conceal a chikee where Mark and his wife lived on a large, raised platform under a thatched roof with sides open to the breeze.

The main house memorializes Jane because she literally built it herself over a two-year period, with advice solicited from plumbers, masons, and electricians. Henry helped with the heavy lifting but it was Jane-built. Completed in 1951 at a cost of some $6,000, half the house is composed of a 50' long screened porch, which is where the family mostly lived. The kitchen features a brick fireplace with a mahogany mantel made from a piece of driftwood. In 1951 there were two bedrooms and a bathroom.[17] The kitchen was not a shrine for gourmets. Jane's cooking consisted of meat, potatoes, and dessert—no salad. And always lots of ice cream. Indeed, sweets were a regular part of any menu. Janet learned to make oatmeal cookies, Maggy vinegar toffee, and Maggy and Bob made fudge. When Janet was growing up, the house not only had no heat and no air-conditioning but also had no fans because Jane did not want to disturb the natural air currents. There were also no interior doors and no telephone until the *Herald* decided their crime reporter had to be reachable.[18] Jane, an expert shot, was in charge of the family rifle.

Mother Jane was not only raising four children and building a house, she was also investigating life on the Seminole reservation and occasionally writing for the *Miami Daily News*. In a truly remarkable exploit, Jane got a story from convict Leroy Horne who alleged that a Miami police officer had acted as a finger man for a holdup gang. Another Jane escapade involved Senator Estes Kefauver and his efforts to fight corruption.[19] As part of a special investigation, his aide, Ernie Midler, asked her to pose as a woman who was unable to have a child and try to buy a child on the black market. Jane stuffed herself into a bra, put on a large floppy hat and a linen dress, donned a fake diamond ring, and set off on her mission driving Midler's blue Cadillac. Jane's exploits in her work in public relations included the creation of the Great Ghost Crab Race, the transport of porpoise Palooza to Cesenatico, Italy, to comfort porpoise Lalla, and arranging for the mayor of Miami Beach to send an alligator as a gift to the London Zoo—for which the alligator responded by biting her. For recreation, Jane walked, with one being an infamous six-day, solo, 104-mile walk along the beach.[20]

Many family and friends gathered on the Reno porch on Sunday afternoons to drink coffee or, more likely, something stronger, and to engage in energetic and never-ending discussion about everything under the sun. Some priority, though, went to politics: local, state, and national. One discussion involved lawyer Robert Welch's use of the law in his duel with Senator Joseph McCarthy. Another concerned *Brown v. Board of Education* (347 U.S. 483, 1954) and how it might diminish the wrongs that existed in a community. Such discussions made Janet think that law was a way to correct wrongs, and that law was an admirable profession.[21]

Janet Reno's mother thought differently; she wanted her daughter to be a doctor. It didn't help mother Jane's hopes for Janet that Henry took her to visit courtrooms, or that Dixie Herlong Chastain (the first woman to graduate from the University of Miami Law School and the first woman to join the Florida Bar), used to sit under the Renos' rose apple tree with Janet and talk about the law, and particularly about the juvenile court system. Janet's thinking about law was also affected by the 1963 case involving Floridians Freddie Lee Pitts and Wilbert Lee who were convicted of murder in a hasty trial and sentenced to death. More than twelve years later, they were pardoned and released after another prisoner confessed that he had actually committed the murders.[22]

Family bonds were close, and the gregarious Renos had a wide range of friends as well, although those did not include people Jane considered self-important, smug, or sanctimonious. No invitation was needed to visit, and there were no locks on the doors. One was welcome any time, any day.

2

School Days

All the Reno children attended Sunset Elementary School, which had neither heat nor air-conditioning. If the temperature reached thirty-two degrees, the girls could wear long pants. Old-fashioned "school marms" presided, and prayers and Bible stories were not seen as unusual.

Sunset was followed by Ponce de Leon Middle School and the new Coral Gables High School. All graduated from Coral Gables High School. Each year for four years the faculty would experience a new and quite different Reno—Janet, Bob, Maggy, and Mark.

Bob was funny and smart and something of a tease. He was the leader who devised games and theatricals for his brothers and sisters. Bob was also a stamp collector and created any number of projects, including a family newspaper. While none of the young Renos pursued a strictly conventional life, Mark's was, perhaps, the most individual. Beginning with a raccoon at age six, Mark always seemed to have at least one pet, which over the years included alligators, opossums, and a five-hundred-pound wild pig named Oink. All the family drank. At age sixteen, Mark and a buddy decided to see what it would be like to be drunk. With siblings present to monitor the event, they proceeded to drink until Mark passed out and his friend got sick.

Mark had a year out of high school, which he spent with his uncle George Wood's family in Bangor, Maine. In 1952 Janet had a year out in Germany. She spent it with another uncle, Roy Wood, who was a High Commission Judge with the Allied High Commission Forces handling civil cases involving American citizens. They lived in Regensburg; Janet noted that the two outstanding aspects of the town were beer drinking and lederhosen. She also told about an experience she had when she was riding circuit with Judge Wood and they passed Dachau; she was told about the hideous events there. That evening, back in Regensburg, she demanded of her German friends "how could you let that happen?" Their response was "just stood by, just stood by." That experience also compelled her to want to be a lawyer.[1] She also told of her respect and admiration for Berliners (West) and her sense of Russia (in East Berlin) as dangerous because it was "frightened." Her fourteen-year-old judgment about the rest of the Germans was that they were prone to follow any leader—possibly even a communist if and when the United States pulled out. When Reno visited relatives in Denmark, she noted that they had no concerns about communists and had even built a ship under contract for the Soviet Union, although NATO did not want Denmark to release it. She noted a certain resentment among Europeans over "rich" Americans, but she expressed appreciation for the Alps, Rome, and the Paris opera, where she saw Gounod's *Faust*. After she returned, Janet's account of her European year was published in the July 13, 1952, issue of the *Miami Herald*, where she concluded that she was probably now ready to travel alone. That year Janet's growing interest in politics resulted in a scrapbook featuring Adlai Stevenson, the Democrats' candidate for president of the United States. He lost to Dwight D. Eisenhower, although Florida did elect Democrat Daniel T. McCarty as governor.

Janet remembered that the route to her junior high school took her past a German prisoner of war camp near Kendall and US 1, and that she was struck by the fact that the men looked so young and also looked just like other people who were free. She remembered the invasion of Normandy, the bombing of Hiroshima, and the death of President Roosevelt. She remembered her mother bursting into tears when a stranger asked, "Have you heard?"[2] She remembered learning how decisions in Washington could affect lives, and how important the Supreme Court was. She particularly remembered the 1950 campaign in which George Smathers defeated Claude Pepper for the Senate by calling him "Red" Pepper, in other words, a man with communist sympathies.

Janet's high school days might be described as quiet and conventional, but things were changing in the United States. In her sophomore year, the Supreme Court's ruling in *Brown v. Board of Education* (374 U.S. 483 1954) held that segregated schools were unconstitutional. In her junior year, Rosa

Parks's refusal to give up her seat led to the Montgomery bus boycott, which ultimately led to a Supreme Court decision (confirming a lower federal court's decision) that segregated public buses were also unconstitutional (*Browder v. Gayle* 352 U.S. 903 1956). Neither decision resulted in immediate and dramatic changes, however. Indeed, in the Brown case the court said desegregation should be conducted "with all deliberate speed," and it was, indeed, deliberate. Still, the legal basis had been laid for important changes that would be won over the next decade by an energized civil rights movement.

The new Coral Gables High School was located on twenty-six acres and boasted 2,500 students and 125 faculty. At the time it was rated one of the best schools in the country, and number one in Florida. At least one former teacher, Vera Porfiri, attributed its success to the leadership of longtime Principal Harry Rath.[3] Indeed, he was famed for holding regular assemblies where he gave motivational speeches urging students to excel in academics. The teacher's parking lot, Porfiri reminisced, was filled with jalopies, while the jam-packed student lot featured many a new car. Porfiri's 1956 salary as a teacher with a college degree was $2,800. Note, too, that Dade County's seven or eight high schools remained segregated.

The inch-thick high school yearbook recounts the lively life of Coral Gables teenagers, much of it revolving around "service clubs." Principal Rath had banned sororities and fraternities when the new high school was opened, but that system of social, exclusionary, and hierarchy-assigning functions continued under the guise of service clubs. Each club had both a faculty adviser and a sponsor from a community organization such as the Coco Plum Women's Club or the Coral Gables Lions Auxiliary. In theory the clubs were open, but in practice they were social cliques. Indeed, a principal function of the girls' clubs was sponsoring a school dance. Janet, who was almost six feet tall at age eleven and whose clothes never seemed to fit, was not a club member.

Karen McCammon, a younger friend of the Reno children, described her own teenage life, which was reflective of a more conventional and citified experience than Janet's—if also a bit later.[4] Growing up on Park Avenue, Karen could walk or bike to school. There was a five and dime near the school and a department store within walking distance. Milk, vegetable, and ice cream trucks plied the streets. School playgrounds were unfenced so could be used any hour, any day. Schools had art, music, and physical education teachers, and a policeman on a horse stopped by once a week. Children were free to "go out and play" returning home only at dark. One route to McCammon's elementary school, Coconut Grove, involved going through "the Black Grove" or "colored town" with its four bars at the intersection of Grand and Douglas. Despite the 1954 Supreme Court order to desegregate public schools "with all deliberate speed," McCammon's Coral Gables High School class of 1,100 had only one Black graduate. However, McCammon remembers the effect of the 1964 Civil Rights Act. Because the act called for the desegregation of public accommodations, a favorite teenage soda fountain shut down rather than serve Blacks. Still, within two years Coral Gables had a large number of Black students who were especially visible on athletic teams, in particular, the football team.

Athletics were not then cool for girls, who detested the bloomer outfits and showers required in gym class. And Girls Athletic Association (GAA) teams for intermural sports weren't "popular." Although parents had to sign a document that their daughters would not be allowed to join a sorority, McCammon acknowledges that the clubs functioned precisely as a sorority and that she and many other girls were unconscious of the events rapidly changing U.S. society. McCammon claims she never knew of anyone using drugs, even marijuana, or of girls having sex, although some girls may have had an abortion. If they did, they would surely have been "dropped." For McCammon and many others at Coral Gables High, the quiet culture of the 1950s extended into the 1960s. But her "normal" existence was not like Janet Reno's.

Reno was not invited or chose not to join Anchor, Beta Cub, Co-Eds, Deb Juniors, Junior Girls, Lete, Omega, Tallet, or Trilon, although perhaps a third of the girls in her class did so. She also was not or rarely invited to a school dance. Janet was, simply, not "popular," although all attest to the fact that she was respected, admired, and had solid friendships.[5] Her yearbook, "Cavaleon," highlights Janet as "most intelligent." It lists twenty-seven other students as "mosts" and "bests" including "democratic," "talented," "versatile," "dependable," "popular," and "sincere." Janet studied hard because, as her mother emphasized, clearly, loudly, and repeatedly to Janet and to her high school adviser: Janet was going to medical school. The adviser, Vera Porfiri, was told to give Janet *no* encouragement whatsoever about something like law school.[6] Perhaps Jane was anxious about the fact that Janet loved her history and government classes. That same adviser, Porfiri, "taught" Janet American history; it was her first year of teaching, and Janet, she admitted, "clearly knew more history than I did."[7]

As was typical in the 1950s, girls took homemaking and boys took shop classes. Smart boys took chemistry, physics, and four years of math. Girls did not; but Janet Reno did. Also, she belonged to the Spanish Club, the National Honor Society, the Future Teachers of America, and the French Club. She was elected to the National Honor Society in her junior year, and, unsurprisingly, she played a variety of intramural sports sponsored by the GAA.

The only team Reno participated in which competed against other schools was the debate team. She served as secretary and then as president of the National Forensic League, the sponsor of the team. Her debate partner was Richard Essen, who would later become colorful and famous enough for his defense of DUIs that he was profiled in the *Wall Street Journal*. The school debate coach, Werner Dickson, may have been Reno's most important high school mentor and was partly responsible for the fact that Janet won the State Extemporaneous Speaking Contest as an upperclassman and went to compete in the Nationals. Reno long remembered the flight from Miami to Albuquerque, a visit to the Grand Canyon at sunset, and then going on to San Francisco. After the competition, Janet flew back to visit an aunt in Los Angeles, then took the bus home to Miami.[8]

Jane Wood Reno had a dim view of debate, which expects participants to be able to argue either side of an issue rather than pursue "truth." Janet thought it was in the spirit of her feisty aunt, Winifred "Winnie" Wood, a member of the Women Airforce Service Pilots (WASP) who had towed targets and ferried bombers in World War II. It was clearly a skill that would serve Reno well in the years to come—and a skill also honed by vigorous family dinner table talk. While Reno's public demeanor was always sober, respectful, and self-contained, family life also made her quite capable of delivering devastating one-liners.[9]

Many high schools encourage students to consider possible future vocations and to write a report on a career of their choice. Reno's, dated 1952, was titled "Nuclear Physics: The Career of the Future." As part of her report she interviewed Benton F. Rogers, the director of personnel at Cornell. She would apply to Cornell and be accepted there two years later.[10]

Janet was a tomboy and deeply devoted to the Brooklyn Dodgers and especially to first baseman Jackie Robinson. Inspired by Don Newcombe, a Black pitcher, Janet practiced and practiced throwing at a batter's figure she had drawn on an old tin shed. She saw the Dodgers on TV only at her grandmother's home since Jane did not permit "mind-rotting" TV in the home.

Janet drove herself and her siblings to school in a little red truck. While she did not "fit in," she did not really choose to. Not popular and not invited to prom, she was, nevertheless, accomplished and respected.[11] A certain detachment might explain why she later attended only two Coral Gables High School reunions, and one of those involved an appearance honoring its by then famous attorney general classmate.

The Reno family had memorable vacations together, often on Plantation Key, which had good beachcombing and sailing. It also included digging in Native American mounds and discovering broken pottery. One year they converted a four-horse trailer for a three-week family tour exploring all of Florida, including Jacksonville, Tallahassee, and Tarpon Springs (where sponges were the economic base until a red tide wiped them out in 1947). Mark remembered a jeep trip to Marco Island, still renowned for its shells and beaches, as a "magic place," where they camped on the beach and had a fish fry for breakfast; they also brought home a dead alligator for Mark—tied to the roof of the jeep. Another year they traveled by jeep to the Smoky Mountains where they stayed in an 1840s log cabin. A bear invaded and destroyed the detached kitchen. The ranger's wife said "shoot it" and handed Jane a rifle. Henry held a light, and Jane dispatched the unwanted two hundred pound visitor. In 1952, Jane took Mark's Boy Scout Troop 69 on a monthlong three-car caravan camping trip to Colorado where they crossed the great divide thirteen times.

The expansive nature of life at the Renos meant friends were almost literally family. Childhood friends often stayed overnight, and the children amused themselves preparing and performing skits or singing "Horace the Peacock Is His Name" composed by cousin Sally Wood Winslow.[12] The old record player ground out country songs, and all knew a variety of drinking songs. There was also just plain talk, and, on some nights, poetry was the concern of the evening. Jane would serve breakfast—often mint chocolate chip ice cream. While the Reno children were growing up and having their friends over, Jane often played seven card solitaire for hours with a can of Busch at her elbow and a cigarette in her hand, and as the children would head out for an adventure, she would loudly declare, "I love you very much."

3

PREPARATION

Cornell and Harvard, 1956–1963

Cornell was a long way from Kendall Drive physically and culturally. More than one thousand miles north of Miami, it is located "high above [Lake] Cayuga's waters" in Ithaca, New York, a town of only thirty thousand residents, then as it is even today.[1] The first freeze can be expected in October, the last in May, and the long winters can bring seventy inches of snow in a year. Opened in 1868 with 412 students, Cornell is a hybrid: both a public Morrill Land-Grant school and a private Ivy League school.[2]

Today there are some fourteen thousand undergraduates and six thousand graduate students, nearly triple the student population of Reno's day.[3] Unlike the other Ivy League schools, women have attended Cornell since 1870; in fact, a PhD was awarded to a woman as early as 1880. Still, when Reno attended, women had their own student government, only intramural sports teams, and dormitory or sorority living was the rule. Indeed, students had sit-down meals that provided employment and cash for students like Janet, who waitressed some fifteen hours a week her freshman year.[4]

For the first time in her life, Reno attended a school with Black American fellow students. Blacks had been attending Cornell since the mid-1880s, and the first Black fraternity, Alpha Phi Alpha, was founded there in 1906. Their numbers, however, were very small. In fact, there is no Alpha Phi Alpha photo in the 1960 yearbook, nor is there a Black person in either the football or basketball team photos. The 1950s have, rightly, been called the era of the Silent Generation, and it was not until a student rebellion in the late 1960s that the composition of Cornell's student body began to significantly change. Today more than a third of Cornell's undergrads are classified as minority students.

When Reno arrived, freshmen wore beanies and were forbidden cars.[5] The Freshman Directory gave instant information about the new students. It was referred to, by men, as "The Pig Book."[6] Sophomores had Cornell sweaters, juniors had blazers, and seniors had straw hats. The class mascot was a St. Bernard—not because of its loyalty or courage—but because of the keg slung under its chin. The women's dorms were sited on one side of the campus across a bridge occasionally barricaded as a prank. Women's hours were 10:30 p.m. on weeknights and Sunday, 12:00 a.m. on Friday, and 1:00 a.m. on Saturday. Not only were sit-down meals served, one was expected to "dress" for Wednesday evening and Sunday noon meals, and at Christmas a formal dinner was held. The fourteen sororities and fifty-seven fraternities played an important social role on the relatively isolated campus. Twenty-five percent of men and 20 percent of women actually lived in their organization's house, but membership was probably double that.

While the men ate at their houses, the sorority women were required to eat in university sponsored dining halls. Students may have studied hard during the week, but the weekends were party time with a substantial amount of drinking at both fraternity and apartment parties. Smoking and bridge were also dormitory activities. In the conforming 1950s, though, Reno's 6' plus broad-shouldered frame did not make her a hot number. Nor did she make an effort to style her hair, to wear makeup, or to follow current fashion. She just burrowed into her education.

Janet Reno's Cornell was awash with possible distractions. Student publications included a literary and humor magazine as well as a yearbook and newspaper. There were fourteen music and drama organizations, including separate women's and men's glee clubs, and some twenty-five other organizations, including Young Republicans (no Democrats), and the Poultry and Parachute Clubs. Among the many academic honorary organizations were Mortar Board, Phi Beta Kappa, and Phi Kappa Phi; Janet belonged to none. Nor was she one of the three women in the Debate Club, although she had starred in debate in high school.

During her freshman year Janet lived in Dickinson dorm's "freshman corridor," where she developed friends who lasted throughout her four years there. During her sophomore year she lived in Sage dormitory. That was the year of student riots over attempts to enforce a prohibition on women's visiting men's apartments.[7] Her junior year she served as president of her dormitory, and in her senior year she presided over the Women's Self-Governing Association—her only yearbook-reported activities. A highlight was an opportunity to introduce Harry S. Truman when he addressed a Cornell audience of some five thousand students. At dinner that night at the Cornell Hotel School, she sat at a table with the university president, Frances Perkins, and Truman who came about to her shoulder.[8]

Those who knew her at Cornell describe Reno as "quiet," "very studious," "modest," "hard working," "down to earth," "well known," "respected"—consistent characteristics that recur also among the descriptions of people who knew her at Gables High, and later at Harvard and in law practice too. But those who knew her well also describe Janet as a challenge seeker, a person of broad interests, and possessing a deep sense of the equality of human beings. And those who knew her very well describe a quick and sometimes quite wicked sense of humor.

As a freshman, Janet was enthralled by Cornell. She wrote to her Aunt Peg in November: "I couldn't have chosen better."[9] She added that the "wonderful people here" had given her "greater faith in the human race than I have ever possessed before." She was thrilled not only by her classes but also by all the free lectures ranging from Confucian philosophy to the works of Sigmund Freud. By the next fall she had become critical. In fact, she made an appointment to see the president, Deane Waldo Malott. Her purpose? To demand that he justify the expense of Cornell given the "unsatisfactory" teaching staff. In a letter describing the meeting, she reported that at the end of the interview President Malott indicated that she should come to him if she had trouble getting a scholarship in the next term. A spring 1958 letter stated that her professors (she was taking chemistry, history, and German) were a "vast improvement over last term's." Even as a young woman, Janet was as direct and forthright as her mother, if, perhaps, a bit more diplomatic. The expense for going home for Thanksgiving or spring vacation was out of the question, but Janet always found something interesting to do. One year she organized a women's raft trip on the Allegheny River.

Reno's college notebooks, one for each class, are marvelously detailed and organized with only an occasional marginal note referring to a fellow student, such as "she's a narrow minded, aluminum type Republican," "an upper-class

Boston Republican," or "she's been invited to Princeton this weekend. I have never seen her so spastic." Various papers prepared for a class show a wide range of interests, for example, "Prehistoric India," "If Thomas Jefferson Were Alive Today," "What Is a Marxist?" (graded 95 and described as "solid thinking"), and "Problem of Verification in Psychoanalysis," which includes extensive handwritten notes from the professor: "quite wrong . . . you are the victim of scientific prejudice, a prejudice typical of our time."

Although she was a chemistry major, Reno was clearly engaged in exploring the political.[10] Other papers include "Soviet Foreign Policy in Western Europe Since 1953," "The Federal Government and Its Role in Our Economy," "Civil Liberties and the Supreme Court," "Judicial Review," and "The Impact of Roosevelt on American Thought" (for a class taught by former Secretary of Labor Frances Perkins and using a text by Arthur Schlesinger Jr.).[11] Her paper on "Brandeis's Influence on the Court's Decision to Consider Social and Economic Influence in Interpreting the Constitution" had a typically uplifting conclusion: "Brandeis's greatness lies in his faith in man, to be ethical, to be informed, and to contribute to his nation. . . . Brandeis used the law to protect man as a spiritual, intellectual, physical entity. Man is the basis of democracy and in protecting his freedoms a greater democracy is evolved."

Cornell Law School held an open house in the fall of Janet's senior year. It argued that the school would be "better" three or four years in the future, but that the upper half of the class would have no problem finding a job. Still, the students were warned that no matter where one went to school "you're going to have to sell yourself personally—name, locale, family, personality make a difference."[12] Harvard was invoked as Cornell's primary rival; it was also Janet's aspiration, although she had doubts that she would qualify.

Janet's college summers were put to good use. After her high school graduation, she worked as a clerk for the Dade County Sheriff's Department, a job arranged by her father. After her freshman year she worked in Miami's Public Safety Department; after her sophomore year she worked in the Placement Division of the County Welfare Department; and after her junior year she worked as a laboratory tech at Miami's Howard Hughes Medical Research Institute. It didn't persuade her that medicine was her calling, and in her senior year she applied to and was accepted by Harvard Law School.[13] When she graduated Cornell, her sister, Maggy, was the only family member there to celebrate Janet's graduation. It was too far and too expensive for her parents, who had four children in private colleges/universities that year.

At Harvard Law School, Janet would be one of sixteen women in a class of 525.[14] One might think the women would experience some camaraderie; if they did, Janet was not part of it, admitting she "might have been characterized as a loner."[15] Dean Erwin Griswold gave the welcoming speech at the orientation. He assured the newcomers that a good job awaited them, and that only 2 percent would flunk out. He urged them to "relax" and enjoy a movie twice a month—but no double features.

Harvard values tradition, and although women had been attending Harvard Law for a decade, the institution was still not used to them. Thus, there was only one women's rest room, hidden in the basement of one of several law school buildings. Some men thought that any woman student had displaced a deserving man, and some faculty members treated women students in ways that Elizabeth Hanford Dole, class of 1965, found "humiliating."[16] Even Dean Griswold, who hosted a dinner for the sixteen women to make them "feel at home," mused that he didn't know what the women would do with their law degrees, that he was responsible for admitting women to the law school twelve years previously, but only because he didn't want to be accused of discriminating.

Although Janet did not have a scholarship, Harvard each year provided her with a series of loans of up to $662. Her first year she also worked. Her employer was Professor Mark DeWolfe Howe who employed her first as a typist and then as a researcher. One of her assignments was to prepare a memorandum for Harvard's Nieman Fellows on the "Difficulties in the Control of Municipal Corruption."[17] The topic was quite familiar to "Janet Reno of Florida," although most of the examples were drawn from New York City. She noted that New York's corruption was not felt because tax resources were currently adequate, and also that Boston's corruption was successful because its many immigrants were politically malleable. While Reno noted that "psychologists must answer why men will inevitably be corrupt," she moralized that outstanding individuals must "assume responsibility and step into the vacuum created by present day indifference" to municipal government, "the most personal" form. Surely these are echoes from Sunday afternoon discussions on the Renos' Kendall screened porch! She sent the Nieman study to the Miami firm of Hector and Faircloth to support her application for a summer job. It bore no fruit, although her rejection letter paternally suggested she might someday become the first woman on the Supreme Court.

Cambridge and the nearby city of Boston provided an urban, and unlike Miami, an urbane life. Her first year, Janet roomed with an astronomer who worked for *Sky and Telescope* magazine at 43 Kirkland across the street from a house where Thomas Wolfe once lived. The apartment was "beautiful and convenient," with a kitchen and two bedrooms—one of which was Janet's study. Her roommate's family provided an iron, a toaster, and a mix master. Janet was elated.[18] She estimated her expenses at ninety dollars a month including rent.

Although her budget was tight, Reno did make use of nearby Boston's cultural attractions. She attended a Boston Symphony concert of Beethoven, and in a letter home described it as "unlike anything I have ever heard," and she pronounced herself as now as devoted to symphonic music as to opera. She quoted from the performance of *A Midsummer Night's Dream* and noted that while she never liked reading Shakespeare, it was a "joy" to watch. But the outdoors woman also explored her surroundings. Once, she took a twenty mile roundtrip hike, the last five miles following the route of Paul Revere.[19] In a letter to "Mummy and Daddy," she described setting out at 6:00 a.m. with a laundry bag slung over her shoulder.[20] Its contents included bread, cheese, and a bottle of wine, as well as band-aids, comb and brush, and a book on the Battle of Lexington. She imagined that battle and diagrammed its events, providing names of participants and even quotes. She detailed the walk through urban slums and wealthy residential areas. She noted the gasoline attendant hurrying to early mass in greasy coveralls and children playing cowboys and Indians in a graveyard. She said one reason for the walk was to try to imagine what it would be like for an army to walk such a route. Would they be tired? Would their feet hurt? Would they be in a mood to pick up a gun and fire?[21] She asked her mother to send the extra copy of *Lee's Lieutenants: A Study in Command* by Douglas Southall Freeman so she could show a friend an example of good historical writing.

Janet was "floating" in "the freest, most democratic place in the world" (according to Felix Frankfurter). There would be no exams or tests until June, "only terribly exciting classes, work, and it's all so much fun." "Everyone is friendly, now relaxed and fun." Still, she noted in a letter home, it didn't seem much like a university plunked down "in this city-like atmosphere."

Reno described her worst moment in law school as occurring during a course on contracts. The professor had described a case in which a drunken Native American had sold his oil interest at an abysmally low price. The question was: What did she think of the court's ruling that upheld the drunken man's right? Reno was unprepared, sleepy, and—she later admitted—a bit hungover, and responded "I'm sorry Professor Dawson, but I haven't decided whether I'm a Goldwater Republican or Stevensonian Democrat." The professor stared, pulled on his mustache, and went on, while the other students burst into laughter.[22]

Her favorite classes were Constitutional Law with Professor Paul Freund, Administrative Law with Professor Paul Batar, Labor Law with Derrick Botts, and Tax Law in which she got her highest grade in law school. Years later, when she was attorney general, she would find her tax professor, Ernest Brown, now working for her![23] While there were plenty of mundane concerns, she found law "the ultimate in learning" and the one thousand years of common law the "greatest product of man's life."

Janet escaped the city regularly. One weekend she and three friends went to Cape Cod for a sailboat outing. They set out about 3:00 p.m., saw a magnificent sunset and ever-changing cloud formations, but were soon becalmed. It got colder and colder. Sometime after 8:30 p.m., they got a tow from a motorboat. She wrote that "never in my life have I been so cold for so long," a statement that must be understood as serious given the strenuous, even risky excursions the Renos were accustomed to taking. Another foray took her to New York City and the new Guggenheim Museum designed by Frank Lloyd Wright. It contained only one painting she liked. She was staying with her Aunt Peg who took her on a tour of Connecticut including a stop at the Litchfield Law School, which was the first law school in the United States and had been founded by Judge Tapping Reeve in 1784, anteceding Harvard by more than thirty years.

Reno joined the campus Democratic Club. That year the Bay of Pigs failure to oust Cuba's new ruler, Fidel Castro, would have lasting repercussions for Miami as would the following year's Cuban Missile Crisis. Closer to home, Eleanor Roosevelt was appointed chair of the Commission on the Status of Women by the new president, John F. Kennedy, and Roosevelt came to Harvard to discuss that status and the status of the world more generally. The next year, Janet would be invited to address the Harvard Law

School Association on the experience of being a woman in the Law School. She would have a lot to say.

Meanwhile Janet's family members were having their own adventures. Her mother continued working off and on for the *Miami Daily News*. In fact, one of her stories about a sickness afflicting children on the Seminole reservation won a "Big Story" award, an award made by a national radio/TV show by the same name.[24] Jane performed other work for the Seminoles whose children were being required to attend public school, where their parents believed they would learn to lie and steal. Jane helped them win a school of their own and was given an honorary name, "Apoongo Stahnegee" (Rumor Bearer). When Smallpox Tommy pinned an egret feather in her hair, Jane cried.[25]

Janet's sister, Maggy, wrote a dramatic account of Hurricane Donna's destruction of the marina where boyfriend Jim Hurchalla's boat survived, but where more than a dozen beautiful, $5,000 boats with 75 horsepower motors did not. The winds were so strong "it makes you think you can fly," she wrote. The waves were dark, the 90 mph winds were frightening, but "I have never seen anything so fiercely beautiful." Returning to Swarthmore early for orientation and her duties as manager of the hockey team, Maggy found that time at college so "nice"—with no classes to distract one, people would talk "indefinitely." That fall her classes included Greek Literature, Comparative Anatomy, and an honors seminar with comfortable chairs, tea and crumpets, and talk . . . sometimes until 1:00 a.m.! Loving school and her professors, Maggy was, nevertheless, terribly homesick. One night she climbed the water tower to paint a message to herself as well as others: "Cheer Up!" And then there was work as a volunteer in the Kennedy campaign. Work, she wrote, is "avalanching." And every weekend was spent with Jim who was at the University of Pennsylvania working on a degree in Mechanical Engineering.

The year 1960 would be especially memorable for Maggy, as she soon discovered she was pregnant. The family rallied round for a November wedding at the Church of the Transformation at 1 East 29th Street in Manhattan. Maggy announced that "shotgun weddings are, indeed, the very best way to get married." She quit drinking and smoking, ate voraciously, and soon reached 150 pounds. She had "a little trouble getting used to being kicked in the stomach," but even as she cooked for her husband and sewed curtains for their apartment, she continued her studies and had time to wish she could be a poet like Houseman or Dickinson, and commented on her reading of Descartes's *Meditations.*

After one semester at Tulane, brother Mark had decided to drop out of college and go adventuring; Maggy gave her hearty endorsement to his plan. Bob, at Tulane, wrote that he was engaged in a profitable business. It involved buying a case of beer for $3.80 then selling the twenty-four bottles for 25¢ each. This grossed $6.00 with a profit of $2.20. A side benefit was the fact that in his zeal to maximize income, Bob claimed that he was himself completely on the wagon. His next project was to try making home brew—so, "Ma, send the bottle capper." While a letter home would casually say "grades best ever," most of the content of his letters referred to non-scholarly activities. One, in particular, provided a long narrative about how he had painted the town red with a woman he met at a wedding and done so by only spending one quarter. It began with the appropriation of two bottles of champagne from the bridal suite, and proceeded into the morning through several penthouses and night clubs. His success, he noted, was because he was "an unabashed moocher."

Law school was lonely for Janet. The handful of women students did not band together.[26] Indeed, those who survived were necessarily of an independent nature. While there was a lot of quite legal discrimination against women in the 1950s and 1960s, Janet didn't think for one minute women "couldn't" or "shouldn't." Faced with rejection, her response was not so much one of anger as to assume that the person was "stupid" and to have no further truck with him (not her).[27]

But she was busy and hardly asocial. Her letters home rated her extracurricular reading: Franz Kafka's *Amerika* and "Boris Godunov" were "ugh," Fyodor Dostoevsky's *Poor People* "beautiful," Nikolai Gogol's *Dead Souls,* a "must." She declared Harry S. Truman a "great man" after reading his *Memoirs,* and noted that she was starting Stendhal's *Charterhouse of Parma.* Janet and her roommate had established a pattern of holding a weekend dinner party—the leftovers providing meals for the rest of the week. As entertainment it was economical, for example, a leg of lamb could be purchased for 39¢ per pound, and the Italian merchants at the Haymarket Square markets "don't even try to gyp you." She found cooking creative, trying new recipes and making baked beans from scratch. They hosted an Italian dinner in their apartment to watch the Nixon-Kennedy debate; attending were one

Democrat (Janet) among nine Republicans. One of the guests was an old friend from Cornell, Roger Kauffman, a brilliant man "who can pronounce all the names in Dostoevsky's novels." "He comes up to my shoulder," she noted. The message was that he was only a friend.

Reno noted that she had enjoyed a day off in the countryside where she had played football, claiming "I'm still good." She reviewed the content of each of her classes in the letter with carbons distributed among the family, noting that in her property class much of the talk was about water rights— "Strange for one coming from South Florida."

The family of law professor Abram Chayes invited Reno for Thanksgiving dinner. Janet judged him as "gay and charming" although "slightly stuffy." Antonia Chayes, a "lawyer in her own right," worked as an assistant to the Dean of the Law School and took an interest in the women students; a good politician, Antonia would later be appointed Under Secretary of the Air Force where she continued her role as a mentor to women.[28]

After filling out a one-page application, Reno was awarded a hefty loan from Harvard for the spring semester. She noted that it was in stark contrast to registration for the Florida Bar, which was an "almost superhuman task" and involved getting fingerprinted. She also deplored the record-breaking winter with an average temperature of 27.2 degrees, but continued hosting dinner parties and reading novels and biographies.[29] She particularly noted Joe McCarthy's 1960 campaign book, *The Remarkable Kennedys*, which described the "uproariously funny" politics of Irish Catholic Boston, even though she found the book's style and accuracy "horrible."[30] According to McCarthy, when Jack first won his seat in Congress, the family celebration included his grandfather standing on a table and singing "Sweet Adeline"— the last Irish Catholic display connected to Kennedy who would later become the first Catholic president of the United States.

By the second semester, Janet had become more accustomed to life in a sophisticated city, and her letters provide enthusiastic details related to her education. Thus, she announced that she never fell asleep in class— "no higher tribute can be paid." Still, she always saw details within a broad picture and essentially asked herself: "Of what is this an instance?" For example, she reflected that one might see U.S. history as one of overcoming tyranny: first the tyranny of foreign powers, then of individual leaders, then of business interests, and, she proposed, it was currently in the process of overcoming the tyranny of labor. In her generation, she predicted, it will overcome the tyranny of government itself.[31]

Second semester is described in two long letters written by Janet, dated February 18, 1961, one to her grandparents and one to her parents. Her classes included the following: Property (the law of historians), Criminal Law (tragic law about the devil in man), Civil Procedure (the law of lawyers), Contracts (the law of the marketplace), and Torts, which she found dreary until she hit upon its analogy to a law drawn from the experience of "four small Reno children in a car waiting for their mother to do the grocery shopping."[32] Contracts was her favorite, because she saw in it an analogy between the creating of democratic legislatures and the act of individual people making an agreement. Moot court that year would focus on the topic of fraud. She described her brief and her oral argument as highly successful. The latter, her oral argument, was presumably polished by her high school debate experience, and the family dinner table and Sunday afternoon discussions on the Reno porch. The Nieman event featuring her research occurred that spring. She found she not only knew more than the journalists—she knew more than the professors. She also observed that the discussion devolved into two "blockheaded" camps: lawyers and journalists who seemed unable to understand each other.

Her general self-education continued. She obtained reading privileges at the Boston Athenaeum, visited the State House to watch legislative sessions, wandered Beacon Hill, and as one did in the 1960s, habituated coffee houses. (Starbucks would not open its first store for another ten years.) A Boston Symphony concert featuring Wagner "finally dissipated" her fourteen-to-sixteen-year-old love of his music. An old friend from college, Margie Seybold, then attending Temple Medical School, came to visit, and Janet went to visit Maggy, whose apartment Janet sketched and described as "haphazardly neat." Maggy, she reported was "so happy," the family must not worry about her. She presented the baby with three books, *Babar, Mary Poppins,* and *The Wizard of Oz.* Janet also visited Mark at Fort Dix before he was sent to Germany. "Don't worry," she said, "I'll bet he even visits the Louvre while he is there."[33]

With the money she got from preparing the Nieman paper, Reno took herself to New York and a "tall girls shop" to do some "hog wild" clothes shopping. As usual, she did not travel home for spring vacation but expressed her yearning: "I've never wanted so much to come home to Miami—not in an immediate sense, but just to come home to stay."

Later in the spring she wrote about a speech at Harvard by a Russian professor who simultaneously asserted "there will be peace" and boasted that the Soviet Union's triumphant (first) exploration of space was a victory for all humankind. She reveled in a talk by Eleanor Roosevelt—and in the chance to sail on the Charles River. She also declared her intention to build a sailboat that summer—a 10′ rooster class for a single sailor. Just now she was busy enjoying spring—a symbol of hope—somewhat diminished by current events such as Cuba, Algeria, and Laos.

Spring, of course also meant exams were only a month away. Janet described herself as working from 8:00 a.m. to 1:00 a.m. and hoped to have a "satisfactory" performance. She already knew that she would not be asked to be on Law Review.

Again expressing the "joy and wonderment" of her past five years of higher education, she urged her parents to save her letters for her granddaughters. She despaired that the Massachusetts legislature was "horribly inept," "gruesomely corrupt," and "superbly confused" but had had hope for the federal government, which would soon be staffed by many Harvard Law School professors. She could understand the attraction. She experienced Kennedy's charm herself. Indeed, one day Kennedy was visiting the Schlesingers only a block and a half from Janet's apartment, and she found herself only fifteen feet away when he came out the door. His "beautiful smile" was compelling. You could just see yourself saying: "Yes, sir." "What else can I do for you?" "Yes, sir, you're right."

The Chayes were among those going to Washington, and Antonia urged Janet to spend a summer there as well. But as Janet wrote to her parents, she preferred to work in Miami, stating "it is my home, my native land . . . and its people are my people." Moreover, it didn't have blizzards—three of them struck Boston in February to Janet's dismay. While snow had had some aesthetic appeal in Ithaca, in Boston, she found, it was gray and slushy and got your feet wet. That year she also met a third-year student named Bob Graham who also loved Florida. He would become both its senator and its governor. Thus were future political ties forged.

In her second year of law school, Janet moved to 46 Avon Hill Street. That fall she continued her hiking, for instance, a seventeen mile trek from Salem to Gloucester ("the most beautiful experience of my life"), visited Quincy, home of the Adams, and its environs, and endeavored an October climb of New Hampshire's Mount Washington, which was thwarted by snow. She also made a trip to Amherst to honor Emily Dickinson, to Bangor, Maine, to visit the Woods with whom Mark had spent a year, and to New Bedford where she learned the skills involved in whaling and scalloping. She also made a special trip to visit her Cornell friend, Bettina Corning, by then Bettina Dudley and living in Albany, New York, because Janet was officially baby Robbie's godmother.

That semester also included what Janet claimed to be the "greatest personal discoveries of my life." Explaining, "I have discovered for myself Japanese art. . . . The Asiatic section of the Boston Museum of Fine Arts is 'paradise'—none of the heavy, dull, florid European art with angels who look like they have cramps and toad-like Madonnas." She continued, "There are tigers so beautiful they can only be compared to Blake's poem. . . . There are lady polo players, Buddhist mystics laughing at the moon, and Confucius at the Apricot altar." She announced. "I shall become rich and become a great collector." She may have been "stunned, amazed, delighted" by her discovery, but she complained/rejoiced that "I have so much to find out." That "much" included history, poetry (Emily Dickinson), literature (Zora Neale Hurston's books and especially those of Isak Dinesen), and philosophy. The latter was inspired by a winter trek across Walden Pond in knee-deep, wind-sculpted snow in 10 degree weather. She described the experience as one in which one was "more alone than you have ever been and yet at one with the world." She noted rabbit tracks, balls of snow hanging from evergreens like Christmas decorations, ice-fishing traps, and the fact that while Concord was lovely, it "seems a bit smug."

Janet's law degree was awarded June 13, 1963. She had graduated in the top 15 percent of her class, but it would not be enough to win a highly desired clerkship or a place in an established firm in her hometown of Miami.

Mother Jane Wood Reno holding baby Janet, 1939. Courtesy of Reno Family Archives.

Janet, c. 1940. Courtesy of Reno Family Archives.

Three-year-old Janet in front of the Renos' Coconut Grove house. Courtesy of Reno Family Archives.

Janet with father Henry Reno holding Bobby, 1942. Courtesy of Reno Family Archives.

Maggy and Janet (on Tony) riding their ponies. Courtesy of Reno Family Archives.

Janet and Maggy adventuring out for a sail. Courtesy of Reno Family Archives.

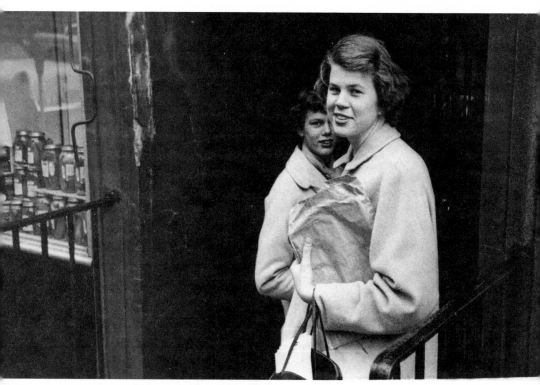

Janet and Maggy, seen here in New York, were able sometimes to visit and travel together during their college years. Courtesy of Reno Family Archives.

Janet in a family game of table tennis, early 1970s. Courtesy of Reno Family Archives.

Robert, Janet, Jane, Mark, and Maggy together, late 1970s. Courtesy of Reno Family Archives.

4

Building a Career

Miami, 1963–1978

Miami was in the throes of rapid and dramatic change when newly minted attorney Janet Reno launched her career. With Castro's rise to power, a host of refugees from the Batista regime left Miami for Cuba, but over the next decade hundreds of thousands of mostly middle- and upper-class Cubans left Cuba for Miami. The CIA supported a failed challenge to Castro known as the Bay of Pigs in 1961. In 1962 the Cuban Missile Crisis resulted in a tacit agreement with the Soviet Union that the United States would tolerate Castro's regime and the Soviets would withdraw their missiles from Cuba.

After those dramatic events, it became clear that Miami's Cubans were in for a long stay, and they began to receive favored treatment by the U.S. government. This included passing the Cuban Adjustment Act that provided Cubans with green cards for permanent residency. But it was not just that Cubans enjoyed privileges that other immigrants did not; they also seemed to enjoy opportunities denied Miami's Black citizens. Indeed, Blacks in Miami referred to the influx as the Cuban "invasion," and took note that one year the Small Business Administration made $1 million in loans to Cubans but only $58,000 in loans to Miami-Dade Blacks.[1] Further, many Cubans were seen as "White" and more welcomed in situations where Black citizens were not. One example is that in Miami in 1962–1963, not one union apprentice out of 1,500 was Black. By 1968 the number had increased to all of four.

On her return to Miami, having forgone an opportunity in Washington, DC, Reno found that most Miami law firms had no interest in hiring a young woman, even one with a Harvard degree. So in 1963 she signed up as an associate with Brigham and Brigham, a firm that had given her a job the previous summer. The focus of the practice was real estate and property law. It gave Reno some experience in the courtroom and made her something of an expert on eminent domain.[2] In one case, she came up against Florida Power and Light (FPL), represented by Talbot "Sandy" D'Alemberte. Janet was incensed at the treatment of her clients by FPL and prepared and prepared for the case. She beat D'Alemberte. Janet soon joined the Daughters of the American Revolution and the American Bar Association (ABA) as she began to collect the many memberships typical of public, especially elected, officials. She also began to work in a variety of political campaigns.

In 1967 Janet joined Gerald Lewis as the junior partner in Lewis and Reno.[3] The professional launch was exciting but began amid personal and national concerns. The year, 1967, was a sad one for the Reno family because her father passed away not too long after a grand thirtieth anniversary party. At the party Jane allegedly asked Henry if he was sorry he had married her. His response? "I wouldn't have missed it for a million dollars."[4] Over the years, he had sometimes found life with Jane exhausting enough that he tried living with Mark in Immokalee, Florida, for a while. He was also known to retreat to a cabin in the Everglades where, in fact, he died of a heart attack, alone except for his five dogs.

Nationally and regionally, racial politics seesawed between highs and lows. For example, Thurgood Marshall was appointed to the U.S. Supreme Court in 1967, and in *Loving v. Virginia* (388 U.S. 1, 1967) that court declared laws banning interracial marriage unconstitutional. The next year, the nation grieved the assassinations of both Martin Luther King Jr. and Robert Kennedy. It was also the year that Miami experienced the Liberty City riots. Tensions had been building from the construction of I-95 through the heart of what was then called Colored Town (Overtown today), which destroyed much of that community and greatly increased crowding in areas like Liberty City. Frustrations finally erupted in riots in August 1968.[5] Republicans were holding their presidential nominating convention on Miami Beach that August, and Black citizens planned a demonstration in Liberty City.

What began with a meeting of only two hundred activists escalated over several days to a confrontation with the Florida Highway Patrol and the Florida National Guard directed by Dade County Sheriff E. Wilson Purdy. Three people died and hundreds were arrested. Purdy and Miami Police

Chief Walter Headley determined that suppression was the only appropriate response. That certainly did not change any hearts and minds, and it may have contributed to a far more serious riot that would occur just over a decade later. While Reno had no role in the 1968 events other than as a citizen witness, she would be front and center during the far more serious 1980 riots because by then she had become Miami-Dade state attorney.

The Lewis and Reno firm was tied to the political sphere, but it was not engaged in civil rights issues. In fact, the reason for its existence was that Lewis had run for and won a seat in the Florida legislature.[6] Blackwell, Walker, and Gray, Lewis's employer at the time, did not permit its lawyers to hold public office. Lewis needed an income, and Janet had worked hard on his campaign. It seemed quite natural that they team up to create a practice as well. The practice was a general one, and one which gave Reno both management and courtroom experience. Her reputation was one of thorough preparation and of expertise in examining, even intimidating, witnesses. It was also one of conscience. In one probate case, the firm was asked to probate a will. It was a large estate and usual practice was to take a percentage of the estate as a fee. Janet observed that the will was quite in order and taking a percentage was not reasonable. They billed by the hour and received a much smaller fee.[7]

In March 1971, Reno became general counsel to the Florida House Judiciary Committee. Its chair was Sandy D'Alemberte, who claims that while driving in his convertible he noticed Reno in the next lane. He called over "Follow me home." Apparently he was impressed by her courtroom victory over him years before. She did follow him home, and he offered her the staff job for his legislative committee. Reno's partner, Lewis, was the vice chair of the equivalent Senate committee and had recommended her for the position. John and Sara Smith, who lived in the same complex as Lewis, had also recommended Reno.

She took the job, moved to Tallahassee, and on weekends often stayed with Sandy's folks in Chattahoochee. D'Alemberte and Reno would become best friends. They sailed together, played racquetball together, and with their families and others, camped in the Okefenokee Swamp. His respect for her would be hard to overemphasize; still, he acknowledged Reno could be abrupt, struck some as rigid, and, perhaps, as having too much respect for law enforcers.

Reno's first personal contacts with D'Alemberte had come through working on the campaigns of Democratic candidates such as Dante Purcell and Claude Pepper. As noted above, she had opposed him in the FPL case. Her first opportunity to work with him, though, was on his committee and specifically on the task of preparing and drafting a constitutional amendment for the reform of Florida's judiciary.[8] That portion of state government had been left untouched in a 1968 rewrite of the rest of Florida's constitution. The new court system was designed to simplify and professionalize. First, it got rid of municipal courts. Second, trials were to be held in county-wide courts with a second tier of state circuit courts for major civil and criminal cases. Third, appeals would go to state district courts and only on appeal from those courts to the Florida Supreme Court. Further, trial court judges were to be elected in nonpartisan elections, while appellate court judges were to be appointed by the governor.

But there was resistance to the reforms from groups such as those serving in juvenile courts who were not necessarily lawyers and not well monitored. In fact, once when Reno was speaking to a group of juvenile court judges there was such controversy and she was shown such disrespect that she left in near tears and later referred to the judges as "dunderheads." Voters, however, approved the judicial amendment that Reno had prepared after many hours of consultation with lawyers, judges, professors, elected officials, and others.[9] An important result was that Reno became well known and well regarded in Florida's governmental/political community.

Congress had recently passed the Equal Rights Amendment, and at Janet's urging, D'Alemberte got it to the House floor where it was quickly passed. Indeed, it may have been the first vote taken in any of the fifty state legislatures.[10] However, opponents in the Florida Senate cited a rule stating legislators could not vote on an amendment unless they were elected *after* the amendment was proposed. That settled that. (Eventually, that rule would be declared unconstitutional, but even so the words have never actually been removed from the Florida constitution.)

With her state constitution assignment completed, Janet entered electoral politics in 1972. A seat representing Miami in the state legislature had opened up when its incumbent was indicted for an insurance scam.[11] Reno beat five Democrats in the primary, and all concerned expected her to win the general election easily, since the district was heavily Democratic.

Instead, she lost by a slim margin. Richard Nixon soundly beat George McGovern in that election, and the choice of presidential candidates apparently rallied Republican voters while discouraging Democrats. Also, Reno may have been so confident about her own candidacy that she campaigned more for McGovern than for herself. It is also possible that Reno's well-known membership in the NAACP cut into her White vote.

Reno felt bad about the loss, but she got advice she never forgot from John Orr, who went down to certain defeat after being the only member to vote for a resolution in the state legislature that condemned the segregation of Florida's schools. He told her, "Janet, just keep on doing and saying what you believe to be right. Don't pussy foot, don't equivocate, don't talk out of both sides of your mouth and you'll wake up the next morning feeling good about yourself."[12] She was also buoyed up by reading a biography of Abraham Lincoln who also lost his first election. Her friend and partner, Lewis, who was by then running for the state Public Service Commission, also lost. However, he soon ran for and won the position of state Comptroller, a position he would hold for many years.

Reno stayed in Tallahassee for a while, working on a revision of the criminal code with a senate staffer. Dempsey Barron, a dominant member of the Senate and conservative from West Florida, objected to what he considered the House impinging on Senate business. Still, he was actually rather charmed by Reno, who seemed to be one of a very few who were not intimidated by him—and who shared with him a love of outdoor adventures and books. In fact, when the finished legislation was to be discussed in the Senate, Barron invited Reno to discuss it on the Florida Senate floor. That broke three taboos: giving the floor to a woman, a staffer, and a House employee.

During this period, Janet helped clean up her brother Mark's record so that he could enlist in the Army.[13] Mark went on to have several marriages and children.[14] He also had several careers. His first was as a member of the crew for a 60 ton, then a 100 ton, then a 500 ton, and ultimately for a 1600 ton ship that plied coastal waters. He won an award for best recruit, then got busted for fighting. He got promoted again and trained as a scout, then went to Officer Candidate School (OCS).[15] After jump school, he chose to leave rather than reenlist and began a series of interesting civilian jobs such as licensed tugboat captain, carpenter, and game warden. Later in life he would enroll at the University of Miami, although he did not finish. He worked in Florida and as far afield as Nigeria. He was a man of irreverent wit (like his siblings), who could enliven any conversation. He and his third wife, Ann, lived on the Kendall property in a chikee close to, but concealed from, the main house. Open sided, it had all the necessaries: a TV, a giant bed, family photos. Nearby small structures included a shed with tools and another with a dressing table and shower.

Brother Bob's life in this period also began taking some twists and turns. After Tulane, he volunteered for the Army and spent his two-year enlistment at Fort Meade writing for the base newspaper, and then returned to Miami and followed family tradition by going to work at the *Miami Herald*. He first reported from Miami, then Key West, where he lived in the Hemingway house before it became a tourist site, and later from West Palm Beach. After a half dozen years, Bob decamped first to the *Times-Picayune* in New Orleans and then in 1968 to New York City to work as a business columnist for *Newsday*.[16] There, he married a Turkish woman, Zeynep Challa Toros, and enjoyed a Greenwich Village bohemian life before moving to Long Island, where the paper was published. Challa did not bond with the Renos, and she and Robert did not come to Miami regularly—not even for the holidays. Still, his family roots were strong, and in a Mother's Day column Bob described the women in his family thus: "I am the progeny of lionesses, not twits, and all the women in my family are bossy as hell." About his mother he said, "If you called her a cow, my mother wouldn't whine and complain, she'd simply bust you in the chops." And "Janny never wrestled an alligator in her life; she froze them with a stare."[17]

While Janet was building her career, she remained devoted to her nieces and nephews. She was solid and predictable; one could be quite sure of what she would think and what she would do. Janet also taught Mark's daughter, Hunter, to treat every single individual with dignity. Result? "The janitors were probably my best friends during my year at Coral Gables High." Hunter, 5'9" at age thirteen, became a successful teenage high-fashion model. Her grandmother, Jane, took a special interest in her, teaching her to drive at age thirteen, then sending her off to piano lessons.[18]

Mark's son and Hunter's brother, Douglas, is a fireman in Miami and has seven children.[19] Janet played an important role in Douglas's life, providing financial support not only for himself but also for his father, Mark, when he was under the threat of financial failure.[20] For instance, Janet lent him necessary funds so that he could redeem his car, which had been towed for unpaid parking tickets. She also put up $25,000 toward Douglas's first home, and, at his father Mark's urging, bought a sailboat that was principally used by Mark himself.[21] Even after she became state attorney, Reno was at the beck and call of family members. One call came at 2:00 a.m. when Douglas's car broke down at Fort Drum 150 miles north. Janet's response? "We'll come."

Janet was a great favorite with Douglas's generation. She could be "scary"—not above dressing as a marauding pirate and wrestling them to the ground—but also tender and would even cry. Sardines was still a favorite family game, and as many as ten kids could squeeze themselves into a thicket to hide from her. Janet was also in charge of "adventures" for her young nieces and nephews. Some involved visits to Seven Springs Ranch, where Mark had built a cabin. There the entertainment was hunting for armadillos and racing horses. When Mark was living on an island in the Bahamas, Janet sailed to visit—once through a violent storm. There was camping on one of Florida's Thousand Islands accessible only by boat and which featured the requisite liquor and invading clouds of mosquitoes.

Janet's responsibility for caring for children eventually extended beyond her immediate family, and the Webb twins are a good example. The Webbs lived nearby on 84th Street, and the two families had been close for many years. Frances Webb, a University of Miami graduate, was a theater critic for the *Miami Herald*. Her husband, Al, was a painter. Al died when his youngest children, twins Daphne and Danny, were twelve. Daphne describes her family as not "normal," and she was right. Al had missed the birth of his oldest child, Ann, because he had gone to Cuba with Jackie Gleason. If the Webbs put on a party, the Rat Pack (yes, the Rat Pack), Tennessee Williams, and Raquel Welch might be among the croquet players. Daphne remembers her father's funeral as involving a good deal of whiskey and a fight between Mark and family friend Walter Froelich after Froelich offered to take Daphne to Germany with him.

Only three years after the death of her husband, Al, Frances Webb died, and Janet Reno, a very busy state attorney, became the twins' formal guardian. It was a hard time. "Uncle" Mark moved into the Webb home for six months and "fathered" to some extent. Despite Mark's efforts, he failed to exercise calm, consistent, parental supervision, and ultimately Sally Wood Winslow, a Yankee, an artist, and an eccentric cousin was assigned to keep house. It was a tough time for all. High school classmates told Daphne, "I heard your Mom croaked." Daphne had some support from her boyfriend, whom she had known since age five and who was Black. When the Miami riots began, though, even her boyfriend told her that if "you come in the area, I will not come to your aid—they would kill me."

Mark continued to take the Webb twins on regular Everglades' excursions with his own children. Daphne particularly remembers wading through water up to her chest to see a Native American mound while covered with mosquitoes, and on another occasion, the sudden appearance of an alligator. She jumped on top of a picnic table throwing her peanut butter and jelly sandwich at the intruder, then looked for the rest of the family. They were snug inside the car.

Janet regularly visited the twins and urged them to "do well" and "don't get in trouble." She also said that, if they did get in trouble, they should come to her. And she was available for such mundane things as standing in the street to help Daphne learn to parallel park. One morning a streaker appeared outside their window. Sally Wood promptly called both the police and Janet. Janet arrived long before the police did. Reno asked the embarrassed officers why it took them so long to get there. A few days later the streaker returned. This time the police arrived almost instantly; further, they were able to arrest the culprit whom Danny had chased down. Happily, Daphne eventually found her niche—the theater—and her drama teacher, Bob Strickland, became a mentor. She successfully completed high school and went on to Tarkio College in Missouri where she majored in drama.

Reno's next professional move was unexpected. Dade State Attorney Richard Gerstein offered her a job. Gerstein was a handsome, popular, and powerful prosecutor, but some, including Janet's father, suspected him of ties to racketeers.[22] Reno was surprised and doubtful. Also, her perception of prosecutors was one that pictured them triumphing with the convictions they had won. She finally accepted the position, however, vowing that her new role would include a guarantee that innocents were not convicted—and that the guilty were fairly convicted.[23] Tom McAliley, a plaintiff's lawyer, had urged her to take the job because she could do a lot to protect innocent people by not charging them. He played on his knowledge that the wrongly accused were always a Reno concern.[24]

One of Reno's first assignments was to develop the Juvenile Division of the state attorney's office. Gerstein said "OK, Reno, you have sixty days to redo and design a juvenile court." She nodded and left. Thirty days later, she threw a full study down on his desk. The study was accepted, the court was created, and she was put in charge of it. Both Gerstein and Reno were no-nonsense characters. When they talked on the phone and had completed the conversation, they simply hung up. No time wasted on goodbyes. When Reno was recruited in 1972, Seymour "Sy" Gelber was serving as Gerstein's top assistant. When Gelber left a year later, Reno assumed the position. Gelber became Chief Judge of Juvenile Court, so contact with Reno, who was prosecuting many cases before him, was renewed. She regularly complained that the weakest judges were assigned to juvenile cases. Indeed, Gelber has observed there was sometimes a "pain in the ass" element to working with Reno. Others have simply noted a certain insistence and persistence in her conduct.

Chesterfield Smith was the president of the ABA from 1973 to 1974 and recruited Reno to serve on the joint International Jurists Association–American Bar Association Commission on Juvenile Justice Standards—providing her with an important introduction to the national reach of the ABA. The commission of some thirty-five members was about one-quarter women. Among them Janet was particularly impressed by Patricia Wald and Justine Wise Polier. The chairman, Irving Kaufman, she found "sort of high-handed." Chesterfield was informal. Once when he spotted Reno at an elegant dinner being held the first night of an ABA meeting, he came up to greet her with "Hello, doll baby." Work on the commission helped make young people and their problems a lifelong concern for Reno.

Some three years later Reno decided to return to private practice.[25] Her new firm, Steel, Hector (he who had previously rejected her for a position) & Davis, where D'Alemberte was now practicing, brought her in as a partner. The big-time clients of that highly successful firm were referred to by Janet's mother, Jane, as the "the big crooks." Another partner was John Edward Smith, who asked Reno to serve on the board of the Greater Miami Legal Services Corporation as part of her pro bono work.[26] Thus would begin Reno's parallel lifetime concern with legal aid for the poor.

At Steel, Hector & Davis, Reno had clients like Southeast Bank, ITT, and FPL.[27] Trial work was a great contrast to her recent administrative duties. Reminiscing about working on the bank case, Reno noted that one gets so involved, so engaged in every piece of what is akin to a puzzle that the case becomes "part and parcel" of you. The ITT case involved a property assessment issue. Reno won, but the verdict was appealed and ITT ultimately lost. The most meaningful part of that case, according to Reno, was meeting the opposing lawyer, "Miss Kate" Walton, one of the first women to be admitted to the Florida Bar. Walton was famous for representing Zelma Cason in a case involving her right to privacy against Marjorie Kinnan Rawlings, the author of *The Yearling*, who had represented Cason in an unattractive way in the novel. Cason did not like the portrayal, and ultimately settled on $1 in damages. Reno noted her approval of Walton's defense of privacy. Walton replied, however, that it was "the dumbest thing I ever did . . . nothing violated it [her privacy] as much as we did" [by pursuing litigation].

It is important to note that even while Janet was building her career, she was developing close friendships with a variety of interesting Miamians. Alan Greer and his wife, Patricia Seitz, were two of them.[28] Greer graduated from junior and senior high school in Miami, and from the U.S. Naval Academy in Annapolis. After service in the Navy, he attended the University of Florida where he obtained his law degree. His career involved forty-six years at Coral Gables's Richman Greer Professional Association, which he helped to found. His first encounter with Reno was on the racquetball court at the home of Sandy D'Alemberte, where Greer and Reno became regular partners. Described as a fierce competitor, even if not highly skilled, Reno, then working for State Attorney Richard Gerstein, was the one to whom Greer turned when he discovered a discrepancy of some $500,000 in the books of Miami's Cedars of Lebanon Hospital. The president of Cedars, Sanford Bronstein, was soon prosecuted, convicted of theft, and sent to prison. At least in this instance, private and public law worked smoothly together.

Patricia A. Seitz was the daughter of Army General Richard Joe Seitz. Like many military "brats," Seitz lived in several places growing up, but she stayed in Manhattan, Kansas, long enough to graduate with a bachelor of arts degree from Kansas State University. She then moved east to earn her law degree from Georgetown University, earning tuition money by serving as a Supreme Court reporter for a Dallas newspaper. After graduation,

Seitz clerked in Washington, DC, and expected to go to Florida the next year with her boyfriend. When they broke up, she decided to go to Miami anyway. Although she had several interviews, no offers came her way. Further, her interview at Steel, Hector & Davis came about only by chance—she impressed someone at a dinner party one evening and was invited for an interview that did not pan out. Back to Washington she went. Sometime later she happened to meet D'Alemberte who encouraged her to come back for another interview; he explained, "Two years can make a difference in hiring." She did and it had. While Reno was the first woman partner at Steel, Hector & Davis, Pat was actually its first woman hire. Firm partner Sandy D'Alemberte did play an important role in the hiring and promotion of women in the firm, but equally important was "forward looking" John Edward Smith.[29]

Because Seitz's specialty was civil litigation, and Janet focused on criminal cases, they were never on opposite sides of a case. They were simply friends, good friends. A friend of Janet's inevitably became a friend of the family. Thus Seitz enjoyed sailing up and down the bay and to the Bahamas with Mark. Her family and various Renos spent one dramatic Thanksgiving in the Everglades with many liquor bottles and an all-enveloping storm. During the downpour Mark and Janet were at the helm of one of the two boats; Janet's only request: "If the boat goes, save the tin of chocolate chip cookies." Often a weekend afternoon would be spent on the Reno porch singing, reading Kipling, and, inevitably, drinking.[30]

During the time both were at Steel, Hector & Davis, Janet had been deputized to "help" Pat in her new role at the prestigious firm and would come by to serve as coach. While insightful, Janet's help was often direct and succinct. One day Pat was wearing a three piece gray suit with a red shirt. Reno commented, "On the mannish side don't you think?" Another day it was, "I have been hearing that you come across as insecure. You need to project confidence." As the two sat together, Pat began to cry. But Janet's was tough love. After Alan proposed, Pat asked Janet what she thought. Reno had two questions: "Is he your best friend?" and "Does he tingle your toes?"[31]

Seitz practiced law in Miami for more than twenty years and, in 1993, became the first woman president of the Florida Bar. In 1996 with Reno's urging, Seitz accepted a position as director of the Office of Legal Counsel in the Office of National Drug Control Policy in the Executive Office of the

President. Her boss was General Barry McCaffrey. Having had a three-star general for a father, Seitz was probably the only staffer who was unintimidated. After eighteen months, with the support of Attorney General Reno and Florida Senator Bob Graham, President Clinton appointed her a U.S. District Court judge; she served until 2012.

Two other close friendships formed during this time were with Janet Canterbury and her daughter Elly. Janet Canterbury, a Miami physician and faculty member at the University of Miami, also lived in a rural setting. Hers included a host of birds and animals and a nontraditional family. Canterbury, a feminist activist, saw many of Reno's actions as feminist, although Janet Reno regularly insisted that she did *not* speak for women, but for all citizens—women, homosexuals, Blacks—and described her "side" as the law. Thus, when Operation Rescue came to Miami to try to close down abortion clinics, Reno sent buses to arrest the many, disruptive protesters. They were taken to the Orange Bowl where Reno gave them a stern lecture, ordering them to leave Miami and "never come back." Canterbury, who knew the family well, noted that while Reno never talked about her dad, she worried about her mother's drinking and her long walks alone on the beach. Canterbury loved the weekend afternoons with her friend, noting that Reno's sense of humor was excellent—but more as a listener rather than as a raconteur.

Canterbury's daughter Elly remembers worrying about what to do when she grew up, and was advised by Janet C. to have a talk with Janet R. about the possibility of becoming a lawyer. Reno's response was that one can "do good anywhere you go. . . . It can be in the law, but it doesn't have to be." She also remembers that Reno always had time for her friends and took time for such mundane but important things as teaching Elly how to play first base. Elly smiled fondly when remembering Janet's proclamations and essays about the need for a shorter work week—she who worked a minimum of twelve hours a day![32]

Private practice lasted less than two years for Reno. This was because her old boss, Richard Gerstein, announced his retirement as state attorney and recommended both Reno and a current assistant, for an interim appointment, one which would last only until the November 1978 election.[33]

Gerstein was considered very, very smart, and his interest in interesting people, both crooked and not, led to many a rumor and even to *Miami Her-*

ald stories suggesting, for example, a market in fixing cases. None of the rumors were ever confirmed. Gerstein was also a promoter of women's careers. At a private meeting at his home with Reno and Edward Carhart, Gerstein had told them that he was going to retire and would be talking with Governor Reubin Askew about his replacement. Janet said "I defer to Carhart." Later, privately, Gerstein told Reno, "You've got to do it, I just don't know whether Carhart can pull the political stuff together to get appointed."[34] Deciding that Janet "stacked up better," Governor Askew appointed thirty-nine-year-old Reno as the first woman state attorney. A glass ceiling had been shattered.

Seitz was with Reno when she learned that she was to become the state attorney for Miami. In a mildly hysterical afternoon, Pat and Janet McAliley took Janet Reno wardrobe shopping for the swearing-in ceremony. Reno was just not much interested in clothes; further, even her best friends believed she could not be trusted to select appropriate, more or less stylish, clothes. Sadly, Seitz was in court defending the *Miami Herald* in a suit pursued by *TV Guide* and missed Reno's Miami swearing in.

5

MIAMI-DADE STATE ATTORNEY

Turbulent Times, 1978–1980

The day after accepting the job as state attorney, Reno went to Public Safety Director E. Wilson Purdy, who was not a fan of Gerstein's, to ask if there was any evidence that Richard Gerstein did anything illegal, and to ask that if there was, it be given to her before the statute of limitations ran out. Nothing was offered.[1]

Reno soon settled into her new office. She was particularly pleased to have Claude Pepper's congratulations as she began.[2] Her office decor reflected her passions. Photos on the wall were of her grandfather, mother, father, her aunt who was a World War II pilot instructor, a niece, a nephew, and a gorgeous color photo of a snowy egret. In contrast, Gerstein's office had featured diplomas, plaques, citations, and photos with his World War II B-17 crew. Reno's office also featured dictating equipment and chairs for staff meetings rather than straight backs and a conference table. Reno's new job also featured a pay cut of $30,000 (down to $41,000) and a weight rise—of at least ten pounds over her racquetball weight of 175.

As part of Gerstein's retirement activities, Reno wrote a letter to him dated September 28, 1978, recalling the changes she had seen in his twenty-one years as state attorney. That included an increase in annual felonies filed from 2,531 to 13,565. She noted, too, the unbelievable pressure of Florida's requirement for speedy trials accompanied by U.S. Supreme Court decisions in *Gideon* and in *Miranda* that greatly increased defendant rights.

When Janet was formally inducted as state attorney, she gave a short speech previewing how she planned to conduct her job:[3]

Miami is at a turning point. If we act together, Greater Miami can be one of the great cities of this hemisphere—a financial capital, a research center, a place to relax and vacation, a place to shop, and a good place to have and raise children.

I commit my office to A) Safe streets and homes (coordinate with police, swift and effective prosecutions, eliminate plea bargaining), B) Atmosphere for legitimate business large and small—stop encroachment of organized crime—not easy, cooperation of all, C) strict enforcement of fire and building codes, D) Progress but not at the expense of environment—pollution control, enforce zoning laws, E) Support community—whoever, whatever color, whatever language—all must FEEL AT HOME AND FREE IN THIS COMMUNITY AND A PART OF THE GOV WHICH SERVES THEM, F) Greatest Duty—make sure innocent people are not charged. Pledge all my energy and effort to work with you in continuing to build a country dedicated and *committed* to what is right.[4]

These guidelines were not quite conventional. The first difference was the emphasis on making sure innocent people were not prosecuted. The second was to ensure the guilty were prosecuted according to the principles of due process and fair play, which did not preclude taking a tough line including no plea bargaining on crimes of violence. Further, Reno recognized that prosecution of organized crime would be unending, and asserted that apparently lesser crimes like prostitution and the use of marijuana were not victimless and also merited prosecution.[5]

One example of what some might find trivial crime involved Emeterio Marino Pijiera, who ran a men's discount clothing store. His suits were extremely reasonably priced and featured tags from stores like Bloomingdales and Neiman-Marcus. Indeed, Pijiera was charged with selling stolen suits, convicted, and sentenced to two years of house arrest. Among his many customers were Dade County Manager Sergio Pereira, who purchased seven suits. He was indicted and suspended from his job, although the case was ultimately dismissed. Another embarrassed customer was John Hogan, who resigned his position as a prosecutor for the state after admitting his lapse in judgment. Reno rehired him, and he again became chief of the Felony Division.[6]

Her sister, Maggy, commented on Janet's appointment, "It's true she's too good to be true. The only failing we know is that she sleeps late on weekends." One reporter complained in an interview that Janet's tone was short. Her reply? "So far all you've asked me are questions that can be answered yes or no."

Reno's new job was demanding.[7] Her office had to review cases brought from more than twenty separate police forces as well as those brought by Metropolitan Dade County police. Further, decisions on prosecution had to be made within thirty days, and any trial had to commence within 180 days.[8] The different jurisdictions had different problems, priorities, and personalities. And, state legislature regularly imposed new policies while providing an almost always inadequate budget. There was never a moment of boredom. Still, over the years, the themes struck in Reno's induction speech would emerge again and again. Along with a commitment to tough law enforcement, there was a commitment to protect the innocent and a grave concern for children. She had emphasized both themes when she worked in the office under State Attorney Gerstein six years earlier, and she would return to these themes after her service not only as state attorney but also after her service as U.S. attorney general as well.

Reno was appointed state attorney in January 1978, but, in fact, it is an elected position, and she had less than a year before she would face running for reelection. Further, the fall 1978 election was only for a term of two years to complete Gerstein's term. If she won, she would have to run again in 1980. She did win the 1978 election against Richard Friedman by a margin of more than three to one. Indeed, after she won the Democratic primary in September, no Republican entered the race scheduled for November, so that was that.[9] In Miami, law enforcement and electioneering do not reside in separate spheres. Throughout her time as state attorney, Reno would be conscious of the election next to come. This did not make her uncomfortable, though, because she saw a commitment to justice both as her job and also as her campaign platform. "Politics" was part of neither.

Reno moved quickly after her January 20, 1978, swearing in. Trudy Novicki, with a new law degree from Vanderbilt, was her first hire.[10] Novicki stayed through her own retirement and saw many changes.[11] Reno began by structuring the office to include three chief assistants. She kept Thomas K. Peterson as her assistant for administration and for the civil and juvenile courts. Two attorneys returned from private practice: William Richey to direct investigations and manage corruption cases, and Hank Adorno who was given responsibility for criminal cases.

George Yoss, who had become chief of the Felony Division at age twenty-seven, was asked to take the position of Deputy Chief and then became Chief of Operations for seven years. Yoss, who became Reno's right hand, has claimed to have always been "whole-heartedly intimidated" by her size, her grasp of the law, her memory, her ability to synthesize data almost as she got it, and by the fact that when he inadvertently hit her in the face in a racquetball charity event, she was unfazed.

Though Yoss has called Reno strong and intimidating, in almost the same breath he described her as a "softie." Example: she ordered the hiring of a candidate whose language was difficult to understand out of compassion, and she reinstated someone she had fired twice before making the third firing final. Sometimes Yoss and Adorno actually took it upon themselves to informally suggest to less competent staff lawyers that they might want to "get out gracefully" before Reno took some action.[12] Some did. Sometime later, one of those lawyers saw Reno at an event and thanked her for pushing him out—"It was the best thing that ever happened to me." Reno was aghast/furious and severely reprimanded Adorno and Yoss for their initiative—with "popping" blood vessels.[13]

The angriest Yoss ever saw her involved another attorney and his parking tickets. Reno had directed all staff to "resolve" any outstanding parking tickets. Some nine months later she discovered one attorney who had not done so. She called him in; he "took the fifth"; Reno picked up a chair and banged it to the ground. He found other employment. Yoss, who claims he had wanted to be a prosecutor since the age of nine, had only one difference with Reno. Budgets were tight and he would have put a minimum of 75 percent of the budget toward prosecution. Reno took substantial amounts for things like victim advocates—social work to Yoss's way of thinking.

Samuel Rabin was another young attorney who had actually started trying crimes as a "certified legal intern." At age twenty-seven or twenty-eight, he became head of Major Crimes, which involved heavy responsibility. Still, he noted that while many of the attorneys were green, many were top graduates, and many came from top schools.[14] Reflecting on the purpose of law and justice, Rabin recalled a 1985 case in which a teacher shot eight people because he didn't like a bicycle repair job done at Bob Moore's Welding

Shop. Obviously deranged, the teacher fled, and a motorist actually killed him by running him down. Janet asked Rabin: "What is your position on charging the motorist with vehicular homicide?" He replied, "the right thing to do" is not to charge; she agreed.

Rabin remembered that Reno made a point of knowing every attorney personally, including much about his or her personal life. He gave an example, "How could she have known about my nephew's tumor?" At the same time, Reno was very much above mere gossip. She was always up to date and interested in her attorneys' cases, but never stepped in to take over a high profile case as Gerstein had been wont to do. She was content to let others take credit and glory. While loyal to a fault and always positive in public, she did not hesitate to privately chew one out, to "slice and dice," Rabin noted. "You knew she was really angry when she had a 'double veiner,' threw a book across the room, or simply slammed her hands down on the desk and rose to her full height."

Interested as she was in people, though, Janet lacked a capacity for small talk. Indeed, one would have to concede that Janet Reno was socially awkward and could not really have enjoyed a lot of social events, but she went anyway. Rabin said that Reno even attended his wedding, four years after he had left the office.

Another one of Janet's core staff was Dan Casey who joined her in 1981 and stayed through 1985. Although he grew up in Pennsylvania and graduated from law school in the District of Columbia, he chose to move to Miami because his wife (who had grown up in West Virginia) was Cuban. He was in the first class of new prosecutors to be recruited nationally and was shocked by the serious cases being tried by Certified Legal Interns. Miami had just been overwhelmed by Mariel refugees, and Casey discovered that its shaky economy was underpinned by a variety of illegal practices.[15]

Casey, along with John Hogan and Richard Schiffrin, became the prosecutors in what would become the famous/infamous 1984 Country Walk child molestation case (covered in chapter 6). Casey, who had previously won a conviction for the rape of a child, had become strongly opposed to having children testify in court. Thus, a new procedure was developed that involved more than eighty hours of taped interviews with children—even a nonverbal two-year-old.[16]

Casey has described the profound impact Reno had on him with her focus on "doing right."[17] That involved indicting police officers even though few convictions were won, and reviewing cases that had been won to be sure no errors had been made. For Reno, there were no shades of gray.

Reno's closest aide was certainly Hogan, whom she met at a Reno family gathering he attended as the guest of her cousin Nora Denslow. Hogan grew up in Massachusetts, received a bachelor of arts from the University of Massachusetts, Amherst, and attended the University of Miami Law School on scholarship. When Reno became state attorney, she invited him to join her. He did, and stayed nineteen years, fourteen of them in the office immediately next to hers. He followed the usual pattern by beginning in misdemeanors, moving to homicide, then to major crime. By the end of five years Hogan had become her chief assistant and would handle many thorny issues.

At the time Reno was sworn in as state attorney, Shay Bilchik was already serving as an assistant state attorney. He would become chief of the Juvenile Division and later chief assistant state attorney, a job involving "the herding of cats."[18]

Reno's state attorney's office was a somewhat formal organization in which she assigned herself the tasks of policymaker and administrator rather than that of courtroom prosecutor. Indeed, she was famous for a (dreaded) little black notebook where she kept track of events and commitments. Thus, if she was promised a memo by a certain date, that promise was recorded and performance expected; errors were to be explained in writing to her.[19] One early and crucial task was recruitment. Turnover was high.

This was because some sought the job to gain experience and planned to leave in three to five years due to the relatively low salaries. It may also have been exacerbated by some who found Adorno cocky and abrasive. In addition, Ed Carhart, who had hoped to be given the position, and a set of his supporters chose to leave.[20] In all, Reno had the opportunity to, and responsibility for appointing about 20 percent of her staff in the first few months. She made a special effort to hire both women and Black attorneys.[21] Indeed, Peterson and Yoss were specifically assigned the task of recruiting Black attorneys. They visited Howard and Southern, Columbia and New York, as well as schools in Boston and Detroit. Seven new graduates were recruited.[22]

Reno began with a staff of some ninety attorneys, each of whom she would soon be able to greet by name. In addition, the support staff numbered almost three hundred. That year the budget was $4.5 million, and the office handled some fifteen thousand felonies. Today the same Miami-Dade office includes a staff of three hundred lawyers and nine hundred support staff. Its budget is approximately $9 million, and it is led by Katherine Fernandez Rundle who was Janet Reno's longtime assistant.[23]

In her first several months in office Reno made a number of headlines. She was appointed to the Council for Prosecution of Organized Crime; she began a controversial crackdown on organized bingo;[24] she served, as has many an ordinary citizen, on a jury in a civil trial; and she subpoenaed hundreds of people in an investigation of the use or misuse of some $160 million of Comprehensive Employment Training Act (CETA) funds. Although the University of Miami had suspended two football players for assaulting a Jewish employee by tossing him into a lake, Reno chose to file charges against them, charges which could bring them a year in jail.

Another early initiative involved the enforcement of housing codes. Rundle was given the assignment. The approach was not the usual misdemeanor charge and a fine of $500. Instead, decrepit properties were declared a public nuisance and repairs were ordered. Rundle even charged the Dade County Housing Department, which managed twelve thousand units. Result? The department was reorganized, and a ten-year plan for rehabilitation costing $150 million was put in place.

The one embarrassing headline involved the dismissal of charges against a number of juvenile offenders, because the Juvenile Division failed to file charges within thirty days following arrest.[25] The Juvenile Division was promptly reorganized.

Carol Ellis's service on a blue-ribbon jury gave her and other jury members the opportunity to meet with Reno every Wednesday over a period of six months. The jury's issues included things like the drug death of a woman, and a pastor whom two children said "put his dick in my p—sy." The jury experience led to a fast friendship between Ellis and Reno who sometimes stopped by the Ellis home on her way back from the office. The two often celebrated their birthdays together since they were only a week apart, and the Ellis children loved a visit to the Renos and the trampoline there.[26]

Reno sometimes said to Ellis, "Let me run this scenario by you." Or, "Tell me the truth, not what I want to hear." Sometimes their conversations turned personal. Ellis once asked Reno if she missed not being married, and Janet responded, "I miss not having a shoulder to put my head on when things are tough." Ellis also recalled that before Reno was to be sworn in as state attorney, Ellis was able to talk her into coming to her home for a proper haircut. After a certain amount of persuasion, Janet also agreed to have her eyebrows plucked—undoubtedly a never before and never again event. Later, when Ellis was leaving her husband, no Miami lawyer wanted to represent her in a divorce proceeding. Janet sent a Christmas card saying, "You have an appointment tomorrow." She had arranged legal representation.[27]

Janet Reno consistently won her elections for state attorney. After her earlier loss for the state legislature, she said, "I lost because I was too busy decorating my office." The lesson? One should be "running every day," thus, she always responded to autograph seekers because they gave her the message that she was "doing something right." But, also important to note, because Reno did not base her decisions on opinion polls, her popularity would fall in the future.

A typical Reno workday went like this: Up at 6:00 a.m. Thirty-minute commute to office ahead of the rush hour, avoiding a serious delay from her Kendall home to town. First order of the day (7:20 a.m.) was tutoring in Spanish. Even though she had studied Spanish in school, Reno and many others found that Miami's Cuban Spanish was very rapid. Further, the last syllable of words tended to go unused. Her morning would involve a review of the most important cases. Lunch was likely to be both spare and at her desk. Afternoons involved staff meetings, follow-up on little black book items, constituent meetings, phone calls, and scheduling of and attendance at public events. At about 3:00 p.m., Reno, like many Miamians, would get a second wind thanks to a cup of Cuban coffee (very small, very strong, and saturated with sugar).[28]

The state attorney is not just a lawyer, but also an elected official; thus, public appearances, community meetings, and speeches were very much a part of Reno's new routine. Her list of memberships and honors grew steadily.[29] Often she attended evening events. Further, she would sometimes return to the office to work late into the night. Friends claim that she kept a sleeping bag there for nights when she worked too late to face the drive home. Although she did not list her home address, Reno did list a home phone number, and often answered her office phone herself.[30] She believed direct contact with the community—her constituents—was important.

While she had a relaxed demeanor and displayed a sense of humor among family and friends, she projected a serious, no-nonsense personality at work. She was her mother's daughter, after all, and she was fully capable of aggressive questioning, of raising or dramatically lowering her voice, of glaring down from her towering height, and, also, of voicing unladylike profanities. She had a capacity for anger—one loyal staffer remembered Reno throwing a pen at him and severely lecturing him while a reporter listened just outside the door.[31] She disdained excuses. It was far wiser to acknowledge a mistake than to try to explain or justify one. Organized, intense, sober, but at the same time caring, straightforward, and principled, Reno's style was very different from that of her predecessor, the colorful and "out there" Gerstein. Some found her too stiff, at least in public, too solemn, too righteous, too exacting; others became loyalists.[32]

Tom Peterson, who was her chief assistant for administration, later became a senior judge. In 1966 he had come to Miami from New York City and Columbia Law School as a VISTA volunteer. He has described the Miami justice system then as almost a caricature, a system run by White men in straw hats and smoking cigars, White jail officers, and Black defendants—a southern system in an international city.[33] He also became involved in a pretrial release program for poor defendants in the Office of the Public Defender, and in the creation of a juvenile justice system—previously, fifteen-year-olds could appear in adult court for even small thefts.

Judge Seymour Gelber, then chief assistant state attorney under State Attorney Gerstein, had hired Peterson for his first real job in 1971, that of creating a Pretrial Intervention Program. By the time Reno became the state attorney, Peterson had been promoted to chief assistant state attorney for administration, and Reno retained him in that position. In an effort to reduce the number of juveniles who even entered the justice system, Peterson took a leave to work in Miami housing projects. His proactive activities included establishing a childcare center, a grocery store, and some health and recreation programs. The efforts garnered a great deal of local support and attention from *TIME* and the *New York Times* as well. Peterson then became a Circuit Court Judge, where he adhered as closely as possible to his motto "Hug a kid; that's where it begins." He and Reno continued to share their concern for juveniles.[34] Among his continuing projects were Troy Academy for delinquent youngsters and Teen Cuisine at the Juvenile Justice Center. Yes, he has said,

Janet was a stiff campaigner—relatively shy and gawky, especially as compared to her predecessor Gerstein, and also to her gregarious sister, Maggy, but she was also a perfectionist, ethical, committed, honest, and loving.[35]

In November 1978, Janet won the special election. Voters may have liked her, but the press was not so laudatory. In "Reno: Year One," Robert Hardin wrote an assessment in the *Miami Herald* after she had only been in office for 120 days. Probably drawing on interviews with supporters of Carhart, Hardin described Reno as tall and imposing but with no criminal experience. Specifically, he wrote, "Reno was innovative, determined and highly flappable. Her temper was already legend." He described her not as Cinderella but as an Alice in Wonderland rushing about to set things right in a chaotic world. Some judges, Hardin wrote, were critical. "When she sets out to solve one problem, she creates two others." Another judge noted "Janet has always thought of this as a business of solving problems. It's not. It's a matter of surviving them." Reporter Hardin noted that no critic was willing to go on the record. Also, some judges did give Reno passing marks. One said that the county was very thin on competent people who would take so much responsibility for so little pay. Another commented, "Frankly, I'd be scared to death of who might be in there if she weren't."

Interestingly, Hardin sent Reno a twenty-five-page draft of the article he had originally submitted to his editor. He wanted her to note that the tone of his original piece was quite different from the one published, and he hoped that he had not lost her "good will." It was true. Many interesting—and humanizing—items had been omitted from the article. One was that two weekends a month were reserved for family excursions, and on several days during the week she saw friends. Also, there was a discussion about her status as an "eligible bacheloress" in which Reno acknowledged that she was currently dating. Reflecting, she went on to say that when you marry your heart should go "bong"—but one should be intellectually happy too. She said, "I want someone who can boss me around—no, not boss me, but not let me boss him around." Hardin also asked Reno: "If the man who waves the magic wand said 'Okay, Janet, here's the perfect man for you and here's the job,' which one would you take?" And Reno replied, "I'd say, 'I prefer to get married.'"

Reno responded to Hardin six days later, "A good writer should do as he thinks right and not fret about criticism."

Another interesting discussion among colleagues concerned conviction rates. Reno concurred with other authorities that no more than one in one hundred charged with a crime was innocent, but acknowledged that twenty to thirty in that one hundred went free. The reason? Human frailty, inefficiency, incompetence, corruption—all more likely in a system overburdened and underfunded. She noted that she had asked the legislature for a budget increase of $300,000. Instead, a new funding formula put her state attorney's office at fourteenth of twenty for funding! Result: those personnel who left were not replaced, and there were no raises for assistants. Another Reno initiative involved direct filing—having an assistant state attorney file instead of waiting for a judge to decide whether a police officer had sufficient cause for an arrest. This was an effort to speed up the process and to weed out "junk cases."

Reno's honeymoon was short. Almost immediately she was confronted with a drug case that led to a conflict with federal law officers, and another case that roiled the Black community and resulted in riots. Those riots lasted three days, claimed eighteen lives, and destroyed $100 million worth of property. The Miami riots came later than many other urban riots, but were among the most destructive and costly of them all. Both events turned an unwelcome national spotlight on South Florida.

Miami drug crimes were, on the one hand, local; on the other, they were national, because Miami was a port of entry and a site for transshipment north. The Video Canary case was one of several in which local and federal officials found themselves at odds.[36] In that case Miami wanted to slowly build evidence in order to arrest and convict a whole network including top criminals. Its key players were an informant, Ron Braswell, and Martin Dardis, who was working undercover from Reno's office. Although Reno went to Washington and worked out a set of guidelines to ensure her Miami office's work would not be impeded, the local officer in charge of Drug Enforcement Agency (DEA) operations believed that the first order of business was to keep drugs off the street. In fact, that officer once threatened to arrest undercover Dardis if he engaged in such activities as helping to unload drugs from a plane; Reno returned the threat. Ironically, the operation would be blown when Reno's office mistakenly issued a search warrant revealing Dardis's identity. Even so, enough evidence had been collected that some sixty-two dealers were caught, tried, and convicted. Among them were Augusto "Willy" Falcon and Salvador "Sal" Magluta.[37]

After serving short sentences, Falcon and Magluta ran a spectacularly successful cocaine business for more than a decade. They were, however, arrested again in 1991, but were acquitted in 1996 by a jury whose foreman had been bribed. That discovery finally led to the conviction of the pair on a variety of charges. Falcon struck a deal and received a twenty-year sentence; Magluta's was 205 years. Ultimately, several of the 1996 jurors and lawyers were also charged with crimes. The national TV audience probably did not realize how close the TV series *Miami Vice* was to Miami's reality.

Miami citizens did. Some, led by Alvah Chapman,[38] formed Miami Citizens against Crime to lobby Washington for support and more federal resources. Vice President George Bush whose son, Jeb, would later become Florida's governor, had an important role in the creation of the multiagency South Florida Task Force [on drugs] that worked well with Miami authorities. Together they began to corral Miami's "cocaine cowboys" who had rocked the city with a drug lord's July 1979 shoot-out at Dadeland, one of Miami's major shopping malls. There would continue to be many arrests and convictions for drug related crimes, but the drug business could not be put out of business, and Black citizens would continue to feel they were not protected by the police.

In January 1980, Willie T. Jones, a White member of the Highway Patrol, molested an eleven-year-old Black girl. The case did not become public until later that year. When it did, the Black community saw Jones's treatment as insufficient. He was allowed to resign from the force, had to undergo psychiatric treatment lasting four months, and had to pay for psychiatric treatment for the child. A larger public agreed that the punishment did not fit the crime, and in July 1980 Jones was indicted for civil rights violations by a federal grand jury. He fled the country before he could be arrested.[39]

But there were other things that angered the Black community. In February 1979, five White, plainclothes officers raided the home of Nathaniel LaFleur searching for drugs.[40] Two men were in the home, schoolteacher LaFleur and his son Hollis. They thought the officers were robbers and resisted their entrance. The officers broke down the door, beat the LaFleurs, trashed the house, and charged 5'5" Nathaniel with battery on a police officer and resisting arrest. No drugs were found. After two months of investigation, Reno announced that the officers had gone to the wrong house by mistake, but had committed no crime. There would be no prosecution. LaFleur sued for $3 million, was offered $50,000, but when the case went to court he was awarded only $20,000 by the Dade Circuit Court. Many, including the county's Community Relations Board, were highly critical of Reno's decision not to prosecute and described the community as "a smoldering volcano."[41]

A September 1979 case involved twenty-two-year-old Randy Heath. Heath was killed by Hialeah police officer Larry Shockley after Heath stopped his car to urinate against a warehouse wall. Heath's sister witnessed the event. Shockley first said Heath had resisted arrest; but during the formal investigation, he said the killing was an accident. The police department announced that Shockley had been suspended without pay pending further investigation. In fact, he was not suspended, and two months after the shooting he actually received a merit increase. Five months after the shooting, the Dade County grand jury cited Shockley for negligence, but found no criminal wrongdoing.[42]

In November, (Black) County Commissioner Neal Adams was arrested for running illegal bingo games.[43] Convicted, Adams got probation, but lost his seat on the County Commission. Then in December 1979 came the arrest of Arthur McDuffie. A Black insurance executive, McDuffie made the mistake of zooming by a police car on his cousin's borrowed Kawasaki motorcycle. A chase ensued. McDuffie stopped. He signaled surrender but was surrounded and thoroughly beaten by a group of White Metro-Dade officers. Indeed, he was so badly beaten that he went into a coma and died five days later. The Metro-Dade officers on the scene tried to make it look like an accident and reported it as such to their superiors.[44] An investigation was launched. Three officers, including the son of a high-ranking police official, were given immunity and gave testimony about the beating. Five White officers were charged with manslaughter and with falsifying reports.

The defense won a change of venue to Tampa. It then eliminated all Blacks and all women during jury selection. The result, then, was an all-White, all-male jury. Moreover, one of the defense lawyers was Ed Carhart, who had only recently lost the appointment as state attorney to Reno.[45] While describing his relationship with Reno as "cordial," Carhart noted that Reno was an exceptional politician with friends in both the legislature and the governor's office. And, though an admirer, he thought she did not evaluate people well, in other words, was a "softie."

While public attention was focused on the McDuffie arrest and the ensuing trial,[46] yet another incident created an uproar in the Black community. It involved "the gold plumbing caper." The story, which went national, was told in some detail by Calvin Trillin in the *New Yorker*.[47] Johnny Jones, a Black man, was the charismatic, popular, and highly successful Miami-Dade Superintendent of Schools. The story involved an attempted purchase by Principal Solomon Barnes (also Black) of some $9,000 top-of-the-line plumbing fixtures using a school district requisition. The fixtures were said to be destined for Jones's new vacation home in Naples, Florida. Alternatively, they were said to be incorrectly ordered for a plumbing course being taught at Barnes's high school. Carol Cherry, a manager at Bond Plumbing Supply, not only notified school district officials, she called a local TV station. To the White community this was just another case of a public official skimming the public coffers. To the Black community it was an unwarranted takedown of one of its most influential members. Jones was convicted of second degree grand theft and sentenced to three years in prison and five years of probation.[48] Jones appealed. One of the grounds was the exclusion of all potential Black jurors from the jury. In February 1985, the 3rd District Court of Appeal granted Jones a new trial.[49] In July 1986, Reno decided not to retry Jones on the plumbing case because key witnesses refused to cooperate.[50]

The McDuffie trial came to an end on May 17, 1980, shortly after Jones's conviction. All the police officers were acquitted in spite of testimony by three fellow police officers and thorough preparation by prosecutor Hank Adorno.[51] Before the day was over, Liberty City (then the largest Black neighborhood) erupted. Cars were torched, stores looted, windows smashed, and three Whites passing through the neighborhood were pulled from their cars and beaten to death. Overtown and other Black neighborhoods soon rioted as well. For three days mobs raged. The Metro Justice Building was surrounded even as hundreds of those arrested were being processed inside. National Guard troops were eventually able to control movement, and a curfew was imposed for the whole county. The toll was eighteen dead—ten Black citizens and eight Whites—hundreds injured, and more than a thousand arrested. Damages were estimated at $100 million. The Miami riot had come late—compared to violent protests in the 1960s in other cities such as Baltimore, Cleveland, Detroit, Los Angeles, Minneapolis, Newark, New York City, Omaha, and Philadelphia—but it was devastating. Many called for Reno's resignation.[52] She refused. Reno believed that in every instance she had conducted her duties responsibly. She argued that a limited number of rioters should not be able to force an elected official from office. Moreover, Reno pointed out, citizens would have the opportunity to vote her out of office in only six months. They didn't, but, of course, Blacks were a minority, so even if they were unanimous in opposition to her candidacy she could have won.

Reno never apologized for the conduct of the trial or for other actions by her office, but she spent hours with different members of organizations in the Black community. She explained the duties and practices of her office and noted that ten of her staff attorneys were Black. In retrospect, Reno believed that part of the problem was trying the case in another city—that if the trial had been in Miami, and advocates for conviction had been in the courtroom and seen the difficulties in proving who had done what and why, or if there had been gavel-to-gavel TV, people might have accepted the verdict.[53]

The night of the McDuffie riots, Reno stayed at the Ellis home. The day after the riots, she took to the streets. Looting continued and buildings were still burning. Reno went to meetings in "dangerous" neighborhoods refusing to wear a bulletproof vest or to take an armed deputy with her, and did not feel scared, but she was concerned.[54] She attended an evening meeting at the Caleb Center in downtown Miami, which lasted until after 11:00 p.m. Her participation and responses there were something of a turning point and taught Reno that if you run into a difficult situation "talk, explain, lecture, talk with action *when* it is appropriate." She continued to ask groups for suggestions, followed up, and reported back on action taken—or, if not taken, explaining why.[55] The riots did not change Reno's focus so much as emphasize the importance of action not promises.[56] Following the riots, Marvin Dunn, a Florida International University professor and community organizer, had called for Reno's resignation. She replied that to do so would contribute to anarchy, that in a democracy, elections were the way to remove people from office. Much later Dunn admitted that he was glad she hadn't followed his advice.

People were upset. Why had this happened? On May 22, 1980, Governor Bob Graham appointed a special committee to investigate the riots. Its report was scathing.[57] Chaired by Irwin J. Block, a partner in Adorno and Yoss, the Vice Chair was James Burke, a young, Black attorney recently the head of the local NAACP. The one Cuban on the committee, Jose Villalobos, wrote a "concurring opinion." He did not dispute or disagree per se, but wished to emphasize that the large number of Cuban immigrants and their economic success were not responsible for the state of affairs in the Black community. Other members were: John H. Gibson, a Black, middle-aged Air Force veteran; William Meadows, a Black minister; Phyllis Orseck, a Black woman active in community affairs; Sandra Sears, a White administrator in the Jackson Health system; and Henry K. Stanford, a White administrator and president of the University of Miami.

The committee's principal finding was that the genesis of the riots was "the failure of society to change the conditions and attitudes which lead to injustice, hatred and lack of compassion, despite the clear warnings of the necessity to do so."[58] The report stated that poverty and unemployment made it impossible to "pursue happiness" and to enjoy "life" and "liberty."[59] The committee reported that government housing went unrepaired, that codes were not enforced in private housing, and that even some high school graduates were functionally illiterate. The report emphasized the widely held perception that the criminal justice system did not provide justice to Blacks, specifically citing the cases of Highway Patrol officer Willie Jones involving his molestation of an eleven-year-old girl and only receiving probation, the grand jury's refusal to press charges against officer Larry Shockley's killing of Randy Heath, and, of course, the McDuffie trial. The report was specifically critical of State Attorney Reno for not acting on the Shockley case herself, in other words, letting it go to the grand jury, when she judged that in fact, the officer had been guilty of manslaughter and, probably, perjury. In the McDuffie case, it criticized Reno for failing to oppose the change of venue and for the prosecutor's failure to interrogate prospective jurors for racial bias.

The report hoped that with its new leadership the county would increase the number of Black police officers, examine possible bias in promotion exams, and consider improvement in community relations through foot patrols and projects like Police Athletic League (PAL) programs. It urged the city, which also had a new chief, to consider programs like PAL and to increase a "street presence." The report then expanded its scope to call for recreation facilities, to critique the use of multi-member election districts, jury pools that included only voters not citizens in general, gerrymandering, evictions before new housing was available, welfare that "enslaves" because any earnings reduce benefits instead of encouraging more earning, and, finally, White backlash.

The committee held eight days of hearings. Reno testified at three of them. One day she was the sole witness. Members were clear that they did not believe that she, personally, was racist, but they did believe that she did not understand the community's perceptions of the justice system, that the community noticed when prosecutors used challenges to remove all Blacks from a jury, that a police officer in the Nathaniel LaFleur suit against the Dade County Public Safety Department refused to take a polygraph or to waive immunity, that there were only seven Blacks out of more than one hundred assistant state attorneys, and that forty Blacks had applied for that position.[60] Reno responded vigorously. She activated a program for the recruitment of Blacks. And she increased her practice of explaining often and publicly the actions her office took and why. It would take time, but ultimately Reno would be seen as a friend of the Black community.[61]

There was a second report on the riots—a more academic one. Governor Bob Graham, the *Miami Herald,* and the U.S. Commission on Civil Rights supported an investigation by Robert Ladner, a former University of Miami research scientist who in 1975 had founded the Behavioral Science Research Corporation. Ladner's study, titled "Community Attitudes and Riot Participation in the Miami Riots of 1980: Social Change, Ethnic Competition and Urban Conflict," began by outlining the dramatic changes Miami had undergone in the two decades preceding 1980. The study noted that the population grew from 1 million to 1.7 million and that the .7 was composed of 700,000 refugees. Further, 40 percent of the population were now Spanish speakers. And while the first refugees were largely White, wealthy, and educated, and while those arriving from 1965 to 1973 were largely middle class, in 1980, the year of the riots, Miami was overwhelmed by the arrival of the generally lower-class Mariel immigrants. For about six months beginning in April 1980, a flotilla of some 1,700 boats had brought an estimated 125,000 Cubans to Miami. Many were younger than earlier Cuban arrivals, and some had been released from jails or mental facilities.[62] The refugees arrived with little in a city recovering from riots and without a lot of capacity to absorb them. Many of the 1960 Cuban immigrants, who were accustomed to and expected a variety of government services, were not enthusiastic about the 1980 newcomers whose arrival accompanied a dramatic increase in a variety of crimes. In fact, because of that increase, the state attorney's office soon doubled in size, and Katherine Fernandez Rundle's career advanced rapidly.[63] One problem was that the new state attorney's job, prosecution, was not a standard law school course. On-the-job training was required, as was support even while the new attorneys were trying cases. Fortunately, Stanley Marcus was soon appointed U.S. Attorney, and the federal and state prosecution systems began to cooperate—especially in the disposition of drug cases. While the state tended to keep murder cases, drug charges related to the same case were often tried in the federal system.[64] Reno often sent armed, "career" criminals to the federal system as well.[65] There they would receive longer sentences than in a state court.

Miami in 1980, then, was stretched and stressed, but the rest of the country seemed pleased to have the amiable Ronald Reagan assume the presidency, and to have Iran and Iraq, both anathema to the United States, at war with each other.[66]

6

MIAMI-DADE STATE ATTORNEY

Building Community, 1981–1992

While Miami's law enforcement demands seemed infinite, Reno did not fail to notice national and even international events. She endured presidential victories of Ronald Reagan and George H. W. Bush, but rejoiced at the appointment of Sandra Day O'Connor to the Supreme Court and was thrilled by astronaut Sally Ride's flight into space.

She was dismayed by Florida's failure to ratify the Equal Rights Amendment (ERA), even though she had written at least one legislator urging support, and was further disappointed when the ERA failed nationally. She wrote Secretary-General Yuri Andropov and later to Ambassador Anatoly Dobrynin, and to U.S. senators and representatives urging that Jewish activist Josef Begun be allowed to emigrate to Israel. She witnessed the U.S. invasion of tiny Grenada, possibly for reasons other than those stated, and the end of the Iran/Iraq War. The Hubble telescope was launched, and the United States and the Soviet Union concluded a chemical weapons treaty. (President Mikhail Gorbachev was forced from office shortly thereafter.)

At home Reno joined an Advisory Council of Barry University, noted the beginning of the Florida lottery, saw the opening of Metrorail, and witnessed the failure to convict U.S. District Court Judge Alcee Hastings of racketeering.[1]

And, of course, Miami would have another major hurricane—this time Andrew—which featured 165 mph winds and destroyed more than 25,000 homes. Because many Cuban families lived close to one another, whole extended families became Andrew's victims.

As we delve into particular actions taken by Reno in this period, it is worth repeating that her public persona was serious, direct, often abrupt, and she felt no need to conceal anger.[2] She didn't try to use the press, and she refused to be used by it. Indeed, she was quite capable of rudely dismissing and/or correcting a hapless reporter. She did, though, honor Florida's sunshine laws. Martha Musgrove, a senior member of the *Miami Herald*'s editorial board, said that Janet in a rage could make the phone melt in your hand—but that she never held a grudge—business would resume the next day.[3]

Reno weathered but probably did not enjoy her first several years as state attorney, ten months as a gubernatorial appointment, and after running unopposed in the 1980 election, two years remaining in her predecessor Gerstein's term. As noted, those years included drama and not a few mistakes. During Reno's tenure violence, corruption, and relationships between the Black community and the police, and to some degree between the police and Reno, were problematic.[4] In December 1982, over a decade after the 1968 Liberty City riots, police officer Luis Alvarez shot and killed Neville Johnson Jr., who was in a video arcade when Alvarez entered to check for narcotics. Alvarez confronted, then shot and killed Johnson, saying that he believed a gesture made by Johnson was to reach for a gun. In May 1984 after a fifty-seven-day trial before an all-White jury of three men and three women, Alvarez was acquitted in a mere two hours.[5] The Johnson family had asked in advance that there be no violence when the verdict was announced, and police deployed and sealed off Black neighborhoods once the jury began deliberation. Thus, there was no repeat of the Liberty City riots, but many in the Black community continued to see the police as armed and dangerous.[6]

Reno was up for election again that fall, 1984, and although she won the primary, challenger R. Jerome Sanford got 71 percent of the Black vote.[7] In the general election that followed, Jose Garcia-Pedrosa, a Cuban Republican, chose to run as an Independent hoping to secure a significant number of Black votes. Reno and Garcia-Pedrosa competed in more than forty debates, giving him ample exposure. Further, the *Miami Herald* endorsed Garcia-Pedrosa, strongly criticizing Reno.[8] Reno had less money and fewer endorsements than her opponent, but she ran an old-fashioned campaign spending hours shaking every hand she could find, including those of a group who had moments before been taunting her by chanting "Reno must go!" Reno won with 40 percent of the Hispanic vote, 72 percent of the Anglo, and 74 percent of the Black vote.[9]

In 1988 her opponent was John Thompson, an activist focused on violence, especially in video games. In one debate Thompson actually handed Reno a piece of paper asking her to check one of three boxes: homosexual, bisexual, or heterosexual. Reno crumpled the paper, put her hand on his shoulder, and is said to have told him, "I am only interested in virile men. That is why I am not attracted to you." Thompson filed a police report claiming battery; the governor appointed a special prosecutor who quickly dismissed the case, but periodically Thompson would assert that Reno was a lesbian.[10] Later, Thompson was ordered by the court to have a psychiatric exam. He passed, but in 2008 was disbarred for "cumulative misconduct."

Reno easily won the contest with Thompson with more than 60 percent of the vote, and this time with the endorsement of the *Herald*. Reminiscing years later, Reno remembered that she began her new term by calling in each lawyer and administrator and asking: "If you were me, what would you do to improve this office"? She took careful notes and incorporated many of the suggestions. She also noted the importance of holding people accountable—in "a fair and respectful way." And, after full notice being able to say, "You've got to improve. Here's how."[11]

Shortly after the 1988 election, the Black community was again protesting police conduct. The 1989 Super Bowl had been held on January 22 in the new Joe Robbie Stadium, and the city and officials had relished the opportunity to flaunt its January sunshine on national TV.[12] The national news was less focused on Miami's sunshine than on another "death by cop." Liberty City erupted.

On January 16, 1989—Martin Luther King Day—a Miami police officer had shot and killed a speeding Black motorcyclist, Clement Lloyd. His passenger, flung from the cycle when the driver was shot, also died. The officer, William Lozano, was convicted on two charges of manslaughter—and his own partner testified against him. However, an appeals court ruled that even though the trial was held some ten months after the shooting, the jury might have been influenced/intimidated by the rioting. A second trial was held in Orlando, and Lozano was acquitted.[13] Also important, the appeals court ruled that no evidence related to police procedure or training could be submitted. During training, officers were specifically told *not* to shoot at a moving vehicle, Lozano had clearly done so, but the jury was not to know this contravened his training. Subsequently, Lozano was fired for violating a police rule that force be used only as a last resort.[14] John Hogan, Reno's right hand, expressed hope that in the future the community would act with restraint to incidents involving the police so that it would be possible to try cases at home, that is, in Miami.

After the 1980 Arthur McDuffie shooting and before the 1989 Clement Lloyd shooting, four on-duty officers had been charged with shooting unarmed Black men. One of them, Officer Robert Koenig, was convicted and jailed.[15] Nevertheless, officers continued to kill suspects.

Meanwhile, drugs continued to flow.[16] In 1981 three assistant prosecutors and three secretaries were arrested for dealing cocaine inside the Metro Justice Building! Another shocker was the arrest of senior DEA agent Jeffrey I. Scharlatt, who was charged with and soon convicted of bribery and obstruction of justice.[17] In 1982 a shipment of $100 million worth of cocaine was discovered in a hangar at Miami International Airport.[18] Some estimated that, because of increased federal efforts, only 75 percent of shipments rather than 85 percent of cocaine shipments were getting through. In a Catch-22, though, the increased arrests overwhelmed the justice system, and Reno finally announced that Florida courts would no longer prosecute federal arrests.[19] The state legislature did give Miami a 1982 boost with a 35 percent budget increase for Reno's office.

Miami's economy was booming, a fact generally attributed to trade and foreign investment. Few openly acknowledged the obvious: drug money was a, if not the, major player in the city's prosperity. Describing Miami as a rogue city, *Harper's* magazine noted that in New York or Washington one asked: "What does he do?" In Miami one asks: "What does he *really* do?"[20]

A *Miami Herald* reporter captured the city's attention by asking eleven civic leaders to provide a twenty dollar bill from their wallets and had the bills tested for cocaine; ten showed traces of cocaine. Among those bills were ones offered by Reno, Jeb Bush (then chair of the Dade County Republican Party), and Catholic Archbishop Edward McCarthy.[21]

A new danger emerged in 1985—crack—a more addictive, violence-inciting, cheaper, and easier to produce form of cocaine. In one twelve-month period, $9 billion worth of cocaine was seized. Profits were tempting enough that even police officers engaged in the commerce. At one point, a group later dubbed the "River Cops" robbed a boat carrying cocaine on the Miami River. Three smugglers jumped into the water and drowned. Their floating bodies provoked enough of an investigation that the role of the police officers was uncovered. They were arrested, tried, and three were convicted—although it took two trials to do so. Another twelve were later convicted of a variety of crimes. Expanded inquiries led to another eighty officers arrested or disciplined.[22] The police needed policing.

In 1986 Reno headed a statewide task force on the cocaine problem. Its recommendations for greater penalties and more prisons—and also for more education and more drug treatment centers—proved too expensive for the legislature and Governor Bob Graham, although the governor did provide money for more prison cells. So did his successor, Republican Bob Martinez. The murder of two police officers by an early parolee had reinforced public support for long sentences and more prisons.

The fact was that Miami was under siege.[23] It was possible to arrest two hundred people for drugs in a single night, jail them, accept a plea, sentence them to time served, and release them in a day or two since there was "no room in the inn." In 1989, with the support of community leaders like Alvah Chapman, who was chairman of Knight Ridder, a special Drug Court was established for the purpose of separating out first time offenders.[24] They were given treatment, counseling, and even job training—all under a watchful eye and subject to random drug testing. Those who successfully completed the program had all charges dropped. The program was so successful it was expanded to include those with more than one arrest and even some charged with felonies. In the early years, more than 90 percent of first time offenders completed the program. The expanded program succeeded with some 60 percent of offenders. The expense of the program was roughly a third of what it would have cost to jail an offender. The program was duplicated all around the country.

It is important to understand that not only did much crime go undetected but also detected crime often went unpunished. One glaring example involved Operation Tick-Talks.[25] That assignment involved close to a year of undercover work and more than fifty arrests including teachers and accountants. The catalyst was an anti-Castro activist/terrorist and drug dealer informant named Ricardo Morales. The operation got its name from a microphone implanted in a clock in the home of Rafael Villaverde. When the clock accidentally fell from the wall, authorities had to act quickly. They had high hopes that they would be putting a host of major players behind bars. Because Morales was considered of doubtful credibility, the case depended principally on the clock evidence. But Circuit Court Judge Gerald Kagan ruled that evidence inadmissible. The wiretaps, he said, were prematurely authorized and rested on an informant with suspect motives. The charges were dismissed.

Miami was not only awash with drugs, it was also awash with guns. State Attorney Reno urged legislators 1) to license gun owners as a car is licensed, including a test on knowledge and proficiency, 2) to register guns, and 3) to require a seven-day waiting period between the time a gun was purchased and the time it was delivered to the customer. The latter was intended to provide time for a check to ensure the purchaser was not a felon, an illegal alien, addicted to a controlled substance, or not eligible for gun ownership for some other half dozen reasons. Reno made her arguments for control over and over again including to groups like the Coalition to Protect Citizens' Rights, which saw no need for such legislation. The National Rifle Association (NRA), though, packed more punch than a mere state attorney, and the Florida legislature ducked regulations.

However, eight years later in 1990, a statewide campaign, "Cool It Florida," was successful in putting one issue on the ballot. This called for a waiting period (but only of three days) between purchase and delivery of a pistol. The referendum passed with 85 percent of the vote.[26] While this might seem a minimal restraint, the Florida Department of Law Enforcement reported that in the first three years, the waiting period made it possible to prevent 27,000 people with criminal records from legally acquiring weapons. It was also possible to identify seven hundred people with outstanding warrants who were arrested when they came back to collect their purchases after the waiting period.[27] Late in Reno's tenure as state attorney, an eighteen member grand jury issued a report urging not only licensing and registration but also liability insurance for gun owners. The report noted that from 1985 to 1992, there had been an average of 337 deaths in auto accidents and 474 by firearms. Florida legislators took no heed, and this time the public was not given an opportunity to act by referendum.

Today Florida is considered one of the more permissive states when it comes to citizens and their guns. First, restrictive local laws are specifically prohibited; gun control is defined as a state issue. Second, Florida was the first to pass a "stand your ground law" in 2005, although now roughly half the states have the same or a similar law. Third, Florida issues licenses for "concealed carry." There are, though, many places in Florida where one may not "conceal carry." These include courts, polling places, and schools; the legislature is regularly lobbied, however, to reduce these exemptions, in particular, the school exemption. Currently, Florida does not restrict certain assault weapons or the size of magazines, nor is there any duty to inform a law enforcement officer who has stopped you that you are carrying a weapon. Ironically, though, Florida is one of only a handful of states that actually prohibit open carry. Florida's law has been upheld several times, but gun enthusiasts have not given up. In July 2017 a writ was filed asking the U.S. Supreme Court to hear the case for open carry. It did not succeed. By 2020 exactly half the fifty states permitted open carry.

Drugs and guns issues may be with us always, but a wide variety of cases, some quite singular, also landed on Reno's desk. For instance, one entailed a fracas involving Saudi prince Turki bin Abdulaziz. The prince had purchased a home on Indian Creek Island and energetically plunged into Miami social life, including making donations to local institutions and organizations. But police were told that an employee of the prince was being held in what amounted to slavery.[28] An investigation ensued.[29] While no "slave" was found at the prince's condominium, a noisy and physical confrontation ended with counter lawsuits by the Saudi family and by the police who said they had been assaulted. After three weeks of furor, the U.S. State Department gave the prince and his family retroactive diplomatic immunity, although the prince clearly was not a diplomat. Further, a splendid dinner honoring the prince was held in Washington, DC, that included Defense Secretary Casper Weinberger, top State Department officials, retired admirals and generals, and members of Congress including Senator Strom Thurmond.

There was another "only in Miami crime"—actually a category called "Agriculture Crime"—and Reno specified that all such cases should be so stamped and copied directly to her. Further, she decreed that no resolution of such crimes was to be reached by negotiation without the approval of both the victim and the arresting officer. (A resolution could be reached by a guilty plea before a judge.) One such case involved two men carrying fishing rods who were arrested at 4:38 a.m. in an avocado grove. Their car, strangely enough, contained burlap bags, and nearby was a pile of such bags containing eight hundred pounds of avocados! They were charged with trespassing and grand theft.

Another headline-worthy incident involved Cuban baseball player Jose Conseco, who was charged with aggravated battery on his wife for allegedly ramming her BMW with his Porsche. He ultimately received probation and community service, but that would be but one of a number of arrests on a variety of charges that, along with steroid use, would mar Conseco's athletic career.[30]

A top crime fighter and a prosecutor has many roles including lobbyist, future political candidate, and future law partner. But some would attribute to Reno another, less usual, role for a prosecutor: social worker. Arguably, Reno saw her role as that of advancing justice, although some might say she would interpret that role rather broadly and project it further into the future than most. Also, Reno's first commitment was to *truth*, which emphasized the importance of not convicting the innocent and also of not obtaining an untrue confession to a lesser crime by threatening the death penalty or a long sentence for a more serious charge. It is true, though, that in arguing for a focus on *fairness*, Reno often spoke to the importance of "affirmative action from the git go" by providing excellent public education and health care to every child. Neither were characteristic of Miami. But Reno would present these themes many times in a variety of venues.

Thus, Miami's chief prosecutor, Reno, took on child abuse, child support, domestic violence, and even slumlords. Raw sewage, leaky roofs, or exposed wires could bring a landlord a fine of $500 and up to a year in jail. Such penalties, though, were considered little more than an annoyance to many property owners. Thus, Reno employed a new tactic: to declare slum property a public nuisance and to require actual repairs; and the repairs would be required even if the property was transferred to a new owner. To Reno it did not matter who the owner was. Indeed, she took on the largest owner of deteriorating property in Dade County—the Dade County Housing Department.[31] It took several court orders, but the result was an audit of the condition of public housing, a ten-year plan for repairs and rejuvenation, and, also important, a reorganization of the (ir)responsible agency.

But Reno did not win them all. Developers had a Miami Beach plan to use tax-backed bonds to redevelop the southern 250 acres of Miami Beach. This would displace thousands of residents and snowbirds in favor of luxury hotels, condominiums, a marina, and shopping malls. Reno's legal challenge lasted more than a year, but the Florida Supreme Court ultimately sided with the developers five to two. But not everything old disappeared as the beach developed. Just to the north some eight hundred buildings were being restored to their 1930s glamour and christened the Art Deco District.[32] It would enjoy both popularity and profitability. The *National Geographic* would describe a walking tour of the district, the neighborhood would be entered on the National Register of Historic Places, and a spirited, annual festival would be overwhelmed with crowds.

While the term "domestic violence" is said to have originated in a 1973 address to Parliament, the issue of "spousal abuse" was put on the agenda by U.S. feminist groups during the 1970s. It did not become a state legislative issue in Florida until the early 1980s. Reno's office, though, was attuned to the issues of family abuse and made the decision that prosecutions could proceed even if the individuals involved opposed prosecution. Tough, yes, but Reno also served on the board of a local women's shelter and understood that abused women might need temporary shelter, financial aid, and health care. A problem was not likely to be solved with a mere courtroom decision. Reno also put some muscle behind the collection of child support by creating a Child Support Enforcement Division. Collections doubled from 1986 to 1992.

Indeed, her efforts led to a rap song titled "Janet Reno" by Anquette that starts "In our town we have a state attorney by the name of Janet Reno / She locks brothers up for not paying their child support / In your town you may have someone just like her." To the tune of "Yankee Doodle Dandy," Anquette continues, "She caught you down on 15th Ave., you tried to hide your trail / She found your ass and locked you up, now WHO can post no bail?" Later, the lyrics state "The proof is here, it's living and breathing / And Janet Reno's makin sure that I start receiving / All the money you makin."[33] That kind of response bolstered Reno during the moments when she may have wished she had not gotten into the nitty-gritty of enforcing the small claims involved in child support, but those claims enabled custodial parents to perhaps pay the rent or buy school clothes for their children.

Janet demonstrated a concern for children in many different ways. One involved the simple matter of ensuring that they were restrained while traveling in a car, as required by law beginning in 1986. In fact, in 1991 Reno went so far as to authorize charges of vehicular homicide against a father after his child was killed in an auto accident. The mother had been holding the child on her lap when the accident occurred. Although the father was not convicted of the felony, the trial attracted a good deal of attention. Indeed, the Florida legislature reacted with legislation imposing a $150 fine and three points against one's driver's license for failing to utilize a proper restraint.[34] Also, Reno announced the creation of a "school" for violators and a fund to help purchase a car seat for those who could not afford one. While in office, Reno served as a mentor for several students in Miami's public schools—something only uncovered when her personal finances were being audited because of her appointment to be attorney general.[35]

Two national news stories about the treatment of children emerged during Reno's Miami tenure. The first featured the appalling and dramatic case of James Richardson. It was a case dating back to 1968 and from another jurisdiction, but Reno was asked by Governor Bob Martinez to review it after a stolen file revealed numerous questions about the way it had been conducted. The second case involved the abuse of children being cared for by a young childcare provider and her husband. In the first case, Reno emerged as probably bringing an injustice to light, in the second, there was a possibility that she had been part of an unjust conclusion.

The Richardson file was taken from the office of John "Red" Treadwell, a former assistant state attorney, by Remus Griffith, a friend of Treadwell's secretary, some ten years after Richardson's conviction. The file did not resurface for another ten years, when a new trial for Richardson began in 1988. Richardson, a poor, Black man had been charged with the death of his seven children by poison.[36] The state's case involved a claim that Richardson believed he had purchased an insurance policy on the children and almost immediately murdered them by poisoning their lunch of rice, gravy, and beans. At the time, Richardson had, indeed, just made a commitment to purchase insurance of $500 per child, $1500 on his wife, and $2000 on himself, although he had also suggested that he might prefer to double the amount of each premium. The agent was so pleased he had Richardson sign two applications, one for each proposal. However, since Richardson did not have the money to pay either premium, the agent said he would return with the applications in a week, take the money, and then submit the one Richardson chose. The agent's statement that made it clear that Richardson was told the policies would not be valid until after payment was never given to the defense.

At Richardson's trial, Judge Gordon Hayes testified that at the hospital, while the children were dying, Richardson told him he had life insurance on the children. However, Reverend Lemuel T. Fagan, who was White, testified that Richardson told him that they had no health insurance, but that he had taken out some insurance the night before that would become effective the following Friday when he had the money for the premium. Richardson also said he had tried to borrow money for the premium from his neighbor, Betsy Reese, who said she could not help him. Fagan's account, which contradicted Hayes, was not provided to the defense.

The third witness to testify about the insurance policy was a reporter, Richard Neelius, who talked with Richardson on October 26, the day after the poisonings. He testified that Richardson told him he had not paid the premium, but that the insurance man told him he would carry him for a few days. A fourth witness, Ruby Faison, had previously said Richardson thought he was covered, but on examination said Richardson said the insurance man would pay the premium. Faison would also tell investigators that on the afternoon of the poisoning she drove Betsy Reese home from the hospital. When she got to Reese's house, she saw children playing in the yard. Faison was alarmed because most families were in a panic about the poisoning and were keeping their children close to home. Reese, though, said she was unconcerned about any possible poisoning. In another interview on the night after the funeral, Ruby said she heard Richardson telling his mother that he didn't think whoever did this intended to kill the children. He said, "I think it was meant for myself and my wife."

Five searches for the source of the poison both in the house and in surrounding areas were made including one at midnight of a shed near the property by the sheriff himself. The next morning, however, a bag of parathion was found in that shed. A neighbor, Charlie Smith, said he had heard some folks talking on the avenue about some poison in the shed and told Betsy Reese, and the two then walked to the shed and discovered the poison.[37] The story was that Reese went inside, looked around, went back out, tore a board off the window, shined a cigarette lighter through the window, and then Smith saw the bag—he reached through the window and pulled it out. The bag was sitting approximately twenty inches from the open door, but Reese claimed not to have seen it when she entered the shed. Also, Faison said that in a conversation two or three days after the children died, Charlie Smith told her that Reese was the one who led him to the shed and that he was frightened about his involvement. Further, in notes he made in a report, Sheriff Frank Cline noted that Smith "expressed fear of Betsy Reese and says that she is a bad woman. I don't believe he would tell anything on her." Frank Schaub, another investigator, told Reno that Charlie "lied all over the place" and maybe even put the poison in the shed himself.

There was more intrigue. Reese said her husband, Johnny King, had gone to Jacksonville with the Richardsons two weekends in a row. He did not return the second weekend. Annie Mae Richardson's sister, Rose, lived in Jacksonville and some thought King was with her. A set of witnesses said Reese wanted King to come back, and one witness, Earnell Washington, said Reese threatened to get Richardson for taking King to Jacksonville—and that Richardson told him that he thought it was Reese who poisoned the children.

The coroner's jury was told by Sheriff Cline that Richardson was responsible for the death of other children in Jacksonville based on a telephone conversation with law enforcement officers in Duval County. Later, police officials said they had not released such information and that further investigation showed Richardson was not involved, and, indeed, was nowhere around when the children died.

Polygraph exams on October 31 seemed to indicate that Betsy Reese and Annie Mae Richardson were not involved in the poisoning, but that James Richardson had brought the bag of poison to the house. The investigation then focused on Richardson although 1) Reese was last to see the children alive, 2) Reese had divided the food into seven portions, 3) Reese had lied initially saying she had not been in the house, and 4) Reese was on parole for killing her second husband over his relationship with another woman. Further, her first husband died under unclear circumstances. The state's investigation of those circumstances included getting the wrong death certificate for Betsy's first husband.

Ultimately, testimony was collected from three jailhouse inmates. The first, James Dean Cunningham, allegedly approached a Black deputy to tell about a conversation with Richardson. His formal interview apparently occurred while Cunningham was under arrest for being drunk, and may actually have been drunk during the interview. Sheriff Cline did use Cunningham as a witness against Richardson, but there were also exculpatory statements made by Cunningham that were not given to the defense.

By the time of the original trial the insurance motivation was discounted by Reverend Fagan and by the agent, Gerald Purvis. Also, it seemed Richardson did not even know what parathion was. Further, Frank Schaub had asked Commissioner William Reed of the Florida Bureau of Law Enforcement for the help of experienced and competent criminal investigators. Apparently authorities thought there was not enough evidence for a trial. However, in late February, testimony was obtained from a second jailhouse witness. And then a third testified: Earnell Washington (charged with assault with intent to commit murder). His own cellmate said Washington told him he knew nothing about the case, but that he was going to use it to get out of jail, which he did after four days of interviews with authorities. Another inmate, James Weaver, gave a long interview that included incorrect information. At the trial he only said Richardson said "I killed my children," but then perjured himself by saying he had never talked to the sheriff. The defense did not know this, and the state did not inform the court of the perjury. In Reno's 1988 investigation, twenty years later, Weaver acknowledged that his testimony was false.

In sum, the original investigation was inadequate. The principal evidence was testimony by three jail inmates, one of whom recanted. Further, that testimony was not only inconsistent, it was undermined by other witnesses. Little attention was paid to Betsy Reese who prepared the children's food, although she had murdered her second husband and some believed her first husband as well! Reno's investigation recommended the release of Richardson. Its impact must partly account for the great care she took as a prosecutor to prosecute only when very certain of guilt—and never just because a conviction could be won. It must also explain the energies she devoted to the Innocence Project after she left the Justice Department.[38]

The second case involved Country Walk, an in-home childcare facility. Its story would be told in a 1986 book, *Unspeakable Acts*, and a TV movie with the same title in 1990. Still later it would become a subject for TV's *Frontline* and national newspapers including the *Wall Street Journal* and the *Washington Post*. The later accounts were strikingly different from the early ones.

Alleged child abuse at the McMartin preschool in Manhattan Beach, California, had created national headlines in 1983 and, many would later say, hysteria about abuse in childcare. The Florida case arose in Country Walk, a Miami suburb, the next year, 1984. Frank Fuster and his sixteen-year-old wife, Ileana Flores, ran a babysitting service there. Fuster could never be described as an admired and beloved neighbor. In 1969 he had been convicted of involuntary manslaughter and served a sentence. Later he was convicted of fondling a nine-year-old and was put on probation. Flores, recently wed to Fuster, was a teenage immigrant from Honduras who ran the service in their home. Crucial to building the case against them was the testimony of and videos made by two University of Miami faculty, Joseph and Laurie Braga, who specialized in the interviewing of young children and whose "Miami Method" for doing so would become well known.[39]

It all began when a mother became alarmed when her son asked her to kiss his genitals "like Ileana did."[40] The case expanded when the Bragas made extensive interviews with Country Walk preschoolers. Tapes of the Bragas' long interviews with the children provide stories of the mutilation of a bird, chants to Satan, monster masks, and the wielding of excrement and crucifixes. Snakes were put in vaginas; so were guns. "Lurid" and "horrific" are the least of the applicable adjectives. Evidence also included a test for gonorrhea of the throat of Fuster's seven-year-old son by a previous marriage. It was deemed positive, although later the (federal) Centers for Disease Control (CDC) would describe the test as unreliable and both parents had negative tests for gonorrhea.[41] But the crucial evidence was a confession by Flores. The couple was quickly convicted. She got sentenced to ten years, served three, and was deported. He received six life terms plus 165 years.

Roughly a decade later, doubts emerged. First, the fact that when Flores pled guilty she also asserted that she was *not* guilty, but was saying so only because it was "in her best interests," had been disregarded.[42] Also, before the trial Reno had visited Flores in jail several times and sat with her during the trial. Both actions were most unusual and could be construed as solace—or pressure. Information would also emerge that Flores, then seventeen but legally still a child herself, had been held in isolation, and, sometimes, she alleged, naked in a suicide watch cell.[43] In several visits to her in jail, Reno personally enlisted her testimony against Fuster declaring that she knew both of them were guilty. In contrast, a woman chaplain who met with Flores in jail concluded she was not guilty.

A 1994 sworn statement by Ileana Flores declared Fuster's innocence was crucial to an appeal by Fuster.[44] The statement, however, was soon undercut by a letter in which, under pressure, Flores denied her statement.[45] But in 2001, Flores contacted *Frontline* declaring both she and Fuster were completely innocent of wrongdoing. Her recantation of her recantation became a part of a *Frontline* report aired during Reno's campaign for governor in 2002.[46] By then, many professionals had become critical of the technique of extended interviewing used in the Miami Method, and the tone of news accounts shifted to cast doubt on the Country Walk case and similar convictions.[47]

Two other child abuse cases prosecuted by Reno were reviewed. One was that of a police officer, Harold Grant Snowden, who was accused of child abuse in 1984. He was acquitted in one case, but found guilty in a second case in 1987. More than a decade later, in 1998, Snowden was freed by a U.S. Court of Appeals, and it was decided not to pursue a new trial. Part of the court's ruling was that a statement that 99.5 percent of what children say about abuse is true had been improper and had influenced the jury. In reporting on the Snowden case, the *Wall Street Journal* commented not only on the apparently unjust conviction of Snowden but also on the effect on children subjected to extended interviews implying they had suppressed horrible events. The *Journal* noted, too, that the cases had cost insurance companies millions of dollars.[48]

In 1991 another related case, that of fourteen-year-old Bobby Fijnje who was nonetheless charged as an adult, resulted in Fijnje receiving a not guilty verdict to the surprise of many. The jury simply did not believe the children's allegations of molestation and abuse. Reno did. Nevertheless, the case was Reno's last of Miami's childcare abuse cases.

Reno was an elected official. Some charged that the Country Walk case gave a boost to her 1984 campaign for state attorney. Many years later, critical *Frontline* accounts coincided with her campaign for governor. If they boosted anything at the time, it was her opponent.

Reno's concern for children was ongoing and resulted in the extra attention she gave to juvenile offenders. While she believed in rigorous enforcement of the law, her perspective was both long range and preventive. Thus, she was responsible for the creation of a Neighborhood Resource Team (NRT) composed of a police officer, a social worker, a nurse, and a housing adviser, which first served West Perrine, a sixteen-block, unincorporated, low-income area, and later other Miami neighborhoods.[49]

In March 1990 the *Florida Bar Journal* published a special issue on concerns related to children. Reno's chapter sums up her long held views. Her piece was titled "To Protect Our Children Is to Prevent Crime."[50] Reno's argument was explicit:

For the last 20 years, this nation has forgotten and neglected its children. As a prosecutor, I feel strongly that we must renew our efforts to ensure swift and certain punishment for those who commit crime. But unless America and its people renew their commitment to their children and the family, all these efforts will be for naught.

Reno connected criminality to poverty, single parents, squalid housing, and lack of health care, but she also noted that busy, affluent parents could be guilty of neglect and lack of supervision too.

Reno argued that it was just common sense to invest in children now and save the expense of prisons later. She then reiterated some dismal Miami-Dade statistics including the following:

Twenty percent of children live in poverty.
Twenty-five percent do not finish high school.
Twelve percent of babies born in one week at a public hospital were
    born to cocaine addicted mothers.
Seventy-five percent of cases in the child welfare system are drug related.

Reno concluded, "Our true innocents—our children." "In the long run the answer . . . must lie in strengthening the American family."

Businessmen needed to be made to realize that children are society's most important form of capital. A concrete proposal? Well, Reno didn't actually recommend it, but she did note that her mother "used to spank the living daylights out of us." Reno did propose a 9:00 a.m. to 2:00 p.m. workday that would coincide with the school day. Educators, of course, were then arguing for longer days, and not even Reno's own office would countenance a shorter workday. Needless to say, the state attorney's office did not go on such a schedule, although Reno did give time off so parents could participate in their children's activities—and if one had no children, time could be taken to invest in children in another way, such as by volunteer tutoring. Still, Reno urged lawyers to direct their pro bono work toward children, and while proclaiming "a crisis exists today," she counseled patience, noting that even action now would produce results only in the next generation.

Reno continued to monitor and take part in efforts to develop a fair and effective juvenile justice system. In 1983 she served on a gubernatorial Juvenile Offender Task Force. The next year she created a full-time center for child victims in her office. In 1986 she created a Child Support Enforcement Division. In 1990 she was inducted into the Juvenile Justice Gallery of Honor. And in 1991 Governor Lawton Chiles asked her to chair his task force on social services.[51]

In a 1991 interview with *Florida Magazine* reporter Charles Fishman, Janet repeated some themes:

You have to trust people.

You have to give them support up front so they avoid crisis.

We should end the workday at 2 or 3.

We should turn elementary schools into family service centers.

Providing prenatal care to every pregnant woman is good for the state.

Fishman's article made it quite clear, though, that Reno was no bleeding heart, pie-in-the-sky official. He noted her clipped conversational style and apparent lack of a sense of humor. But he reminded his readers that while she might talk like a social worker, she is a big-city prosecutor of "sinewy . . . settler stock." Fishman summed Reno up as: "She's the law in a town filled with exuberant outlaws." Noting the abundance of gold jewelry, mahogany tans, and luxury cars in Miami, Reno pondered with Fishman the source of the money being spent.[52]

Another characteristic of Reno's administration was concern for the victims of crimes and for witnesses to crimes. Thus, a team was charged with supporting both groups.

Reno was well known throughout the state, but among professionals she had become known nationally as well. Thus, she was appointed to an ABA Special Committee on Criminal Justice in a Free Society led by Sam Dash, once a Philadelphia district attorney and made famous as Chief Counsel for the Senate Watergate Committee.[53] Edwin Meese, who believed justice was not being served by the *Miranda* and other decisions expanding the rights of those charged with a crime, had initiated the creation of the committee. Published in 1988, the committee's findings did *not* confirm Meese's, and much of the public's, suspicions of excessive leniency. In fact, the committee began its report by insisting that the public should understand that only a small percentage of criminal actions ever enter the justice system; in particular, only half of felonies do so. The committee unequivocally concluded that constitutional protections were *not* the reason for so few successful prosecutions. What it did find was that the criminal justice system was woefully underfunded and understaffed.

The committee's second major finding was that the system was overwhelmed with cases related to drugs. Janet Reno had been struggling with both issues; now the ABA committee had lent its trumpet to the two problems. Its recommendations emphasized 1) education with the belief (or hope) that support for funding would follow, and 2) further study of how best to control drugs.

An ABA Commission on Racial and Ethnic Diversity in the Profession had existed since 1984, but after the 1992 Los Angeles riots, Reno's friend and then president of the ABA, Sandy D'Alemberte appointed a special task force to specifically study minorities in the judicial system. Its findings, "Achieving Justice in a Diverse America," were made public in 1992 but not published until 1994. Not surprisingly, it urged diversity at every level of the justice system—from cops on the beat, to defenders and prosecutors, to juries and judges, too. It critiqued private firms as well as governmental organizations. And not surprisingly, given that Reno was on the task force, it emphasized the importance of examining (and doing something about) the needs of children in poverty.[54]

The committee spun off a working group chaired by retired judge A. Leon Higginbotham. That group offered a report that was expanded to include a wide range of "unmet needs" of children and their families. They included after-school programs, access to health care, and safe and clean housing. It also urged reform of the welfare system.[55] Progressive to be sure, but not as radical as the proposal Reno had put forth in the special issue of the *Florida Bar Journal* focused on children.

Yes. Janet Reno was a tough prosecutor in a county riddled with crime. At the same time, she energetically pursued and paid for programs her critics said were best left to social workers. In 1992 she ran for state attorney unopposed. By then she had held office for more than a decade and was well known and honored throughout the community.[56] But she was not to stay long. President Bill Clinton needed a woman nominee for attorney general, and Janet Reno would be his third, but winning, choice.

7

ATTORNEY GENERAL, 1993–2001

Conducting the Nation's Business

On March 12, 1993, Janet became the first woman attorney general of the United States.[1] She would, incidentally, also become the first person whose color photo would grace the front page of the *New York Times*. Reno's nomination occurred only after the Hollywood Women's Caucus, led by songwriter Marilyn Bergman and by entertainer and director Barbra Streisand, had extracted a promise from presidential candidate Bill Clinton that a woman would be appointed to lead Treasury, State, Defense, or Justice. Since men had already filled the first three positions, Clinton needed a woman for Justice.

Reno's nomination came only after two attorney general nominations of well-connected and accomplished women, Zoe Baird and Kimba Wood, were withdrawn. Baird and her Yale Law School professor husband had hired a Peruvian couple as nanny and chauffer, even though they knew they were illegal immigrants. Senators and the public were outraged. Wood and her *Time* magazine correspondent husband had hired a woman from Trinidad. They had helped her get a residency permit and did pay the proper taxes, but the Clinton White House foresaw a confirmation problem and withdrew the nomination.[2]

Soon thereafter, Reno casually mentioned to her friend Carol Ellis, "I have to get home. Bill Clinton is phoning me."[3] Why? Because her friend Mary Doyle, a Miami Law School professor, and a member of Clinton's transition team, had reactivated support for Reno as attorney general, and the president was interested in exploring her candidacy. Reno had formerly told

Doyle that her mother was seriously ill and that she could not even think about a presidential appointment. Sadly, however, Jane Reno had just died, and the day before her funeral, Doyle secured Janet's permission to propose her for attorney general.

At Jane's funeral, Reno's eulogy included a favorite nursery rhyme, "Wynken, Blynken, and Nod." She also noted that Jane "was responsible for the most excruciating moments of my life. But as I look back . . . almost all of her outrageous foolishness was directed at puncturing the pomp and arrogance of this world."[4] One condolence letter described Jane as "a force of nature, rugged, bright and a rare bird, free and an independent spirit who tried to do the right thing but in her own way." It was true. Jane had even sold an acre of the family land after retiring, and traveled—to Australia and New Zealand, the Galapagos, Greece, and Persia. Jane's ashes were scattered in the bay while family members drank and recited her favorite poetry including Shakespeare, Swinburne, and Spender.

Longtime family friend Daphne Webb happened to be the one to answer the phone when the White House called the Reno home to explore the possibility of Janet Reno's nomination as attorney general. (Reno was in the bath.) After she had called back, Daphne was told that Reno would have to leave town in a few days but she was not to tell anyone anything about the call. It couldn't be kept a secret, though. John Hogan and John Smith soon appeared at the home, and the phone began ringing, and ringing, and ringing.

Soon there was a request for someone to address possible support from women's groups; among others Anne Lewis, the former wife of Reno's former law partner, was asked to respond.[5] A hint that Reno thought a nomination might be possible was her going out to buy a winter outfit at Saks. The next day, a Sunday, Senator Bob Graham called to say he had just seen President Clinton and that Reno should be prepared to come to Washington immediately. Monday morning Reno called Saks saying she needed her new outfit, which was being altered, right away. It arrived at her office by noon. At 1:00 p.m., White House Counsel Bernie Nussbaum called inviting her to Washington and asked her to bring 1) a list of people who did not like her, 2) a list of people who did like her, 3) her income tax and medical records, and 4) an account of everything she had ever done wrong.[6] Nussbaum had instructed Reno not to let anyone know she was coming, so she had assistants buy her plane ticket, tried to be inconspicuous, and flew to Washington.

On Tuesday, Reno met with Clinton's vetting committee from 9:00 a.m. to noon. The only problem, Vince Foster said, seemed to be that she paid far too much in taxes. Reno replied that she made it a point of not doing anything "fancy" on her tax returns and that she had a 2:30 p.m. flight back to Miami. Foster replied with a smile, "You aren't going anywhere," so Reno lingered while committee members pursued any possible negatives. One probably involved John Thompson's 1988 charge that she was a lesbian and another involved the search warrant served on a member of the Saudi royal family. Foster then explained that Webster Hubbell, a close friend and former law partner of Hillary Clinton, was currently working in the attorney general's office and would like to meet with her. That proceeded well. Reno was reassured, noting that Hubbell had helped to create Arkansas's Ethics Commission and had served as State Chief Justice there.[7] In the evening, she met President Clinton himself in the Oval Office. Reno was impressed and charmed to learn that a friend from Cornell, Diane Divers, by then Diane Blair, and both a professor of political science and close friend of the Clintons, was another person who had recommended her appointment.

Then-Senator Joe Biden was chair of the Senate Judiciary Committee. He had urged Clinton to make no mistake in his third nomination—and when Reno's name came to Biden's attention, he was supportive. This, even though as Florida state attorney, Reno had testified before his committee about the creation of a national drug policy coordinator some years before, and in the hearing had chastised Biden for using the foreign sounding term "czar." Biden definitely remembered her.

The interview with President Clinton himself was followed by even more searches for a negative. Queries were made about cases prosecuted and grand jury investigations. Opponents like Jose Garcia-Pedrosa were called.[8] Her longtime mentor Sandy D'Alemberte was in Washington following an ABA meeting and soon found himself serving as her press agent as curiosity about Reno and her possible appointment grew. One lovely summary of Reno's qualities came from Florida's attorney general, Bob Butterworth, who was quoted as saying "Janet Reno's not Mother Teresa, but she's probably the closest you'll get."[9]

While the announcement of her candidacy was mostly greeted warmly, the old charges that she was a lesbian reappeared and Queer Nation members held a demonstration demanding that she "come out." The old drunk driving rumor surfaced, and the NRA announced its opposition, but most Washingtonians found the statuesque, plain, and plain-spoken woman from Florida refreshing.[10]

Foster told her to prepare for an announcement the next day, Thursday, and to "prepare some words." Reno said "Words? I haven't been offered anything." Foster replied "Well, assume that you have. But don't assume it." (It had, though, already been put out on the wire that she was being considered.) Thursday afternoon, Reno was ushered into the dining room off the Oval Office. Soon the president emerged, came up to, elbowed her, and said "Don't blow it"—her first official indication that, in fact, she had been offered the job. At the news conference that followed, crusty reporter Helen Thomas asked her position on abortion. Reno didn't hesitate: "I am pro-choice." Clinton was warned. Reno was direct and clear in her statements. She was no hedger.

The White House then began an even more thorough screening and interview process. Bank records and tax records were explored. Positions on abortion and the death penalty were queried. Persistent efforts to uncover something negative failed. A lengthy interview with the president himself was followed by even more searches for the negative.

Reno gave a short acceptance speech after President Clinton announced her nomination. It was not very law and order. At the same time that she called for "strict and certain" sentences for violent criminals, she called for diversion programs and "a fresh start" for the nonviolent. She pledged to restore civil rights enforcement as a top priority, and pledged to do "everything I can" to protect children from abuse. She said she hoped to make the law make sense to citizens and business by minimizing bureaucracy. And Reno, the outdoors environmentalist, promised to use the law to make sure "the waters, the land, and the skies of this nation are protected."[11] She concluded that she wanted to help President Clinton "put the people first." Her agenda clearly extended beyond law enforcement to one which others had long claimed mimicked social work.

The *Miami Herald*, enthused that her "unquestioned character" would restore "rectitude" to an office that had lost it under the leadership of Nixon's John Mitchell and Reagan's Ed Meese. While Reno firmly insisted that the job was apolitical, this was by no means an established tradition.[12] John Kennedy, for example, appointed his own brother, Robert, as attorney general.

Senate confirmation was next. Reno flew back to Miami to gather material for the process.[13] Again, her friends Pat Seitz and Janet McAliley helped her shop for appropriate outfits. When she returned to Washington, she underwent an intensive and extensive preparation. In particular, she needed an education on federal jurisdiction. John Smith and Trudy Novicki came from her Miami office to help in the prepping. Her Washington tutors were Jamie Gorelick and Ron Klain, now working for Clinton, but were the recent Chief Counsel for the Senate Judiciary Committee. Klain escorted her as she visited each of the committee members. Substantive discussions were held on controversial issues and on issues new to her, such as an a qui tam action, which rewards whistle blowers whose testimony leads to a conviction. Gorelick coached her on administration policies, the workings of the Justice Department, and the crucial role of career staff.[14] After three weeks of study and briefings, the confirmation hearings began.

Reno was told it was usual for family members to be present for the hearings. Brothers, uncles, and more came. In particular, Maggy came and stayed with her. Reno remembers that the two of them took a walk one night from her accommodations to the Capitol and then to the Lincoln Memorial. As Reno read the Gettysburg Address, a pigeon pooped on her. Her sister took the occasion to announce "that pigeon is doing the best possible thing for you; now you won't get too big for your britches."

In a way that relaxed Reno. She felt her previous experience working with the federal government would be helpful and decided that one theme of her presentation would be improving the relationship between the federal and local governments. A second theme she would emphasize would be prevention, especially in the face of a rising youth crime rate.

While Democrats were expected to support Reno during the confirmation hearings, it was important to be prepared for Republican queries. This meant being informed, practicing the give-and-take of a hearing, and considering how best to handle "hot potatoes." Reno *was* well informed, her handlers gave her practice in give-and-take, and Reno didn't "handle" hot potatoes, she just said what she thought. The hearings lasted several days, and much of the time was taken up by statements by senators and other witnesses. Reno's opening statement before the Senate Judiciary Committee was disarming. The theme was "I want to remember." She wanted to remember the Everglades, women, civil rights, children, and the many citizens who had touched her life and to whom she had committed herself to always pursuing justice.

On the afternoon of the third day, Reno was in the Executive Office Building watching C-SPAN when North Caroline Senator Jesse Helms proclaimed, "Now, I understand that Ms. Reno takes care of her mother and that she is an old maid. And I understand that she supports choice. . . . Well, I think she is a woman of great character and I'm supporting her although our positions don't matter [sic]." A vote was taken that afternoon, and her nomination was approved by the committee 18 to 0. The next day the Senate confirmed her with a vote of 98 to 0.[15] She was sworn in officially that afternoon and again the next day at a White House ceremony with family and members of the Judiciary Committee in attendance.[16] When Reno returned from the Washington confirmation hearings, she found her home filled with floral tributes.

Some forty family members trooped to Washington for Janet Reno's swearing in. Daphne Webb was up until 3:00 a.m. the night before preparing lists of the gathered clan and their social security numbers so they could be cleared by security. Bob Reno's daughter, little Janet, held the Bible. The ceremony was held in the White House in the Roosevelt Room. Afterward, Al Gore asked Daphne if she would like to see the Oval Office. "Yes!" she replied. Daphne did see it, but was too timid to cross the threshold. She met Ruth Bader Ginsburg at the party that followed, and Nora Denslow told Mark, "I think that guy in the corner is taking the coats." "That guy" was actually Ted Kennedy. Ann Richards came to the house where Reno was staying, but Daphne and others had no idea who she was.[17]

The ensuing celebration was briefly marred by a controversy generated by Mark over the particular beer being served: he had wanted one with a black label, and was enraged that one with a gold label had been purchased. It turned out that it was the right beer, just put in the wrong box.

Reno's appointment came late, which meant she missed the retreat and orientation for new cabinet members. Moreover, she was plunged immediately into managing the siege in Waco, Texas.[18] She had few administration contacts—and no time to develop them, even if she had been inclined to do so. She had been engaged in law enforcement for years, but Washington was foreign territory as were its ways. Except for her college and law school years, and for a year and a half in Tallahassee, she had lived where the family called home, South Dade. There she had many long-standing and deep friendships.

One involved the McAliley family. Janet, a Miami activist and school board member, was Janet Reno's age, but equally important were McAliley's children Chris and Neal.[19] Chris worked in the U.S. attorney's office in Miami on issues relating to the environment. Periodically she went to Washington on business, and on one occasion stopped by Attorney General Reno's office for a visit. Janet greeted Chris sorrowfully: "Your daddy is very sick. We have two flights booked for you to Tallahassee." Reno bought the ticket, sat on the couch with McAliley until time to go to the airport, and went there with her in her official Lincoln Town Car. Chris's father died two days later. The funeral followed in two days, and without announcement Reno "just showed up" in Miami. Reno had, in fact, been "mothering" Chris since she was a child. She taught her scuba diving and took her "frogging" and camping. In eighth grade, Chris was to work as a page in the state legislature for a week. Terrified by the flight from Miami, Chris cried en route—Reno consoled her, but also teased her about it for years afterward.

Neal McAliley closely observed Reno at work in Washington.[20] Although he thought her a micromanager and socially awkward, he also noted that she was routinely underestimated and should be credited with an authenticity often missing in the DC governing class.[21] He also noted that even though she didn't engage in Washington social life, everyone knew who she was. Neal was a Harvard College and Berkeley Law graduate. He arrived in the Justice Department five months before his "godmother" (Reno) arrived. He called her office to let her know that he was in DC and received a call back in five minutes. "Let's have dinner tonight at 701 Restaurant." Reno continued her Miami habit of ignoring proper channels and would call anyone in the chain for a briefing. McAliley clearly recalled being asked for a briefing late in the day when he had not yet had a chance to brief his own boss. And stress? She responded, "I just do my best, and, if necessary, stand at attention with my hands at my side and wiggle."

The public was curious about the new attorney general as were Washington insiders. While she was well known in Florida and nationally among members of the ABA, and even though she was a Harvard Law alumna, she was an unknown quantity to most in the new administration, to those from the other forty-nine states, and to the permanent regime in Washington—civil servants, lobbyists, members of the press, and leaders of non-governmental organizations (NGOs). A fellow cabinet member, Donna Shalala, a serious networker and people person, described efforts by herself, Alice Rivlin, and others to include Reno in DC social life, and particularly in the women's network.[22] Reno wasn't interested. She rarely attended Katherine Graham's famous dinners or even White House events if they were not obligatory.

Some six months after her appointment, the *Los Angeles Times* managed to secure an interview and then to provide an account of Reno's first steps.[23] It described Reno as "expansive and warm" and as an "indefatigable handshaker" when meeting the public. It noted her "passionate prose" offered in a soft, deep voice with a southern lilt, and that she had become a folk hero, the most popular member of, though not within, the administration. There she was seen as a lone wolf, one who took firm positions and never traded votes or gave chits to other cabinet members. She believed that her role was to be a lawyer for the people, not President Clinton's loyal soldier. Nor was Congress spared her unvarnished views, for instance, on gun control.[24] Chair of the Senate Judiciary Committee Joseph Biden once observed that "good political judgment is not her strong suit." Staffers found, as they did in Miami, that she could be brutally blunt.[25] One staffer described a meeting of twenty new political appointees who Reno was to address. She allegedly walked in, announced "we will work together as a team," and walked out—no greeting, no questions. With 95,000 employees under her direction that might have seemed an appropriate allocation of her time, but the new hires surely expected a bit more of a greeting.[26]

Her longtime mentor Sandy D'Alemberte explained to the *Times*'s reporter that Reno believed in redemption—that people could be saved. Former police officer and former prosecutor Judge Stanley Goldstein described the many "social work" programs Reno began in Miami such as the Drug Court over which Goldstein presided. An emphasis on balancing punishment and prevention, and on "certain" punishment rather than on length of punishment, were her mantras. These positions would not mesh well with Clinton's call for more police officers and for boot camp for young offenders. Further, that fall Congress would consider then approve a bill to add 50,000 more cops, to shorten the time for death sentence appeals, and to add the death sentence as a possible penalty for fifty additional federal crimes.

Once in office, Reno had a lot of positions to fill. She proposed that the president nominate, but that she have a veto, and also that she be able to make suggestions for some of the positions.[27] Confirmation by the Senate would, or in some instances would not, follow.

John Hogan and five other members of her Miami staff followed her to Washington.[28] When Reno was appointed attorney general she asked Hogan: "What do you want to do, and when are you coming?" He suggested two months; she said two days; he arrived in a week. As he entered the lobby of her office, a senior staffer queried "Are you going to like Atlanta?" Yes, he was almost immediately dispatched to investigate the shipment of large amounts of money by the CIA to President Saddam Hussein. This involved eight months of work, but no illegality was uncovered. On his return to Washington, Hogan became Chief of Staff. Hogan returned to Miami to Chesterfield Smith and Holland and Knight just before the Monica Lewinsky and Elián González dramas. His later work involved the defense of major corporations facing a variety of federal charges.

One failed nomination of a Department of Justice (DOJ) staffer was that of University of Pennsylvania Law School Professor Lani Guinier as Assistant Attorney General for Civil Rights.[29] A graduate of Radcliffe and Yale Law School, Guinier had served in the Civil Rights Division of the Justice Department during the Carter administration and worked in the NAACP Legal Defense Fund during the Reagan administration. The stumbling block came from the interpretation of some of her academic writing in which she discussed "race-conscious" districting and other possible ways of ensuring participation of minorities. Her arguments and the uproar were too much even for Senators Ted Kennedy and Carol Mosley-Braun. Both urged Clinton to withdraw the nomination, and he did. A second choice for the same position, John Payton, was also withdrawn. Although civil rights organizations initially supported Payton, a number of Black members of Congress were incensed by his "noncommittal" response related to the issue of the new Black majority, electoral districts—from which a number of them came. He also had to acknowledge that for years he had not exercised a rather hard won right—to vote!

Another withdrawn nomination was that of Gerald Torres to be Assistant

Attorney General for Environment and Natural Resources. Torres would have been the only high-ranking Hispanic at DOJ. While some disliked his writing related to "critical theory," the main difficulty was the Federal Bureau of Investigation (FBI) case involving two of his former associates for fraud. Torres did accept a position as deputy assistant attorney general in the division and also served as counsel to Reno.

Reno announced the appointment of her top team in early April.[30] The appointments included Webster Lee "Webb" Hubbell from Hillary Clinton's Little Rock Rose Law firm as associate attorney general and link to the White House; Carl Stern, longtime NBC law correspondent, as director of Public Affairs; Drew S. Days III as solicitor general; and Philip Heymann as deputy attorney general. Heymann, however, quit within months of assuming his position. He was succeeded by Jamie Gorelick, who was, in 1997, replaced by Eric Holder who, in 2009, would become the attorney general for President Barack Obama.

Heymann's departure was announced at what the *Times* called an "extraordinary" joint news conference. He and Reno agreed that there was a lack of "chemistry" and that differences in style prevented effective functioning as a team. They agreed that there were no significant philosophical differences and that there was no precipitating incident. Insiders said that Reno's habit of keeping many balls in the air and checking on each regularly through notations in her little black book frustrated and embarrassed Heymann, whose assignments often weren't completed as soon as she expected.[31] Heymann, a Harvard Law School professor, had held important positions in the Kennedy, Johnson, and Carter administrations and had eagerly accepted the position as number two at DOJ assuming that he would be the department's policymaker. Under previous leadership he had enjoyed near independence, but apparently he lacked the flexibility/ability to work for a very directive boss.

Philip Heymann violated the norm for quiet departures.[32] Immediately after resigning, he publicly condemned the administration's proposed crime bill. Less than a month later, he gave the *Los Angeles Times* an interview discussing the attorney generals he had known: Robert Kennedy, Griffin Bell, Ben Civiletti, and Janet Reno. While commending Reno for adding the dimension of prevention to considerations of violence, and for emphasizing the importance of giving every child a "chance," he wondered if an inspiring vision would yield an effective program. He also made it clear that there was a "lack of structure" for the relationship between the White House and DOJ, which he found a very ineffective and often a demoralizing way of working.[33]

Jamie Gorelick was then working in the Pentagon. When she was asked to consider moving to the attorney general's office, one of the people she contacted was Heymann. This led her to discuss with Reno just what her responsibilities would be and just how the office would be organized. Things would have to be different.

Under Gorelick's direction, a DOJ news summary was issued daily consisting of key articles from the *Wall Street Journal, New York Times, Washington Post, Washington Times,* and *USA Today.* Typically, the summary covered some dozen topics with three to ten items for each topic. The full articles were attached so there could easily be more than fifty pages to read. There was also a "Weekly Supplement" that included items from other sources. Gorelick's top staff of about a dozen would meet twice a day. Those meetings were informal, jokes were made, and hierarchy ignored.[34] Gorelick's relationship with Reno was relaxed enough to be able to tease her about always wearing pastels and to call her "sweet," which Reno would inevitably deny. When they were discussing a knotty issue, one of them would often ask: "What would our mothers think of that?" Reno thought often of her mom; and, perhaps, felt she was fulfilling some of her mom's own dreams. Gorelick, like others, emphasized Reno's interest in children and recalled her spending the White House Easter Egg Hunt reading *Voyage to the Bunny Planet* to a rapturous circle of children. (The Bunny Queen in the book is appropriately named Janet.)

Another sticky wicket involved the director of the FBI, William S. Sessions. Sessions, a Reagan appointee, was midway through a ten-year term.[35] On the day William P. Barr left the office of attorney general, he presented the report of an internal ethics investigation begun during the summer. It was provoked by a copy of a letter from author Ronald Kessler and by an anonymous letter accusing Sessions of a variety of illegal behavior, for instance, charging the government for the cost of a security fence around his home and for flights to visit relatives. It was even alleged that he kept an unloaded gun in the trunk of his car so that it could be claimed as a full-time law enforcement vehicle; this yielded a significant tax benefit.[36] Sessions had not been favored by George H. W. Bush's Attorney General Dick Thornburgh, and his relationship with Thornburgh's successor, Barr, was not much better. Further, his style and priorities were not appreciated by many of the FBI's old hands.[37] In his long career, Sessions had been considered a straight arrow, a Boy Scout.[38] He was considered and believed himself to be a man of exceptional integrity. He believed he had followed the rules in every instance, and that a proper investigation would clear him of any serious wrongdoing.

It was Janet Reno's responsibility to consider the report and take action, but as soon as she was sworn in, she was confronted with the aftermath of the (first) World Trade Center bombing and the ongoing siege of the Branch Davidian compound near Waco, Texas. Not long after, the FBI uncovered a plot to bomb the United Nations, and the Holland and Lincoln Tunnels. And then there was a neo-Nazi plan to spark a holy war in Los Angeles. Thus, there was a substantial delay before Reno could examine the 160-page report on Sessions and decide on the proper course of action.

Reno herself was fastidious, even hyper-meticulous, about ensuring that nothing could be construed as favoritism or inappropriate in her dealings with others. Bad luck for William Sessions. Ultimately, she came to the conclusion that Sessions would have to leave and made an appointment to see him.[39] She spoke with him about the charges and indicated that he should resign. He refused and was fired by President Clinton the next day. At a press conference, Sessions, who clearly believed he had been doing his job and doing it well, spoke vigorously about the importance of an independent FBI and said he would continue to speak about the need to protect it from both internal and external efforts to politicize it. Later, Reno would find herself sturdily resisting what she believed were efforts to politicize her own office.[40]

Reno made herself available to the press once a week—a rare practice among her fellow cabinet members. While she was as closemouthed about issues being worked on as she had been in Miami, the weekly meetings kept her well up on what was on the mind of the press and presumably on the mind of the public. Reno also gave many a talk, and they were purposeful. Messages were delivered. For instance, on November 5, 1993, eight months into her "incredible adventure," Reno addressed CIA personnel telling them she believed a new spirit was afoot. She noted that *TIME* magazine had written such a positive article about her that her brother-in-law had sent her a banana advising her to go the middle of Pennsylvania Avenue and "carefully execute my descent from grace in a controlled fashion." More seriously, she noted that Watergate continued to cast a long shadow, and that Congress had been creating new programs, then telling states to take them over without financing them, and that the states then passed the responsibility on to communities, which left citizens "with their backs to the wall." Reno often emphasized the importance of federal agencies working together at the community level, remembering that in Miami they were "spitting" at each other. In a talk December 14, 1993, at a national conference on Organized Crime/Drug Enforcement, she again emphasized that there must be an end to turf battles and announced that Louis Freeh of the FBI would lead an Office of Investigative Agency Policy to make that happen.

When she became President Clinton's attorney general, Reno would be an energetic supporter of the Brady Handgun Violence Prevention Act. That act was named for James Brady, an aide to President Ronald Reagan, who was severely injured in 1981 during an assassination attempt on Reagan. Congress did pass an act, but it had only one provision—a five-day waiting period between purchase and delivery of a handgun. Further, the provision was to expire at the end of five years. The argument was that by then computers would have access to such comprehensive records that an instant check on a purchaser's record would be possible. At a press conference, Reno urged licenses for handguns analogous to driver's licenses, as she had proposed early on in her career, and again stated her opposition to the death penalty, although she had, in fact, had occasion to request it. During a Q&A, Reno was told that there were stories that she was "overwhelmed" and "not fully in charge." "Not true," she answered. Asked what surprised her most, she replied, "Nothing really," in her usual abrupt way. "Any goal?" "To explain the work of DOJ in 'real words' not 'government gobbledy gook.'"

In a December 13 speech, Reno addressed the fact that court proceedings cost too much and took too long and that the ABA itself said that many defendants had no access to representation. In addition to funding, Reno suggested the possibility of training non-lawyers to fulfill the role of representation in some kinds of cases. At another event, the National Newspaper Association's Governmental Affairs Conference on March 10, 1994, Reno specifically asserted her commitment to open government and to a new policy of "presumption of disclosure." She also noted that trying to respond to 600,000 requests a year was expensive and a burden. Still, she said, she was committed to change but noted that it would be a bit like turning an aircraft carrier—slow.

A first step toward that change, she said, would be to include a copy of the Freedom of Information Act in every employee's next paycheck. Further, responsiveness would become a part of an employee's performance rating. Because a huge backlog existed, she asked reporters to focus their requests and assured them that DOJ would expedite items of exceptional interest. Reno went on to note that in Miami she had had no press officer, and returned all calls herself. Her newspaper father had taught her the importance of the press, although in confrontational moments she occasionally had to remind herself that the press was just "doing its job"—an important one. She concluded by saying that she hoped that when she left office, the department's relationship to the press would be one of "respect, openness, and mutual regard."[41] In a March 16, 1994, talk at the National Press Club, Reno declared disclosure "the new norm," that she hoped she was living up to her father's standards, and would the press please stop reporting that she wrestled with alligators!

While Reno's investigation of fellow cabinet members (and President Clinton) may have made her something of a pariah at cabinet meetings, her independence made her something of a hero to others, especially DOJ career staff who cherished her independence. Reno's interest in a challenge to Virginia Military Institute's exclusion of women, in protection for abortion clinics, in motor voting, in enforcement of the American Disabilities Act (ADA), and in nondiscrimination in lending was real. In the last two instances the DOJ took care to publicize its legal action in order to get others to voluntarily change their behavior. Similarly, her efforts to get federal, state, and local law enforcement to cooperate with each other, and her championing of gun control and drug courts were important to her but not particularly visible to the public. Nor was the significant amount of time she was engaged in international travel and negotiations.

The press gave some year-end coverage to Reno. *Vogue* featured a photo by Annie Leibovitz of Reno's hands in an August 1993 article titled "The Unshakable Janet Reno," *USA TODAY* (January 28, 1994) proclaimed it "a rocky first year" citing the resignation of Philip Heymann, a *New York Times* article quoted career lawyers as questioning her competency, a *Washington Post* article described "disillusioned supporters," and a CBS piece called her a "loose cannon." She was, though, credited with tightening immigration rules, integrating agencies such as the FBI and DEA, and announcing guidelines to ensure employees were not discriminated against.

Bill Clinton's summary of Janet Reno on a *Larry King Live* episode was: "She's got a steel backbone, and she understands what really works." On the upside, Sara Lee Corporation gave Reno a "Frontrunner" award that year. The other winners were poet Maya Angelou, Lorraine Hale, and Linda Alvarado. A serious mark of Reno's success was the clue "Janet of Justice" in a *New York Times* crossword puzzle.

Reno's years in Washington did not lead to any improvement in what others saw as her fashion sense. Even after her Washington years, an April 15, 2004, *Washington Post* column by Robin Givhan rhapsodized over the appearance of those testifying before Congress about the September 11 terrorist attacks. Givhan described the men as displaying the conscientious grooming of a television anchor or job applicant, freshly starched, and every hair in place. She described Condoleezza Rice's beige career suit and Madeleine Albright's stern black blazer. And then there was Reno and her "fashion subversiveness." "Frumpy," Givhan wrote, "is too simple a description. Her suit was the color of mud—the sort of soft muck formed by rain water and ashy city soil. Her jacket hung loosely, and the skirt reached midcalf. No scarf, no jewelry. Her small, wire-rimmed glasses were of the sort covered in full by a typical health insurance policy"—but Givhan did detect a possible use of geranium pink lipstick.

Reno's nephew, Douglas Reno, tells a story about one of her visits back from her post in Washington. The family went to Joe's Stone Crab Restaurant where there was a long, long wait anticipated. Janet Reno sat down. Douglas whispered to the maître d,' who quickly ushered them to a table. When they entered the room, those dining stood in recognition and approval.[42] Douglas noted that she relished her DC job, but remained very much herself, saying to Senator Orrin Hatch, who was interrogating her during a Senate committee hearing, "Senator Hatch, you don't have to be so harsh." Douglas also noted that she spoke at his 1999 Firefighter graduation ceremony. After expressing her respect for those who responded to chemical or biological attacks, to violence and tragedy as well as to fires, she repeated what was almost a mantra: "I love this city, I love its people, I love what it means to so many. It means hope, and freedom and opportunity."[43]

While Reno had several pressing issues on her plate/desk, drawing from her experience she established several priorities.[44] One was developing partnerships with state and local law enforcement agencies, in particular concerning violent crime. In developing the DOJ agenda she invited members of the Senate Judiciary Committee to attend meetings—and they did. Her emphasis on cooperation came from experience of gangs operating across jurisdictions and engaged in local, state, and federal crimes. The goal was not to just pick off the low hanging fruit, it was to use a variety of charges in a variety of jurisdictions to incapacitate a whole criminal operation. Further, Reno consistently emphasized that prosecution and conviction are important, but law enforcement also had to focus on prevention and on the causes of crime. Reno had long been familiar with crime: petty crime, major crime, organized crime, white collar crime, juvenile crime, international crime—Miami had had it all. As attorney general she found that the country seemed to think *it* had it all too. Congress's response was the bipartisan 1994 Violent Crime Control and Law Enforcement Act.[45]

The bill provided funding for 100,000 new community police officers and $9.7 billion for prisons. While it provided $6.1 billion for crime prevention, and while there were some limitations on the manufacture of assault weapons and on high capacity munition magazines, and while there were funds for domestic violence hotlines and women's shelters, and while victims of crimes were authorized to speak at the sentencing of their assailants, the thrust of the legislation was for more enforcement and more severe punishment. For example, the death penalty was attached to some sixty crimes, the "three strike" law called for life in prison without parole for those convicted of three felonies, fifty-two new offenses were subject to the death penalty, and children as young as thirteen could be charged as adults for certain violent crimes. It also ended the practice of letting prisoners apply for Pell grants to support work for a college degree.

Reno had no qualms about being a law enforcer, but she also strongly supported efforts emphasizing education, prevention, and rehabilitation. Thus, she joined forces with Secretary of Commerce Ronald Brown and Secretary of Health and Human Services Donna Shalala in efforts to fight drugs. This included support for the expansion of drug courts such as those she had established in Miami. And, while the 1993 Brady Bill had imposed background checks and a waiting period for gun purchasers, Reno, with her usual focus on juveniles, asked the Division of Juvenile Justice and Delinquency Prevention to prepare a report on how to reduce gun violence.[46] The division was led by Shay Bilchik, who had been Reno's chief assistant for administration in Miami and came to Washington with her to continue his work on juvenile issues. *Promising Strategies to Reduce Gun Violence* was issued in 1999. The report noted that in the United States every day 93 people die of gunshot wounds and an additional 240 are wounded. In 1996, 54 percent of gun deaths were suicides and 41 percent were homicides.[47] The report noted that 25 percent of American adults had a gun. It then provided a series of "profiles" from a set of U.S. cities where people seemed to be doing something right. Listings included Seattle's safe gun storage and Maryland's Shock Mentor Program in Prince George County. The idea was to provide a "toolbox" for communities to adapt to their own situation.

Happily Reno found DOJ had resources she never had in Miami; it was a veritable gold mine.[48] She also marshaled the energies of leaders in the Centers for Disease Control,[49] Health and Human Services, Education, and Labor. And she mobilized the talents of women within DOJ such as Jamie Gorelick, her deputy attorney general; Doris Meissner, commissioner of the Immigration and Naturalization Service (INS); Ellie Atchinson, head of her Office of Legal Policy; and Lois Schiffer, who headed Environment and Natural Resources. Reno rarely talked openly about advancing women per se, but did feel women had a special faculty in staffing and in implementing situations. An example, she thought, was the leadership that women in the Civil Rights Division provided in investigating the church arsons in Tennessee and Alabama in the mid-1990s.

Reno's department also served as an enabler for the work fellow Floridian Carol Browner was doing as head of the Environmental Protection Agency. One example was the prosecution of Royal Caribbean Cruise Line for pollution, which ended in conviction and an $18 million fine.[50] A second example involved charges under the Clean Air Act against the Tennessee Valley Authority (TVA) and seven other electric utility companies for failure to install the best pollution control technology. In that case a final resolution was not reached until 2011.[51] Another case involved the elimination of the use of Freon, which was believed to be destroying the Earth's ozone layer. Freon is the commercial name for a chlorofluorocarbon organic compound also known as CFC. The DOJ won eighty convictions and collected more than $58 million in fines.

While Doris Meissner was doing an excellent job, immigration had been and continues to be a thorny issue. During Reno's day, the focus was on illegal immigrants crossing into the United States along the southern border. She emphasized that the United States is a nation of immigrants and asked: "Why do we draw the line now? Fences and armed patrols won't solve the problem. People need to come to make money to send home—and we need them in a variety of industries. Further, they need to be able to turn to law enforcement when they are victims." One example of the latter she indicated was victims of domestic violence. Under Reno, the process for achieving naturalization was cut from twenty-eight months to six. Almost seven million immigrants applied for citizenship—more than in the previous forty years combined![52] At the same time, Reno was committed to enforcing the law, which meant repatriating thousands of illegal immigrants. Indeed, after changes in the immigration law in 1996, there was a four or fivefold increase in the number of detainees and returnees. A principal focus was the essentially open southwest border.

Janet Reno appeared to bear both external and internal criticism with equanimity. Perhaps she was assisted by a piece of needlework in cross-stitch that hung on her office wall, capturing a quote from Adlai Stevenson: "The burdens of office stagger the imagination and convert vanity into prayer."[53]

Reno approached something else with equanimity—a diagnosis of Parkinson's. She had noticed a slight shaking of her left hand during the summer of 1995.[54] In October her doctor gave her the diagnosis. She spent three weeks learning all she could about her condition and concluded that it would not interfere with her work. Thus, on November 16, she called Clinton's Chief of Staff, Leon E. Panetta, to alert him that she would be announcing her diagnosis at a news conference later that day. (She didn't think she should "bother" the president himself with the news.) She noted that she felt fine and that she was taking Sinemet, which controlled the hand shaking, and when asked if "strain" increased the symptoms, noted that the shaking had actually ceased while she was testifying during the Waco hearings. She noted that Parkinson's would not interfere with her weekend walks along the Chesapeake and Ohio Canal, and that she had thus far covered 72 of the 187 miles—115 to go!

The response was rapid and remarkable. Within days, she had received some 250 personal letters to which she sent handwritten responses. They came from across the country: from Chicago and from Tallulah, Louisiana, from the mighty and the low, from intimates and strangers. Many sent prayers, others said "me too" and thanked her for her announcement on behalf of her (500,000 to 1,000,000) fellow sufferers. One of the latter was Harvard law professor Louis Loss who wrote "Welcome to the club!" One came from Edward Carhart and another from Congresswoman Pat Schroeder. In her response to Schroeder, Reno noted that the Congresswoman had been the very first to offer support when her nomination as attorney general was announced.

The wife of Mo Udall wrote; the Chief of the Rochester Police Department wrote; a member of Nichiren Shōshū wrote, saying that while the organization was "not politically correct" it had some remedies to recommend. Sheila Anthony wrote: "You showed your usual spunk in meeting adversity head on, and I've no doubt you'll get the better of Mr. Parkinson before it gets the better of you. I'm in awe of your courage." While Reno was not churched, she did write some letters similar to the following: "I look to God for my strength and I pray. My Presbyterian grandmother used to say that God helps those who help themself [*sic*] and I am trying not to let him down."

There were a host of letters offering cures or at least relief. Some like that from "certified spiritual healer" Gene Whipp gave testimonials to his healing powers including his capacity to provide a protective aura to surround a woman threatened with violence by her husband. Susan Ward of the Holistic Animal Center of Arizona offered three or four remedies. Donald Rose diagnosed "electro striction" and sent a crystal set to deal with the "migration of magnetically charged fields." Tara Deane urged Reno to explore the Science of Ayurveda in Kerala, India, noting that British royalty, oil sheikhs, and even Dr. Deepak Chopra had found help through Ayurveda. Stanley Levin from Hawaii recommended a pallidotomy by a Swedish neurosurgeon and attached accounts from the *Wall Street Journal* (February 22, 1995) and *Neurology* (vol. 43, nos. 1–7 [1993]). One wrote a passionate letter about the costs of medicine for Parkinson's, saying her great-aunt had to set aside more than a third of her monthly $850 income for medicine. Others lamented the low level of federal funding for Parkinson's, arguing that in 1994 Parkinson's allocation was only $30 million while that devoted to multiple sclerosis was $158 million and to HIV $1 billion.[55] Reno answered them all.

But the focus, as always for Janet Reno, was work. Ninety-five thousand employees! A budget of $17 billion! A lot to administer. As others had done before, and at the urging of Jack Brooks, who was Chair of the House Judiciary Committee, Reno's office had asked all ninety-three (largely Republican) U.S. attorneys to submit their resignations. But replacing them took time. Vetting was time-consuming, so priority was given to the most important districts, for example, to the Southern District of New York where Mary Jo White was quickly confirmed. The process continued for some time under the management of the assistant attorney general in the Office of Policy Development. Also, an Attorney General's Advisory Committee of U.S. attorneys chaired by Tom Korbut was important to establishing priorities—and to raising issues of concern to the attorneys.[56]

Reno did a bit of reorganizing. By 1996 the Department of Justice organization looked like this.

There were five bureaus under Reno: the U.S. Marshals Service, the Federal Bureau of Investigation, the Federal Bureau of Prisons, the Drug Enforcement Administration, and the Office of the Inspector General—each with some degree of visibility and some degree of independence.

There were six "lawyering" divisions: Antitrust, Civil, Civil Rights, Environment and Natural Resources, Taxes, and Criminal.[57]

The solicitor general was/is responsible for representing the DOJ in cases before the Supreme Court. The inspector general's mission is to "detect and deter waste, fraud, abuse, and misconduct" in the department. Most of the other units are self-explanatory.

While much of the attention given the DOJ focuses on court decisions, the budget tells a rather different story. In 1996 over 30 percent of the DOJ budget went to Community Oriented Policing Services, and 20 percent to U.S. Marshals. Just 20 percent went to U.S. attorneys scattered across the country, and a mere 10 percent went to the prosecuting divisions of DOJ.

Three of the most high profile cases under Reno involved the Branch Davidian cult siege in Waco, Texas, the impeachment of the sitting president, Bill Clinton, and the custody of a Cuban child, Elián González. These

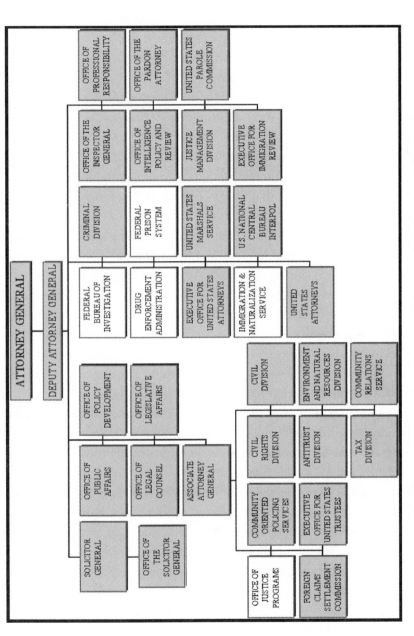

Chart from Audit Report 97-33. Management's Overview, U.S. Department of Justice Office of the Inspector General. https://oig.justice.gov/reports/plus/a9733/a9733p1.htm.

cases will be examined in the next chapter. While other cases may have been equally, if not more, significant, they were not headliners.

While the attorney general's focus was on the United States, Reno did have a responsibility to combat international crime. In the summer of 1994, she traveled to Denmark and Sweden, and in November she attended the World Ministerial Conference on Organized Transnational Crime in Italy. This was followed by the first Summit of the Americas meeting, which was held in Miami. The Miami meeting produced a broad and ambitious Plan of Action with twenty-three items.[58] The year was capped when Reno attended, as a U.S. representative, the inauguration of Brazil's new president, Fernando Henrique Cardoso, a distinguished scholar and statesman. His election seemed to confirm that Brazil had, indeed, recovered from its dark days of dictatorship (1964–1985).

Two trips were made to Canada in 1995. One for the signing of an Asset Sharing Agreement that provided for the sharing of assets seized in a criminal case, which could then be used to combat crime. The second was for a conference on Counter Terrorism. In 1996 Reno traveled to France to sign an extradition treaty, to Hungary for the dedication of the International Law Enforcement Academy and for a Summit on Eastern European Organized Crime, and to Puerto Rico for the Governor's Drug Conference. It was Mexico, though, that more than any other country claimed Reno's attention. In 1993 she attended a NAFTA conference in Mexico City, and with Senators Barbara Boxer and Diane Feinstein, both of California, visited Tijuana to announce new border initiatives. In other years she would attend the inauguration of a new president, Ernesto Zedillo, and another time participated in a Mexican Independence Day celebration.

By the end of Reno's service, the United States had signed some sixty new treaties related to law enforcement with countries ranging from Austria to South Africa to South Korea. The United States also signed a variety of multilateral conventions at the United Nations and the Organization of American States concerning terrorists, transnational corruption, drug trafficking, and trafficking in firearms.

Back home, there were a number of foci. One was antitrust cases. Ever since Teddy Roosevelt, Americans have had a soft spot in their hearts for the trust-buster. Reno had had no experience with corporate colossi before arriving in Washington, but Justice took on two major antitrust cases during Reno's tenure. The first involved American Airlines (AA). Airline deregulation in 1978 had led to competition and an expansion of low-cost carriers. Over time, though, the hub system had led to consolidation, higher prices, and, some thought, illegal monopoly.[59] In 1999 the DOJ brought a case against American Airlines. Some low-cost carriers had entered the Dallas–Fort Worth market where 70 percent of all flights were being flown by AA.[60] In response, AA cut ticket prices and increased the number of flights on routes the small airlines were flying. After the small airlines were pushed out of the Dallas–Fort Worth picture, AA raised its prices and cut the number of flights. Justice charged American with predation, monopolization, and attempt to monopolize. Justice lost.[61] Today more than twenty airlines fly out of Dallas–Fort Worth.

The second antitrust case involved Microsoft, which began before and ended after Reno's tenure. Microsoft, a wildly successful company, was led by the brilliant, brash, and, some would say, belligerent Bill Gates.[62] A 1994 interview in *Playboy*, subtitled "A candid conversation with the sultan of software about outsmarting his rivals," offers a quote calling Gates "one part Albert Einstein, one part John McEnroe, and one part General Patton."[63] In the interview, Gates claimed that "I never criticized a person. I have criticized ideas. If I think something's a waste of time or inappropriate, I don't wait to point it out. I say it right away. In real time. So you might hear me say, 'That's the dumbest idea I have ever heard' many times during a meeting." Already future oriented, Gates noted that the computer made it possible to have direct democracy in which citizens make the decisions rather than representatives (elected officials). He didn't think it a good idea, though.

Gates with a buddy, Paul Allen, sold his first computer program at age fifteen for $20,000. His parents insisted that he attend college, and he went off to Harvard after scoring 1590 out of 1600 on his SATs—as he was happy to tell anyone who didn't already know. He didn't stay long. At age twenty, he and Allen formed what would become Microsoft. Three years later the company's income for the year was $2.6 million. Gates was a product genius, but unlike many others in the new industry, he was an equally astute, and driven, some would say ruthless, corporate strategist. He argued that innovation would only be sustained if there were financial rewards—a position at odds with many in the computer community at the time. He sought and he received huge financial rewards. He has been near the top of

Forbes's "wealthiest" since his early thirties, and by age forty-five was said to be worth $101 billion.[64]

In the beginning of the 1990s, competitors, some of whom believed they had been taken advantage of, complained of monopolistic practices by Microsoft. This led the Federal Trade Commission (FTC) to begin an investigation. One important question involved whether Microsoft's dominance in computer operating systems was being used to stifle competition in software. After the FTC deadlocked at 2–2, Reno's Department of Justice took up the issue in 1993. One specific concern was the bundling of Internet Explorer (software) with Windows (an operating system). Microsoft argued Internet Explorer was just a "feature" of Windows. DOJ argued that it was a separate "product." In a 1994 consent decree Microsoft agreed that products could not be tied to Windows.[65] The decree also included some restrictions on Microsoft's contracts with computer makers and stated that price could not be contingent on buying another product. In 1995 the consent decree was thrown out and then reinstated. Shortly after, Windows 95 was launched to much acclaim. But Internet Explorer had been bundled.

In 1997, encouraged by Microsoft competitors like Netscape, Oracle, Dell, and IBM, Senate hearings on monopolistic practices in the industry were led by Senator Orrin Hatch, Republican of Utah. DOJ piled on with a request that Microsoft be charged with civil contempt, and a judge enjoined the bundling. Five months later another judge voided the injunction, and a month later the Court of Appeals ruled the 1995 consent decree did not apply to the new edition of Windows. DOJ and twenty states plus the District of Columbia then filed an antitrust suit against Microsoft.

The trial *U.S. v. Microsoft* began in late 1998. The brainy and deeply involved Gates's depositions featured many an "I don't know." Twice, evidence tapes submitted by Microsoft were found to be doctored. It was almost as though Microsoft didn't think the proceedings were serious. The judge's decision came in two parts. First were the findings of fact. The judge did not hesitate. Microsoft was guilty. Later he would say that Microsoft executives had, "proved, time and time again, to be inaccurate, misleading, evasive, and transparently false. . . . Microsoft is a company with an institutional disdain for both the truth and for rules of law that lesser entities must respect. It is also a company whose senior management is not averse to offering specious testimony to support spurious defenses to claims of its wrongdoing."[66] After a delay, the judge gave his decision concerning his "conclusions of law." He ruled Microsoft should be split into two entities. The appeals court accepted the lower court's facts. However, the appeals court was not sure that previous antitrust law assuming the per se illegality of tie-ins was easily applied to a network industry like Microsoft.[67]

The two sides then went to work on a settlement. In November 2001, an agreement was reached. The government gave up on the division of Microsoft into separate entities. Microsoft agreed to share its application programming interfaces with third-party companies and to appoint a panel of three people who would have full access to Microsoft's systems, records, and source code for five years in order to ensure compliance. However, the DOJ did not require Microsoft to change any of its code, nor did it prevent Microsoft from tying other software with Windows in the future. On November 1, 2002, Judge Colleen Kollar-Kotelly released a judgment accepting most of the proposed settlement. Nine states (California, Connecticut, Iowa, Florida, Kansas, Minnesota, Utah, Virginia, and Massachusetts) and the District of Columbia (which had been pursuing the case together with the DOJ) did not agree with the settlement, arguing that it did not go far enough to curb Microsoft's anti-competitive business practices. However, a number of states did accept the terms of the settlement, and on June 30, 2004, the U.S. appeals court unanimously approved it, rejecting objections that the sanctions were inadequate.

Microsoft's obligations under the original settlement expired on November 12, 2007. However, Microsoft later "agreed to consent to a two-year extension of part of the Final Judgments dealing with communications protocol licensing, and that if the plaintiffs later wished to extend those aspects of the settlement even as far as 2012, it would not object. The plaintiffs made clear that the extension was intended to serve only to give the relevant part of the settlement 'the opportunity to succeed for the period of time it was intended to cover,' rather than being due to any 'pattern of willful and systematic violations.'"[68]

Issues related to abortion mobilized passionate debate and passionate action as well—ever since the Supreme Court's *Roe v. Wade* decision in 1973—and they continue unabated. Most of the debate and action occurred at the state level, but Reno had to deal with one issue almost as soon as she became attorney general. She was sworn in on March 12, 1993, two days after physician David Gunn was murdered outside a Pensacola clinic that offered abortions and the same day that the *Miami Herald* editorialized that "Killing Cannot Be Pro-Life."

The day after the physician's murder, confirmed but not yet sworn in, Reno vowed to do "whatever is within our federal authority to prevent any physical conduct that in any way interferes with access to abortion clinics."[69] The public was with her. Congress passed the Freedom of Access to Clinic Entrances Act in just over two months. Gunn's murderer, Michael F. Griffin, was convicted and sentenced to life in prison in less than a year.[70] Alternative metal musician Marilyn Manson recorded "Get Your Gunn" critiquing the murderer, but others like Paul Jennings Hill, who issued a "Defensive Action Statement," supported him. Just over a year later a second doctor, John Britton, was murdered outside the same clinic. A third physician, Barnett Slepian, was slain in Amherst, New York, in 1998, and a fourth, George Tiller, in Wichita, Kansas, in 2009.

Immigration, another key issue facing Janet Reno, has long been a feature of life in the United States. In the late nineteenth century, the flow began to feature central Eastern and southern Europeans including many non-English speakers as well as Catholics and Jews. WASPs (White Anglo Saxon Protestants) began to feel the country was no longer "theirs," and Congress reacted with legislation. The first action, in 1917, required a literacy test for those over the age of sixteen. In the early 1920s, national origin quotas were established based on the 1890 census. Specifically, the law limited visas to 2 percent of each nationality already in the country. The purpose and effect was to greatly favor northern Europeans.

With the beginning of World War II, security became a third force driving immigration law. Aliens were required to register, internment camps were created for people of Japanese origin (including U.S. citizens), and enforcement of immigration law was moved to the DOJ.[71] Also, provision was made for the admission of agriculture workers who did work that citizens did not want to do.

While national origin quotas were removed in 1965, overall limits remained, and preference was given to the reuniting of families and to skilled workers. Thus ended any hint of a policy related to the inscription on the base of the Statue of Liberty that reads: "Give me your tired, your poor, your huddled masses yearning to breathe free" from a poem by Emma Lazarus titled "The New Colossus." Today's policy favors those who have relatives in the country and those who are already favored. For example, it is possible to get an immigrant visa by investing $500,000 in an enterprise employing ten workers.[72] One other group got special treatment. Reno issued an order allowing individuals who had been persecuted for homosexuality to come to the United States citing the Toboso-Alfonso decision. Narrowly construed, the ruling applied to homosexual identity, not to conduct, which was actually illegal in at least a third of the states at the time. (The last sodomy laws would not be struck down until 2003.)

When Reno assumed her new job, immigration had yet again become a political issue. By then, most immigrants were from Mexico, the Caribbean, and Central America, but a significant number were from South America and Asia. Miami-born Reno was well acquainted with the issues, and as every Miamian knew, there was a great disparity between the welcome given Cubans who arrived without documents and the deportation of those of other nationalities who similarly lacked documents.[73] Officials also knew that many residents were in the country illegally. Indeed, it was estimated that more than 8 percent of the U.S. population was foreign-born, that more than a million new immigrants were arriving each year, and that a quarter of those were illegal immigrants.[74]

The American public had become intensely focused on the issue of immigration after the 1993 bombing at the World Trade Center that killed six and injured more than a thousand.[75] The public's alarm led state politicians to demand federal moneys for costs related to immigrants—legal and illegal—and to demand closure of the southern border, which was, simply, porous. It was crossed, circumvented, and tunneled. Some new arrivals claimed asylum; still others came on tourist visas and then disappeared.

By 1996, the Pew Foundation estimated that there were 6.8 million unauthorized immigrants in the United States. When Reno visited the southwest border, she traveled some distance on horseback and had the experience of having rocks thrown at her. Clearly the border was not controlled. In a February 8, 1996, talk about "Operation Gatekeeper,"[76] Reno noted that she was appointing a Personal Special Representative for the southwest border, that the INS had recently had a 24 percent increase in its budget, that there were 1,000 new agents on the border, and that $140 million had been allocated to deport criminals and $63 million for worksite enforcement.[77]

That fall, President Clinton signed the Illegal Immigration Reform and Immigration Responsibility Act and the Antiterrorism and Effective Death Penalty Act. They were the toughest immigration bills yet, providing for "expedited removal" and requiring that any asylum claim be made within a year of arrival.[78] The law could be applied retroactively and provided that even individuals with legal permanent resident status could be deported for a past "aggravated felony"; that definition was expanded to include even tax evasion and failure to appear in court. Penalties for offenses were increased, accepting government benefits such as student loans was made illegal, and enforcement funds were increased. The new law seemed to require deportation of some 300,000 Central Americans who had fled civil war and government oppression in the 1980s. Under the previous law these refugees were qualified to apply for permanent residence if they had been here seven years, were of good moral character, and would suffer hardship if deported.[79] The new law exempted only those who would suffer "extreme and unusual hardship." When a DOJ Board of Immigration Appeal said the law was law and that it would be applied retroactively, Reno suspended enforcement in order to review the cases one at a time.[80] It was estimated that 40,000 Nicaraguans, 190,000 El Salvadorans, and 70,000 Guatemalans were affected. In a public speech supporting the North American Free Trade Agreement, Reno stated that ultimately the solution to the problem of illegal immigration required "a richer, more stable, more competent Mexico."[81] The problem of illegal immigration from other countries was not mentioned.

In spite of these and further efforts, the Pew Foundation reported that by 2014 there were an estimated 11.3 million unauthorized immigrants, who were 3.5 percent of the population and 5 percent of the labor force. Also by 2014, the successor to the INS, the U.S. Citizenship and Immigration Service, had 19,000 employees and a budget of more than $3 billion.

There was another immigration issue on which Reno took a clear and public position. It involved the citizenship status of a child born in this country to noncitizen parents. She whole-heartedly supported the Fourteenth Amendment to the Constitution that says that a child born in the United States is, by definition, a citizen.[82] There were and continue to be vocal objections to this law without much notice taken that it is a constitutional not a legislative matter. And without much notice that there are two quite different situations. Many baby citizens are the children of noncitizen parents of modest means, often Hispanic or Caribbean, who work and live in the United States, some for many years. Others are the children of wealthy women sometimes called "birth tourists" who come only for a matter of months, stay at an expensive "maternity tourism" hotel, and leave with a U.S. birth certificate for their "anchor baby." Attaining such citizenship is so prized that in 2014 federal agents closed fourteen Los Angeles maternity tourism hotels.

Tobacco became another target issue for Reno. At a news conference on September 22, 1999, Reno announced that the DOJ had filed a lawsuit against Philip Morris International and other major cigarette manufacturers to recover federal dollars lost because of the companies' intentionally misleading and fraudulent behavior. Seven years later, on August 17, 2006, Judge Gladys Kessler issued a 1,683 page opinion holding the companies liable for violating the Racketeer Influenced and Corrupt Organization Act (RICO) by fraudulently covering up the health risks associated with smoking and for marketing their products to children. "As set forth in these Final Proposed Findings of Fact, substantial evidence establishes that Defendants have engaged in and executed—and continue to engage in and execute—a massive 50-year scheme to defraud the public in violation of RICO." This was a victory, but it was preceded and enabled by suits brought by more than forty states that revealed information the companies had tried to keep secret. The feds were not in the lead.

The Tobacco Master Settlement Agreement (MSA) was entered in November 1998 originally between the four largest United States tobacco companies (Philip Morris, R. J. Reynolds, Brown and Williamson, and Lorillard—referred to as the "Majors" or the "original manufacturers") and the attorneys general of forty-six states. The states settled their Medicaid lawsuits against the tobacco industry for recovery of their tobacco-related health-care costs, and also exempted the companies from private tort liability regarding harm caused by tobacco use.[83] In the MSA, the original participating manufacturers (OPM) agreed to pay a minimum of $206 billion over the first twenty-five years of the agreement. The companies agreed to curtail or cease certain tobacco marketing practices, as well as to pay, in perpetuity, various annual payments to the states to compensate them for some of the medical costs of caring for persons with smoking-related illnesses. The money also funded a new anti-smoking advocacy group called the American Legacy Foundation that is responsible for such campaigns as the Truth. The settlement also dissolved the tobacco industry groups Tobacco Institute, the Center for Indoor Air Research, and the Council for Tobacco Research.

Cyber issues also became serious during Janet Reno's term. She began to try to educate the public on issues related to computers, encryption, storage of intellectual property, and espionage, and she emphasized the importance of training being given to DOJ employees. In 1998 the National Infrastructure Protection Center was founded in the FBI.[84] Inside her own office she created a special unit of prosecutors, the Computer Crime and Intellectual Property Section. The issue was tackled in myriad ways. The Cybercitizen Partnership taught children about online ethics. InfraGard emphasized the exchange of information between industry and law enforcement. The Internet Fraud Initiative tackled exploitation of consumers. And the Intellectual Property Fraud Initiative worked with law enforcement to combat piracy and counterfeiting of intellectual property. In fact, the DOJ won the first criminal copyright conviction under the "No Electronic Theft" Act for unlawful distribution of software. Internet Crimes Against Children Task Forces around the country were created.

In 1997 Reno went international calling on the Senior Experts of the P-8 Group on Transnational Organized Crime to address cybercrime.[85] Reno was particularly hopeful that the group would address the issue with "common sense" and find "practical" solutions. This would require training law enforcement in how to collect evidence and identify hackers, and contemplating how laws might have to be written to provide for their prosecution. The issues were clear; solutions were not.

The DOJ created a small unit headed by Scott Charney who managed the cyber issue for the attorney general. By the time he left in 1999, the Computer Crime and Intellectual Property Section would be well established.[86] By 2000, cybercrime had become such a major concern that on February 15, 2000, FBI Director Louis J. Freeh sent a memo to Reno listing these urgent goals: the elimination of the backlog of computers to be searched; the protection of the nation's information and other critical infrastructures; the capacity to detect cyber criminals around the world and bring them to justice; the creation of a technology center supported by government, academia, and industry to provide expertise and tools to federal, state, and local law enforcement to assess "digital evidence"; and the adoption of an organizational structure that ensured technical and legal excellence in handling the full range of cyber matters. At a Cybercrime Summit in June, Reno participated in a dialogue with industry leaders. Her concerns were how to protect the public and enforce the law in a way that "fostered privacy and civil liberties" while allowing the internet "as little inconvenience as possible."[87]

Terrorism was another issue on the attorney general's plate as well. While the FBI pursued foreign terrorists, collecting transcripts from the conversations of suspects around the world, it is important to remember that terrorism can be completely homegrown.[88] The bloody incident at the Branch Davidian compound in Waco had led the DOJ to establish a behavioral center to address ways of talking down a situation.[89] But the April 1995 domestic terrorist attack in Oklahoma City gave no time for negotiation. The bombing of the Alfred P. Murrah Federal Building killed 168 and wounded more than 600. The front was torn from the federal building and damaged as many as 300 other buildings. Timothy McVeigh, the culprit, was actually in jail having been stopped for a traffic violation and then arrested for unlawfully caring a handgun. He had had some assistance from Terry Nichols, who he had met while serving in the Army. Both were survivalists, and weapons were a basic part of that culture. Both were appalled by the Waco event and also by the Ruby Ridge shoot-out at the home of survivalist Randy Weaver in Idaho in which Weaver's wife and son were killed. McVeigh received a death sentence,[90] Nichols 168 consecutive life sentences, and Michael Fortier, who knew about the planned bombing but did not alert authorities, received a twelve-year sentence. The reaction of Congress was to sign the Antiterrorism and Effective Death Penalty Act the following year.

The longtime issue surrounding civil rights continued to be imperfectly enforced. At a Southern Christian Leadership Conference (SCLC) event in Detroit on August 12, 1996, Reno acknowledged that while laws had been changed and progress made, the journey was not complete. She referred to the church arsons, possibly two hundred in number, to the ongoing investigation of police departments, to the new (fair) requirements for lending, and to the monitoring of voting rights. And efforts such as quotas and affirmative action were controversial and under attack (for instance, the cases of *Hopwood v. Texas* and *Adarand Constructors v. Peña*).

Deval L. Patrick, who would later become governor of Massachusetts, was the first Assistant Attorney General for Civil Rights under Reno. As a Black American, he understood the issues as both legal and moral. He once described being trapped in a stereotype as having people "look right through you." At his swearing in, he vowed to act "with sufficient resolve and with wisdom." "We cannot and will not fail. . . . Let us begin." Patrick's concerns included bombings of churches and abortion clinics. "Motor voting," which allowed people to update their voter information when they updated their automobile registration, became a quickly realized goal.

A major focus of Patrick's was on the issue of lending discrimination practices aimed at minorities. Discrimination in renting, buying, and financing housing became illegal under the 1968 Fair Housing Act. Lenders were not to charge more to Blacks or to other minority borrowers. But a case brought against Chevy Chase Federal Savings Bank went further, saying whole neighborhoods could not be "redlined," that is, be denied services by simply not operating there. The result? In 1992 Chase had made thirty-six loans in a particular tract. In 1994 it made 229. In addition to ending red-lining, the ending of discriminatory evaluation of applications and discriminatory pricing of loans resulted in an increase in loans to Asian Americans by 56 percent, Hispanics by 43 percent, and Native Americans by 27 percent.[91]

Then there were civil rights infractions occurring in the hotel industry. Blacks were not necessarily welcomed as guests. The Adam's Mark hotel chain was sued by the DOJ, but also by the State of Florida and by a group of private plaintiffs for discriminating against non-White guests. The latter claimed Black guests were discriminated against at a Black college reunion held at the chain's Daytona Beach hotel. One settlement included an $8 million award, about half to the reunion guests who were discriminated against, and much of the rest to four historically Black colleges in Florida. A second agreement concerned the use of an outside monitor, Project Equality of Kansas City, Missouri, which would ensure compliance with the agreement for the next four years.

An ally of Patrick's in all these activities was Drew S. Days III, a Yale Law School graduate and faculty member who had worked for eight years for the NAACP Legal Defense and Education Fund and in the Civil Rights Division of DOJ during the Jimmy Carter administration. Days was appointed solicitor general by President Clinton, a position that represents the administration in cases before the Supreme Court. Days disagreed with Reno about an interpretation of pornography in *United States v. Knox*, but they were consistent allies on civil rights issues.

Then there was the issue of fundraising. A century-old law forbade fundraising on government property. Republican House Speaker Newt Gingrich and Judiciary Chair Henry Hyde plus Senate Judiciary Chair Orrin Hatch launched an investigation of fundraising in the White House. President Clinton said he had done so, but only in the residential quarters, so no law was broken. Vice President Al Gore admitted that he had made calls from his office but said it was "soft" money, in other words, not for himself, so not covered. In his reelection campaign, Gore received $100,000 from a Buddhist temple. Then there was Johnny Chung, a businessman who gave a $50,000 check to a Hillary Clinton aide and another $360,000 to the Democratic National Committee. There was James Riady, an Indonesian, who contributed funds to Clinton through other contributors. There was Charlie Trie whose $450,000 was returned. And John Huang, who visited the White House over seventy times, had only half the money he brought returned.

In a *Miami Herald* piece of September 13, 1997, Sandy Grady noted that just after Reno cleared the White House of raising money at coffees, forty-four videos appeared showing campaign contributors being feted at the White House. Nothing illegal was shown, but Reno was "mad," Grady wrote, and continued, "the gulf between Reno and the White House is as wide as the Grand Canyon." Grady's article concluded: "With so many enemies she must be doing a good job." On October 9, 1997, Carl Hiaasen would say it more plainly: "An honest chump is still a chump." And likened Reno to "a bowling pin who keeps setting herself up."

Janet Reno continued her work regarding juvenile justice issues. On March 18, 1996, she gave a speech at Canisius College, in which she argued the importance of juvenile justice on the grounds that it not only enhanced public safety but also that young people were the next generation of workers. She even said youth violence was a number one danger. The remedy? Families, neighborhoods, and the city itself. Indeed, remedies should begin before the age of three when conscience developed. School and after-school programs were needed. And when crimes were committed, the sanctions must fit the crime—and severe sanctions should be given to a person who put a gun to another's head.

Reno's predecessor, Barr, had begun the Weed and Seed program in 1991.[92] The program targets specific neighborhoods where it "weeds" out gang and drug activities. It then "seeds" it with appropriate services and development projects. Law enforcement, members of the community, service agencies, and nonprofits collaborate in a variety of efforts to revitalize the neighborhood. By April 1999, Reno was able to report that such efforts had led to a significant reduction in juvenile crime in an address she gave to the Coalition for Juvenile Justice.[93] Still, Reno iterated and reiterated the need for more, including after-school activities, health-care coverage, model courts for child abuse and neglect similar to those for drugs, and many other programs. She also noted that research and evaluation would be important as innovative programs were begun.

By 1996, the DOJ was taking on the issue of organized crime in a five-year project called Heaven's Gate. It aimed at La Cosa Nostra and was intended to convict members of the Gambino and Genovese families and their allies in the Teamsters and Longshoremen. Drugs and the Russian, Colombian, and Sicilian gangs who supplied them, were a focus as well. A crucial tool would be asset forfeiture through RICO proceedings.

But Reno was just as concerned with the issue of actual violence, and she had her staff prepare a report (released February 5, 1994) reviewing the history of television violence, reforms then being discussed, and agreements that had recently been made with cable and network officials. The issue had become a matter of public debate with a 1972 Surgeon General's Report that linked media violence and aggressive behavior. Debate ensued but CBS, ABC, and Fox couldn't agree to create joint standards. Pressure continued, for instance the presidents of the American Academy of Pediatrics, the American Psychological Association, the Society for Adolescent Medicine, and the American Psychiatric Association called for a "partnership" to lessen the effects of violence in films, television, music, and video games.

President Clinton asked Hollywood glitterati to reflect on the effect of TV violence at a Hollywood fundraiser for himself. Attorney General Reno began to explore the issue and let her concerns be known. However, the industry now included numerous cable networks that were not necessarily in accord with the networks, but they, too, were eager to avoid legislation on the topic and so agreed to the creation of an independent monitor and a rating system. Cable went further than the networks to agree to a block-ing technology, parental advisories, and responsible scheduling. Reno's staff noted that media was in a process of rapid change, and that it would be im-portant to try to anticipate future changes. The report also included statis-tics on the prevalence of media violence noting that two-thirds of children ages ten to thirteen could identify Freddy Krueger, a movie villain, but only one-third knew Abraham Lincoln had been a U.S. President. Reno's office concluded that a wait-and-watch policy was best.

Scrutiny of television may have seemed a bit precious to some, but there was one large issue that was not: terrorism. The September 11, 2001, attack on the World Trade Center had made every American uncomfortably con-scious of the possibility of terrorist attacks on home soil. It mobilized fed-eral officials. The FBI began to collect transcripts of suspects' conversations from around the world. Some individuals who raised grave suspicions were detained even if there was not enough evidence for an indictment, or there was evidence, but it was classified and thus unavailable to the subject and his counsel—if any counsel existed. One example was Anwar Haddam, an Al-gerian Islamic leader who had just been elected to Parliament when the Al-gerian Army staged a coup in 1992. He fled to the United States and applied for asylum in 1993, but was arrested in 1996 and held on "secret evidence" for four years. Released in 2000, he was never charged with any crime.

A December 2001 review based on classified evidence involving foreign nationals listed fourteen cases, six of them involving a group of Iraqis ar-rested in Nebraska. All but one had been released from custody by the time of the review. In the case of the Iraqis, an agreement was reached that they would leave the United States but would not be returned to Iraq.

A trickier case involved Yaser Esam Hamdi who, born in Louisiana, was a U.S. citizen. Captured in Afghanistan with members of the Taliban, he was declared an "illegal enemy combatant" by the Bush administration. That status permitted the government to hold him until the conflict was over. Three years passed with no charges, but, finally, in 2004, the U.S. Supreme Court ruled that as a citizen, Hamdi had a right to due process. A bargain was soon struck. Hamdi was released on condition that he leave the country and renounce his citizenship.

Joseph Padilla, a Puerto Rican and thus also a citizen, was suspected of planning to release a dirty bomb. In 2002 he was arrested, and first charged as a material witness. His status was then changed to "enemy combatant," and he was placed in a military prison. The changed status meant he could be detained until the conflict was over, in other words, indefinitely. Four years later his attorneys managed to have him transferred to the U.S. District Court in Miami. There he was found guilty of conspiring to kill in overseas jihad, and of funding and supporting overseas terrorism. He appealed the sentence of seventeen years and four months as excessively long. In 2014, the case finally came to an end—but with the conclusion that the sentence had been too lenient! It was raised to twenty-one years.

By 2003, the ABA had prepared a report recommending that U.S. citizens and residents designated as enemy combatants have meaningful judicial review, not be denied access to counsel, and that clear standards concerning "enemy combatants" be established by the Congress in coordination with the executive branch.

The attorney general's scope for "the Nation's Business" encompasses a wide range of issues. Some might be tempted to narrow their vision and focus on the most serious. Reno tried to do it all. Further, she added to the mission. She did not shrink.

8

ATTORNEY GENERAL, 1993–2001

Three Dramas

Janet Reno was no drama queen, but her tenure as attorney general was filled with crises. The first involved events that came to be known as the Waco Incident/Siege/Tragedy/Massacre. A second involved the impeachment of her president, Bill Clinton. A third concerned the fate of Elián González, a Cuban child rescued at sea, and whether or not he should be returned to his father in Cuba.

The Waco drama went national with bloodshed and a siege just before Reno was sworn in as attorney general. But the story actually began in 1929, when a group led by Victor Houtoff split from the Seventh-day Adventists, renamed themselves Davidian Seventh-day Adventists, and moved to a ranch in Elk, Texas, near Waco. At Houtoff's death, his wife, Florence, assumed leadership. The group shrank drastically. After the apocalypse that Victor Houtoff prophesied failed to materialize, a second split occurred, which led to the 1955 creation of yet another group known as the Branch Davidians, led first by Benjamin Roden and then by his wife, Lois. At her death in 1984, a struggle for leadership erupted between her son, George Roden, and Vernon Howell (later to be known as David Koresh) who she had allegedly designated as the next leader. The struggle erupted into gunfire in 1987, and Howell/Koresh was tried for, but not convicted of, attempted murder. Five years later, Roden killed a fellow Davidian, was declared insane, and was institutionalized. Howell/Koresh took over. Less than a decade later he would preside over something very much like an apocalypse.

The Branch Davidians settled at seventy-acre Mount Carmel Center

Ranch. As the years passed, the group's beliefs became more and more unorthodox. Indeed, Koresh issued an audio tape, "New Light," that directed men in the group to become celibate and declared that he had been charged to procreate with the women—a group that included females as young as twelve years old.[1] Koresh also asserted that only he could interpret Holy Scripture.

Life in the group came to the public's attention in February 1993 when the *Waco Tribune-Herald* began a series on the Branch Davidians describing them as a cult practicing child abuse, polygamy, and their establishment of an arsenal. In fact, the Bureau of Alcohol, Tobacco, Firearms and Explosives (ATF) had been monitoring Mount Carmel for some time, but it was the newspaper story about child brides that led the ATF to get a warrant to search for illegal weapons and a warrant to arrest Howell/Koresh as well. Action began on February 28, 1993.[2]

Reno would be sworn in as attorney general within days; she was to have a heavy responsibility thrust upon her. This is because the ATF raid turned deadly. Four of its agents were killed and more than a dozen wounded. Five or six Branch Davidians died at that time. Because federal agents had been killed, the FBI then assumed responsibility, and so began what developed into a fifty-one-day siege. Some seven hundred law enforcement officials participated in the effort to end it. At any given time 250 to 300 FBI officials were present as well as officials from other federal, state, and local agencies.

In the next several weeks fourteen adults and twenty-one children did leave the commune, perhaps because Koresh believed they lacked sufficient resolve. His own resolve became evident, however, after he failed to keep a promise to surrender if he was allowed to broadcast a religious message by radio. He then said he would come out after Passover; he didn't. He said he was analyzing the message of the seven seals in the New Testament and would come out when finished, but he refused to suggest a possible date that that might happen. Promises Koresh made to his own attorneys were broken, and assessments by behavioral scientists concluded that he would ultimately not comply with government requests. In determining a course of action, the government had to deal with the possibility that Koresh might instigate a mass suicide, or that he might launch an attack possibly using children as shields.[3]

After more than a month and a half of negotiations, there were no signs that the remaining Branch Davidians were weakening in their resolve or running out of water or other necessities. The FBI decided it was time to act. It had already cut off all means of communication for the cult except by phone, and that only with the FBI.[4] Pressure had been applied by patrols of the perimeter with (Army) Bradley fighting vehicles known to most of us as tanks, by cutting water and power, and by bombarding the compound with loud noises to prevent sleep. Ultimately, the plan was to use tear gas to force the cult members into the open. The increased pressure had led eleven more Branch Davidians to emerge; they were promptly arrested. Eighty-five members remained in the compound. The FBI grew impatient. Reno consulted President Clinton who remembered a 1985 siege in Arkansas that was resolved after only four days. He approved the FBI's plan, although he made it clear that the decision was Reno's.[5] The two sieges were quite different. The Waco siege had already gone on for a month and a half, and Koresh had broken many a promise. The FBI's plan was to insert tear gas step-by-step until the occupants emerged through the single available exit. If children were used as shields or in any way exposed to danger, the raid would be suspended. If the Branch Davidians fired their weapons, a full-bore attack would begin.

On April 19, 1993, the FBI lobbed nineteen gas canisters into the Branch Davidian living quarters. No one emerged. Instead, the occupants immediately began shooting at FBI agents. The agents did not fire in return, nor did they use their weapons at any time during the struggle. Soon a series of fires erupted; these quickly consumed the compound and more than seventy human beings inside. While nine people escaped, some, including several children and Koresh, were shot in "mercy" killings; the rest died as a result of the fire.

In the aftermath, controversy abounded and would continue.[6] Janet Reno, as was her wont, immediately took responsibility for the decision to use tear gas, but asserted that the fires could not have been set by the canisters, and were, instead, the actions of the Branch Davidians themselves.[7] The House Judiciary and Appropriations committees swung into action. Chaired by Democrats, neither committee was trying to play "gotcha," but they were intent on finding out just what had happened, and what could be done to ensure that nothing like the conflagration would happen again.[8]

In Neal McAliley's estimation, Reno emerged as a star during the congressional hearings on Waco. When Congressman John Conyers of Michigan began "I, for one, am not going to be nice to you," Reno retorted with spirit: "You will never know what it is like. . . . They were killers. . . . four FBI officers had been killed." That changed the nature of the discussion.

Reports were prepared for the Treasury[9] and Justice departments, by the attorney general's office itself, and by independent groups such as the Anabaptist Mennonite Biblical Seminary. In an attempt to provide a clear and comprehensive account that would put all issues to rest, former Senator John C. Danforth was asked to prepare a definitive report. It was issued in November 2000. It took more than a year to prepare, cost $12 million, and involved sixteen lawyers and thirty-five investigators. The report found that some FBI agents had lied, and that four hours previous to the firing of tear gas into the living space, some canisters with the ability to ignite had been fired—but not into the building. The report flatly asserted that federal agents were not responsible for the fires that erupted in three different locations inside the compound, and it provided transcripts that suggested gasoline had deliberately been poured in several locations by Branch Davidian members.

The Danforth report also concluded that agents had not directed gunfire at individuals or at the compound, and that agents had not illegally used the military in civilian law enforcement, although the Bradley vehicles had been borrowed from the military. Thorough it may have been, but the report did not lay Waco issues to rest. The libertarian CATO Institute almost immediately issued a study casting doubt on the report, and books have continued to explore the nature of the Branch Davidians, the possibilities of negotiation, and the overreach of authorities. In December 2000, a committee led by Representative Dan Burton of Indiana issued a report casting doubt on the accuracy of Danforth's findings.

Janet Reno was deeply saddened by the death of children and felt the whole affair could only be described as a tragedy. Her status in Washington, though, changed dramatically. From being unknown, she became the best-known member of President Clinton's Cabinet—and one with a strong approval rating.

The second drama involved the impeachment—but not the conviction— of President William Jefferson Clinton. No presidential administration has been able to completely avoid scandal. Some scandals, though, have been more grievous than others, and some have been more energetically exploited by opponents. The Reagan administration had scandals in Housing and Urban Development, in the Environmental Protection Agency, and others related to the savings and loan industry. The big scandal, of course, was Iran-Contra, which touched members of the administration at the highest level.[10] The George H. W. Bush administration, which followed Reagan's, was itself relatively untainted.[11] However, Bush pardoned high-level Reagan officials—both convicted and not yet tried—in particular, those who were involved in Iran-Contra, an activity in which he may himself have been involved.

Reagan's attorney general, Ed Meese, saw himself as the president's lawyer. Indeed, he was so sufficiently enmeshed in the Iran-Contra scandal that he was forced to step down. In contrast, Attorney General Reno saw herself as the people's—not the president's—lawyer. She was herself scandal free, but had to deal with a variety of charges against her president, Clinton, who would become the second U.S. President to be impeached.[12]

In the wake of Nixon and Watergate, Congress in 1978 passed the Ethics in Government Act with requirements related to disclosure of the finances and employment history of a variety of officials and with a clause related to lobbying after leaving office. Also important was the creation of the Office of Special Prosecutor, which five years later, when it was renewed, would be retitled the Office of Independent Counsel. Either Congress or the attorney general could bring charges under this act, but the independent counsel was to be appointed by a panel of three federal judges and was given a charge with no restrictions on budget or on time.[13]

Republicans in general were not happy about the office, although President Reagan did sign its 1987 reauthorization.[14] Republicans were, however, able to prevent a second reauthorization when the legislation lapsed in 1992. However, Republicans quickly changed their minds when Bill Clinton won the presidency and a hint of scandal emerged in an attorney general's investigation into what would come to be known as Whitewater. Thus, with the enthusiastic support of Republicans, and support by both Attorney General Reno and President Clinton, the Independent Counsel Act was reconstituted in 1994. A number of investigations soon commenced. In fact, five members of the presidential cabinet underwent investigation. Bruce Babbitt, Secretary of the Interior, was investigated, but not indicted. Alexis Herman, Secretary of Labor, was investigated, tried, and acquitted. Henry Cisneros, Secretary of Housing and Urban Development, was convicted, but only of a misdemeanor and was later pardoned by Clinton. Ron Brown, Secretary of Commerce, died in a plane crash while an investigation was in progress. Michael Espy, Secretary of Agriculture, was tried and acquitted. The big drama, though, involved the Clintons themselves and the various investigations conducted by Independent Counsel Kenneth Starr.[15]

Starr was a star. After graduating from high school in San Antonio, he entered Harding University, a Christian liberal arts school in Searcy, Arkansas. He soon moved to George Washington University, where he received a bachelor's degree. While there he, a registered Democrat, participated in activities such as anti–Vietnam War demonstrations. Continuing his upward track, Starr went to Brown University for a master's degree and then to Duke for a law degree. He first clerked for a federal appeals court judge and then for the Supreme Court's Chief Justice, Warren Burger.[16] His next step was to join the Washington, DC, office of a Los Angeles law firm, Gibson, Dunn and Crutcher. A member of that firm, William French Smith, was appointed attorney general by Reagan and soon thereafter Starr became counselor to Smith. Two years later, Reagan appointed Starr as a federal appeals court judge, and when George H. W. Bush became president, Starr left the court to become solicitor general. When Bill Clinton took office, Starr retreated to the practice of law.[17]

Then came the death of Vincent Foster and the Whitewater scandal. Attorney General Janet Reno appointed an independent counsel, Robert Fiske, to explore both Whitewater, a proposed real estate development in Arkansas, and also Foster's death. Foster had been a partner, like Hillary Clinton, in the Little Rock firm of Rose Law. His career had been highly successful. And with two others from the Arkansas firm, he went to Washington with the Clintons. His position was that of Deputy White House Counsel.[18] Fiske issued an interim report finding no problems related to Whitewater and, also, that Vincent Foster's death was a suicide.[19]

On the very day that Fiske's report was issued, the Independent Counsel Reauthorization Act was passed, which required that the independent counsel be appointed by a panel of judges from the Washington, DC, Federal

Appeals Court.[20] Reno asked that Fiske be appointed in order to complete his investigation, which had involved lawyers, physicians, FBI agents, and DNA experts among more than one hundred witnesses. The judges' panel, instead, appointed their former colleague, Kenneth Starr, to complete the investigation. And so began a long saga, one which would culminate in the impeachment of President Clinton.[21] In addition to the Fiske investigation, two congressional committees, the U.S. National Park Service, and the FBI had all concluded that Foster committed suicide. After three more years of investigation, Starr, too, concluded that Foster's death was a suicide.[22] Even so, conspiracy theories related to Vincent Foster continued to circulate, and Starr was just warming up.

Something else had been warming up: the World Wide Web. It entered the public domain in 1993, and by 1994, twenty-five million households, including the Clinton White House, were online.[23] This service has enabled communication between dissidents, conspiracy theorists, and just plain troublemakers to keep unproven (and proven) dramas alive. In fact, in spite of the many investigations, new Foster stories continued to be posted more than two decades later!

Whitewater was complicated. It was a development project that the Clintons had invested in with James and Susan McDougal when Bill Clinton was attorney general of Arkansas. The project failed and was dissolved in 1992. At that time, the Clintons reported a loss of $40,000. In the interval, the McDougals had founded Madison Savings and Loan, which also failed. Both McDougals were found guilty of fraud related to that failure. After it had taken over the failed bank, the Resolution Trust Corporation (a federal agency) sought to subpoena the Clintons. There were questions about Hillary Clinton's legal work for Madison Savings and Loan. (Subpoenaed records about that work took two full years to be "found on a table in the White House."[24]) There were also questions as to whether or not Bill Clinton, in 1986 while governor of Arkansas, had pressured a local banker, David Hale, into making a fraudulent loan to Susan McDougal.[25] And there were questions as to whether some of that loan money went to Whitewater and to pay Clinton campaign debts rather than to Madison Savings and Loan.

Whitewater sent several of Clinton's Arkansas associates to jail. One, Webb Hubbell, was convicted and sentenced to twenty-one months prison time for overbilling clients. He would later become a particular target for Kenneth

Starr who believed that, with sufficient pressure, Hubbell would provide evidence against the Clintons. He didn't. After three indictments by Starr, Hubbell was ultimately convicted of only one misdemeanor for which he received probation. The Clintons were never charged with a crime related to Whitewater, but once Starr's team started investigating the land deal, it found more and more to investigate—not about Whitewater, but about Bill Clinton and his presidency. For example, Starr investigated the improper acquisition of FBI files by a White House staffer. However, it was Clinton's relationship with intern Monica Lewinsky that would ultimately lead to his impeachment.[26]

When Bill Clinton began his move to the national scene, allegations about some of his behavior in Little Rock became national headlines. For example, during the 1992 presidential campaign, Gennifer Flowers announced that they had had a twelve-year affair. Three days later, with Hillary at his side, Clinton denied such an affair on *60 Minutes*. Soon thereafter, Flowers produced tapes that appeared to confirm that there was, in fact, a relationship.[27] The little case that grew, though, was that of Paula Jones.

In 1991, Danny Ferguson, a state trooper, brought Jones to a hotel room where Bill Clinton, then governor, allegedly propositioned her and exposed himself. She told intimates about the incident, but did nothing until 1994. By then Clinton was the president of the United States. Two days before the statute of limitations would expire, Jones filed a sexual harassment lawsuit with Little Rock attorney Daniel Traylor.[28] When Traylor realized he would be up against well-known Washington attorney Robert S. Bennett, he called for help. Washington lawyers Gilbert K. Davis and Joseph Cammarata responded. Conservative critics of Clinton saturated the talk shows as the case proceeded. Three years later, in May 1997, Jones was offered a settlement, but by then Susan Carpenter-McMillan, a conservative activist in California, was acting as Jones's spokesperson, and she persuaded Jones to reject the settlement. Jones's attorneys then resigned, believing they had accomplished their purpose. Donovan Campbell from a small Dallas firm that dealt with a variety of conservative causes then took up the case. Next, in 1998, Judge Susan Webber Wright dismissed Jones's case saying she had not suffered damages. After Jones began an appeal in a higher court, the two sides agreed to settle at $850,000 with no admission of guilt and no apology. But President Clinton's ordeal was by no means over.

A former White House employee, Linda Tripp, who knew Clinton had/

was having an affair with Monica Lewinsky, told Jones's lawyers about it, and when those lawyers were deposing Clinton, they surprised him by asking about Lewinsky. He denied having relations with her.[29] The deposition was on January 17, 1998. But rumors abounded, and Clinton denied such an affair to his top aides, to PBS's Jim Lehrer, to his cabinet, and on January 26 to a national TV audience.[30] But Starr knew the truth, and Reno had already given him permission to investigate the possibility of perjury and obstruction of justice related to testimony in the Jones case. Starr immunized Lewinsky, who had falsely denied any affair, and in addition to her testimony obtained the famous, semen-stained, blue dress. On September 9, 1998, Starr delivered his report to the House of Representatives, which promptly released it to the public. It included a photo of the blue dress and 3,183 pages of testimony. Starr concluded that there were eleven impeachable offenses. The House considered four charges and referred two to the Senate for trial. The Jones case had taken four years to complete. In contrast, impeachment charges were brought in December 1998, and by February 1999, Bill Clinton had been tried and acquitted. Conviction required sixty-seven votes. There were fifty votes for a charge of obstruction of justice and forty-five for a charge of perjury.

But the ordeal was still not over. In April 1999, Judge Susan Webber Wright found President Clinton guilty of civil contempt of court for misleading testimony in the Paula Jones case. The judge fined him and referred the issue to the Arkansas Bar Association, which revoked Clinton's license to practice law for five years. Also, Clinton resigned from the U.S. Supreme Court bar after his disbarment there became likely.

Drama three involved a Cuban child, Elián González. On Thanksgiving Day 1999, fishermen Donato Dalrymple and Sam Ciancio found five-year-old Elián floating in an inner tube some sixty miles from Miami. The boat that he and his mother had boarded to flee Cuba had capsized, and eleven passengers, including his mother, had perished. A cousin and two great-uncles who lived in Miami took Elián in and celebrated his escape—from death and from Cuba. A state court granted one of the uncles temporary guardianship, but Elián's father, Juan Miguel González-Quintana, whose ties to Elián were strong, asked the Cuban government to assist in Elián's return to him in Cuba. On December 5, the Cuban government formally requested the child's return. A saga began.

The Immigration and Naturalization Service (INS) then began an inquiry to ascertain the relationship between Elián and his father and requested an interview and proof of paternity at a meeting in the U.S. Interests Section in Havana. At a December 16 news conference, Reno expressed hope that all issues would soon be settled, and on January 5, 2000, INS Commissioner Doris Meissner ruled that Elián's father had the authority to speak for him on immigration matters, that Elián should be returned to his father, and ordered it done by January 14.[31] The relatives declined. Further, they won temporary guardianship from a state court with no hearing scheduled for months.

Predictably, Miami's Cuban community erupted in indignation and opposition—of course, no child should be subjected to the horrors of the Castro regime! Then began legal proceedings, demonstrations, and a press frenzy. The Miami relatives sought custody and asylum for Elián and refused to honor any order that would remove him from their home. Immigration attorney Spencer Eig stepped forward to file a lawsuit asking U.S. District Court Judge James L. King to grant Elián asylum. At one point, Eig even announced that, because Castro was said to have threatened that a commando team would come to Miami to kidnap Elián, the family would be keeping him at home. All this, even though Reno had written to Eig on January 12 stating that Elián's father was the sole authority regarding the child's status, and that he had not requested asylum for Elián.

While a child custody issue is normally a state issue, immigration and the asylum claimed on Elián's behalf were federal issues, and a Florida court had ruled, therefore, that Elián's status must be decided in federal court. Thus, the State of Florida had passed along a very hot potato, and Attorney General Reno soon became even more involved in the case. This was not surprising, since she was both a devoted Miami native and also possessed a special concern for children. She also appreciated the passion of many of Miami's Cuban exiles who were demanding that Elián remain "free" by staying in Miami. Still, again and again, Reno described the controlling issue as being the bond between parent and child.

The Miami relatives disregarded the INS ruling, and the controversy went national. In late January, Elián's two Cuban grandmothers requested permission to visit. Escorted by officials of the (U.S.) National Council of Churches, they flew to the United States hoping that Elián would be given to them so they could take him back to Cuba. In Miami they stayed at the home of Sister Jeanne O'Laughlin, the president of Barry University. The Miami relatives, however, flatly refused to surrender Elián. Further, Sister O'Laughlin, who had been selected as neutral in the controversy, changed her mind and publicly expressed her view that Elián should stay in the United States, as did a second nun, Peggy Albert, a trained child psychologist.[32] Indeed, O'Laughlin appeared in public with Senator Connie Mack who was sponsoring a bill to give Elián U.S. citizenship. When the issue went congressional, both the grandmothers and the custodial relatives began roaming congressional offices pleading their case.

Senator Mack had expected to have instant and positive action on his bill, but he found that his colleagues were not all in agreement. Speaker Dennis Hastert, an Illinois Republican, had supported Mack at first, but then decided that a decision should not be rushed and should be considered by the House Judiciary subcommittee, which considered immigration. Maxine Waters, a California Democrat, stood with Grandmother Mariela Quintana and declared her support, claiming to be surprised that a nun—a nun who was supposed to be neutral—would change her position.[33] In the Senate, there was even less support for Mack's efforts. There, Senator Chuck Hagel, R-Nebraska, fought to keep the issue off the floor, and Senator Trent Lott, R-Mississippi, backed off a plan to have an immediate vote. Janet Reno, eager to find a resolution, agreed to meet with Elián's custodians. However, that meeting was canceled, although INS hoped to reschedule it. Meanwhile, support was developing for letting Elián return to his father and Cuba. Indeed, a rally and march were held on February 19 saying "Enough is Enough."

On March 21, 2000, a federal court upheld the decision to return Elián to his father—and Cuba—and to deny him asylum. The INS also moved to terminate Elián's relatives' custody. On March 23, Elián's father formally requested immediate reunification. The next day, Kendall Coffey of Coffey, Diaz and O'Naghten, sent a six-page, single-spaced, passionate letter asking that the issue simply become one of determining the "best interests of the child," that it be done outside the court system, and with no appeal permitted.[34] Elián was now very much national news. ABC's Diane Sawyer taped an interview with him, and even small papers like Colorado's the *Rocky Mountain News* provided readers with byline accounts. On March 29, Lazaro González, Elián's relative who had custody, agreed to surrender Elián if: 1) the legal process requires it, and 2) psychologists say returning to Cuba will do no harm to the child, and, 3) the child agrees to the return. The third provision was clearly unacceptable.

That same day, Janet Reno gave a lengthy opening statement at her regular press conference about the strength and value of Miami's Cuban community and her confidence that law would be honored even though the mayor of Miami-Dade County, Alex Penelas, had indicated that Metro-Dade police would not be used to control any unrest related to Elián. Reno also told a story about a boy whose father was terribly injured in an accident and whose rich Aunt Lucy took him in, a lovely moderate woman; she did everything right by the boy. Six weeks later when the father, now severely disabled, asked to take his son back, the aunt argued that she could do much more for him and that the child would be psychologically damaged by upsetting his new routine; the boy should stay with her. Reno saw an analogy and argued that none of us doubt that he should be returned to the father. Further, she argued, we all know "perfectly wonderful" people who have come to this country who were raised in Cuba. As to asking a six-year-old to choose, Reno told another story about her weekend visits to her grandmother's house where she was treated to a movie, ice cream, and card games—and cried and hid when her mother came to take her home.

In early April, Elián's father, Juan Miguel González-Quintana, arrived in the United States with his wife and infant son to take Elián home. González-Quintana issued a statement "To the American People" deploring "the cruel psychological pressures aimed at influencing Elián's personality already weakened by the terrible trauma." He noted that Elián had been paraded and exhibited at public rallies and had participated in an extended TV interview, that González-Quintana's phone calls to Elián from Cuba were managed by those caring for him, and that his requests for information about Elián's medical care and medicines had been unanswered. On April 7, the INS's Michael Pearson told Lazaro González the transfer must occur, and that a team of psychologists will meet with him on April 10 to determine the best way to accomplish the transfer.[35]

Janet Reno flew to Miami on April 12 and met with family members at the home of Sister Jeanne O'Laughlin. It ended in an angry walkout about midnight. Meanwhile, Elián's father, now in Washington, DC, asked why nothing was happening—he had been there a week. The next morning, the

13th, Reno directed Lazaro González to bring Elián to the Opa-Locka air-port by 2:00 p.m. in order to transfer the child to his father. He didn't. In-stead, González released a video in which Elián said, "Dad, I do not want to go to Cuba." The April 16, 2000, *Miami Herald* reported González as saying, "The child stays here. . . . They will have to pry Elián out of my arms."[36] The *Herald* article also quoted psychiatrist Paulina Kernberg as saying Lazaro was "a man of many contradictions," stating that, "one minute he will be charming, then he goes into an outburst," for example, referring to Reno as "that old bitch hag."

The parole of Elián to Lazaro González was officially revoked on the 13th; González no longer had any authority to keep Elián. On the 19th the Elev-enth Circuit court ruled Elián must remain in the United States until all state and federal appeals were completed. Thus, the father's custody was upheld, but he could not take the boy out of the country until every legal issue had been resolved.

The issue drew in senators as well as members of the House. These included Trent Lott, Bob Graham, Robert Torricelli, Bob Smith, Paul Coverdell, Jesse Helms, Jim Bunning, Larry Craig, Arlen Specter, Orrin Hatch, and Robert Menendez.[37] Bob Butterworth, the Florida attorney general, and his fellow cabinet members cautioned against a return to a communist country, and Rep-resentative Lincoln Díaz-Balart, long a supporter of Reno, was confounded by the "incomprehensible Goebellian nature" of her actions and asked: "How could you be doing this, Janet?" Dr. Marta Molina, a recently arrived Cuban doctor who had been granted asylum, filed an affidavit describing the Castro regime's indoctrination practices that could involve severe penalties. Molina said that on his return, Elián would be given a blue bandanna and asked to swear allegiance to Los Pioneros. Their slogan? "We will be like Che." His mother, she asserted, would be labeled a traitor, a "gusano" (worm) for trying to go to the United States. Only a few politicians, among them Representative Nydia M. Velazquez (New York) and Maxine Waters (California), urged that the child be reunited with his father in Cuba; so did Joan Brown Campbell, former secretary-general of the National Council of Churches.

The U.S. relatives continued to make proposals; at one point, as reported in the April 21, 2000, *Los Angeles Times,* they even agreed to meet with Elián's father with Elián in Washington—on the condition that Elián would afterward return to Miami with them. The INS began preparing for a raid.

Surveillance began. White vans were leased and equipped with puncture-proof tires. A diagram of the interior of the house was prepared. Drills were practiced. Then the president of the University of Miami, Tad Foote, brought Cuban leaders and attorney Aaron Podhurst together for yet another attempt at forging a bargain. Reno agreed, but said one thing was not negotiable. Elián was to be returned to his father. The Miami Cuban leadership began lengthy discussions about how to reach an agreement to give Elián to his father, but the final proposal did not, in fact, offer a handoff. It proposed a shared custody with the families living in a single location in Miami and with facilitators who would help the family do what was "in the best interests of the child." Foote, at least, had hopes. But federal authorities read the proposal as a further stall and one which did not explicitly give the father custody and the ability to exercise his parental rights. Federal authorities didn't even share the proposal with the father.[38]

The drama reached its climax when President Bill Clinton authorized a raid to seize Elián and give him to his father.[39] At dawn on April 22, 2000, after more than six weeks of negotiations intended to reunite father and son, some 130 INS agents led by eight armed men, at least one of whom carried a submachine gun, seized Elián. News photos of heavily armed men taking custody of a wailing child appeared in the national and international media. Reunited, father and son flew not to Havana, but to Washington, DC, where the legal wrangling would continue.[40]

The day after the seizure/rescue was Sunday, Easter Sunday. Reno explained the reason for the action called Operation Padre as the sacred bond between a father and his son supported by law "as well as common sense." The talk shows gave the raid and Elián's story prime time. *Face the Nation* had an extensive interview with INS Commissioner Doris Meissner, and a shorter one with Jose Pedrosa, the attorney for the Miami relatives who argued for the child's right to claim asylum. Miami's Representative Ileana Ros-Lehtinen and Representative Charles Rangel of New York spoke briefly. Rangel argued that it was time to take a deep breath and get on—that it was a pleasure to see the smiling son reunited with his loving father. Congresswoman Ros-Lehtinen supported the view that the only concern should be the best interests of the child and that that was appropriately decided in a state family court. This was also the position taken by Vice President Al Gore and George W. Bush, both campaigning for the presidency. The *Wash-*

ington Post supported the action. The *New York Times* argued still more time would have been appropriate. Someone flew a small plane over Little Havana trailing a banner "America loves Janet Reno."

Meet the Press interviewed Eric Holder, deputy attorney general; Representative Tom Delay of Texas; Manny Diaz, attorney for the Miami González family and Gregory Craig, attorney for the father, Juan González-Quintana. Holder noted that negotiations had been going on for four or five months, that the raid involved only eight people, and that it took just three minutes. Representative Delay said he was outraged, sickened, and ashamed. He was clear that the issue was custody and belonged in family court. Diaz too, argued family court and best interests.

Demonstrations and counterdemonstrations ensued. One of the more dramatic demonstrations occurred in late May when Janet Reno was invited to be the keynote speaker at a celebration of Florida's first 150 women lawyers in Bal Harbour. The Cuban Bar Association withdrew its support, and Miami Beach lawyer Rosa M. Armesto asked the Florida Supreme Court to stay the celebration on the grounds that it would be "political." The court didn't. The Sheraton dinner for some eight hundred attendees proceeded while a similar number of demonstrators marched outside. Some protesters were organized by former Cuban political prisoners, Mothers Against Repression, and the Democracy Movement. Other groups, though, supported Reno, while a third set of marchers called for "Justice for Haitians."

So much of the news coverage was dramatic and featured those determined to keep Elián in Miami that it is worth quoting at some length from a letter written by Jacqueline Mendez to Janet Reno on April 24, 2000. Mendez, thirty-three at the time, had been living in Miami since 1969; in other words, she had been brought to Miami at age one or two. In the letter she notes that her parents feel "very strongly against Castro," but that she is not "tainted" herself. She described the demonstrators as "so tainted and scarred by Communism that they cannot separate it from their souls. They cannot make clear and rational judgments . . . involving Fidel Castro." She described the protesters including her parents, Gloria Estefan, and the Miami relatives as fighting not for Elián but against Castro. Now the community, she notes, is dismissing the smiling photos of Elián with his dad as "false and doctored." Mendez added that while many Cubans felt Elián was "seized," her belief was that he was rescued, and was pleased that it was done quickly, efficiently, and without harming anyone. She concluded that she was "proud of my government and proud of you and the President. Please don't be hurt over this matter. You did the right thing."

The Eleventh Circuit Court of Appeals had emphasized that Elián must not go anywhere beyond the reach of U.S. courts, in other words, the Cuban Embassy, until all legal issues were settled. That occurred on June 28 when the U.S. Supreme Court declined to hear the case. Elián's drama had begun on November 25, Thanksgiving Day. He was returned to his father in April just after Easter. Two months later, the Supreme Court chose not to act. Elián's father was confirmed as his guardian and as properly speaking/acting for him. Father and son promptly returned to Cuba.

Reno issued this statement: "All involved have had an opportunity to make their case—all the way to the highest court in the land. I hope that everyone will accept the Supreme Court's decision and join me in wishing this family and this special little boy well." Reno's approach had been to give all involved the opportunity to make their best case.[41] It took seven months. Years later, Neal McAliley asked her about the Elián incident, which had also broken the unity and invincibility of Miami Cuban leader Jorge Mas Canosa. Janet Reno only regretted the length of time it took to resolve the case, replying "I should have gone in earlier."

That summer, after things had quieted down, Sister Jeanne O'Laughlin wrote Reno a gracious birthday letter thanking her for honesty and integrity and expressing remorse if she had caused the attorney general pain. O'Laughlin went on to say that she was sure Reno was the greatest attorney general who had had to face the complexity of modern life, and that she knew Miami "will welcome you home for you are loved." She wished Reno "good health and happy days" and wrote that "I look forward to your return home." Reno responded that O'Laughlin had caused her no pain and repeated one of her personal mantras involving Harry Truman's assertion that doing right "was easy. The difficult thing was figuring out what right is."[42]

At the end of her service as attorney general, Reno ran for governor of Florida against Jeb Bush. Much of Miami, once her devoted political base, bitterly opposed her, and she lost in the Democratic primary.

9

Home Again

As the new George W. Bush administration assembled in Washington, Janet Reno returned to Miami and the family homestead. Her fellow cabinet member, Donna Shalala, had prepared for a post-administration life. Indeed, she would become the new president of the University of Miami. Reno had not prepared; her sense of duty required full-time attention to her job as long as she held it. Nevertheless, one might logically expect that a recent attorney general would receive at least an honorary appointment at the University of Miami Law School. Wrong. The president, Shalala, and former dean Mary Doyle were not able to overcome, or were unwilling to test, the fury of Miami Cubans over Reno's return of Elián to his father in Cuba. The chair of the university's Board of Trustees, Carlos de la Cruz, may have been worldly and sophisticated, a Phillips Academy–Andover and Wharton School graduate, as well as a Miami Law School graduate, but de la Cruz's board was thought unwilling to approve any link whatsoever between Reno and the university. Later, though, in 2004, Reno would become a Visiting Fellow at the Law School's Center for Ethics and Public Service.

Reno's first public appearance after leaving office was on *Saturday Night Live,* where she had been spoofed several times before in a series of skits titled "Janet Reno's Dance Party." But her first important "after" appearance was at a Harvard Women's Leadership Summit in April 2001. In her opening remarks, she referred to the *Saturday Night Live* skit and its reminder that it is important to be able to laugh at oneself and to laugh together as well. She also told the assembled women the story of her mother building the Reno home—the home that lost just a single shingle in Hurricane Andrew—and repeated for the nth time the message that one can do anything one really wants to do if you put your mind to it *and* it's the right thing to do.

Only then did Reno turn to the topic for the day: women's leadership. Her advice was: 1) put people first, for example, the poor mother of four in an apartment with a leak from the apartment above, the eighteen-year-old regularly racially profiled, the seventy-two-year-old abused and neglected; 2) figure out how to raise children in a safe and constructive way that leads them to solve problems, make peace, and rejoice in beauty; 3) ensure health care; 4) work with businesses, schools, and the community to end violence—it is not just the job of the police and courts; 5) pay teachers; 6) master and think through the use of new technologies; 7) enable someone without much money to be a serious political candidate; and 8) ensure access to the justice system. And, finally, she stated: "We must bring peace to this world." After these few and modest charges, Reno concluded by urging those assembled to never forget their families and recalled, first, the teenage twins whose care she inherited, and, second, the care she gave her mother—at home and until she died in her arms.

At her mother's funeral, Reno's talk had recalled Jane Wood Reno's capacity to insult and to embarrass—the company had held its breath, but after the family burst into laughter, the rest of the gathering did so as well. Reno's mother had been a stickler about integrity, and when Janet first met with politicians from newly democratic Eastern Bloc countries, she echoed her mother by reiterating again and again the importance of integrity. She noted that that would require paying officials appropriately—neither too little nor too much. The latter seemed to give her eastern audiences pause. Later Reno would express doubts about the impact of her talks. It was pretty clear that at least in some of those countries, integrity in government was not a primary value.

Another important appearance was before the National Press Club. There Reno addressed the Black community's distrust of law enforcement. She recalled the recent killing of Amadou Diallo and noted that even a U.S. attorney believed he must carefully instruct and remind his Black American son about the caution and respect it was vital to exercise in any interaction with a police officer, because officers were "armed and dangerous." Reno also noted, though, that hundreds of police officers had been killed in the line of duty, and she urged communities to focus on a movement toward "Effective Policing" because "every American must respect the law, but the law must [also] respect every American." Reno acknowledged that many police and a significant set of citizens felt fear in each other's presence. She remarked that good community policing would include police accountability, the hiring of more minority officers, a citizen's correctly feeling safe to complain, and, most importantly, police being willing to acknowledge the transgressions of fellow officers. Reno also revealed that household data were currently being collected on "crime victimization" and that those data would include questions about police stops and police use of force.

Reno spoke and spoke and spoke. Among her April speeches, she addressed the members of the Department of the Navy's Office of General Counsel; she spoke at the U.S. Border Patrol's 75th Anniversary Celebration (topic: National Missing Children's Day); she presented at the National Association of Drug Court Professional's Conference on Mental Health; she addressed a meeting of Chief U.S. District Judges; and at a DOJ "Police Integrity Conference," she cited a recent survey on policing, "Facing History and Ourselves." And she was written to as well. For example, Pete Seeger wrote on behalf of Kim Loy Wong, a steel band leader from Trinidad. Wong, who had lived in the United States for more than forty years was convicted of marijuana possession, served three years, and was about to be released—and deported. Seeger wanted to know what could be done? Four college men signing themselves as "Future Senators" proudly noted that they had gotten into a fist fight with some guys who were "bad mouthing you," and would she please send them a photo?

Not long after returning to Miami, Reno rode the metro downtown to answer a jury summons. She was more than willing to serve, but the presiding judge was her longtime friend Patricia Seitz who promptly excused her. Reno's admirers then persuaded her that another Bush—Jeb, the current governor of Florida who would soon be up for reelection—was vulnerable, and that she would be the perfect replacement.[1] The election would be held in the fall of 2002, some eighteen months away, but first there was the matter of the Democratic primary.

Ten individuals filed for the primary; Reno's strongest opponent was an attorney named William McBride, who had recently stepped down as leader of the law firm of Holland and Knight.[2] McBride grew up in Lees-burg in central Florida, a town of about 10,000, where he was proclaimed Mr. Leesburg High by classmates. As a senior, he attended Boys State where he was elected governor. He moved on to the University of Florida, where he graduated as a member of the prestigious Blue Key honorary society. After serving three years as a Marine Corps officer, some of it in Vietnam, he returned to the University of Florida for law school. Chesterfield Smith, then president of the ABA, became a mentor to McBride and not long after graduation, McBride joined the Tampa office of Smith's Holland and Knight law firm.

July polls showed Reno running thirty points ahead of McBride.[3] How-ever, many Democratic leaders had already committed to McBride even though he had never before run for office. Holland and Knight had ex-panded from ten to thirty offices under McBride's leadership, and the firm was not only well known throughout Florida but also known nationally as well. In contrast, Reno's Florida career had been almost exclusively in Mi-ami, and she had been out of the state for eight years. Thus, much of the smart money was on the political novice, William McBride.[4] Undaunted, the Reno team plunged in for her first statewide campaign untroubled by cartoons circulating that showed her head on the body of Arnold Schwar-zenegger or that of Xena, Warrior Princess.

Described as a "mom and pop" operation, Janet Reno's campaign was low budget and involved dozens of relatives described as being, like Reno, "tall, independent, liberal, outspoken, and a little quirky." The team did include one Democratic pro, Mo Elleithee, as manager.[5] The tone was set by Reno's plan for a fifteen-day tour of the state behind the wheel of her 1999 red Ford Ranger pickup truck.[6] It was launched on February 26 near the state line with its first stop Pensacola, followed by stops in Fort Walton Beach, Santa Rosa County, and Panama City. Reno went through Chat-tahoochee and Quincy, then stopped for a variety of appearances in Tal-lahassee before moving on to Perry and Gainesville. A primary theme for Reno (and McBride too) was the (very) low standing of Florida's public schools.[7] Success in reversing that low standard would require investing not only in the schools, Reno argued, but also in pre-kindergarten pro-grams as well. She deplored Bush's failure to advance programs for health care, particularly for seniors and for children, and for failing to even use the large amounts of federal funds available to Florida. Her third issue was care of the environment.[8] Reno's trip was casually programmed; stops were often announced only a day in advance, and crowds were often small until she arrived in South Florida.

In June she led McBride by 28 percent.[9] For three days "President" Martin Sheen of TV's *The West Wing* joined the campaign—giving it some extra media play.[10] The Elián controversy, though, clouded her prospects for the essential Miami vote.[11] Reno was also criticized for authorizing the Waco, Texas, attack. Further, it was unclear whether she should flaunt her Clinton credentials or flout them.[12] And then there were always some who focused on her palsy.

The quirky campaign even held a "Janet Reno Dance Party" fundraiser at Level, a then-hot Miami club—admission twenty-five dollars.[13] As one columnist pointed out, ordinarily the "door snobs" would have taken one look at the squarest woman in America, her dowdy black dress, sensible shoes, and bobbed hair, and sent her packing. "Watching what Reno will do next is now America's guilty pleasure of the summer," according to the same columnist. And people were watching—and joking. David Letterman quipped that Reno was hosting a dance party at a night club where she was the guest of honor—and also the bouncer. Geeky, off the wall, and ill-dressed as Reno may have seemed, in some ways what were apparent political liabilities actually worked to her advantage. They reinforced the fact that she was, in fact, very intelligent, very caring, and not into big money.

Campaign items included T-shirts silk-screened by her sister, Maggy, attendance at the Oscars, and hobnobbing with Elton John. Reno's campaign issues, iterated again and again, were education, the environment, pensioner benefits including health care, and the foster care system.

As soon as Reno filed her campaign papers a team of volunteers had swung into action.[14] They were led by Susan Vodicka, who rallied some fourteen of Reno's most committed supporters in a September 6, 2001, memo emphasizing the importance of centralizing campaign efforts and reporting progress in creating a "virtual campaign office," in other words, a phone answered by Janet's recorded voice and a website.[15] Other concerns were creation of a team to develop a public policy platform, a team to work on scheduling, and one to develop a "comprehensive money strategy." The next week, Week Two, reported that a bank account was being created to receive campaign funds, a team was being prepared to research issues, and a press briefing had been scheduled at Jackson Memorial Hospital where Reno and several doctors would discuss Parkinson's.[16]

As the campaign progressed, a staff member provided an October 4, 2001, analysis of the subjects addressed in phone calls, emails, and letters to the campaign over a three-week period. The listing included the staffer's rating from one to ten as to the topics' importance and relevance to the campaign. High scores went to gays seeking asylum in the United States, children exposed to violence, education reform, people with disabilities, and Florida's Department of Children and Families (DCF). Low scores went to airline security, the 9/11 attack, and revisiting the Florida 2000 election results.

As the campaign proceeded, the press began to assess Reno's prospects. Some thought she might win the primary but would lose to incumbent Governor Bush. Others, like the *Orlando Sentinel* on November 3, 2001, proclaimed her "larger than life," and said of Bush, "Dude's in for a fight." In an interview in the *Weekly News,* a paper serving the gay community, Reno was clear that civil and human rights should not depend on a vote.[17] At the same time, she argued that one should not refer to "the gay and lesbian vote" as a "bloc," even while urging a "forceful and persuasive turnout" when gay issues were being debated. There were critics, though. John Rivera, president of the Police Benevolent Association (PBA), critiqued Reno's performance as state attorney and a Miami businessmen's organization for even inviting her to speak.

Voters probably do not realize how much research is done by candidates in their efforts to learn what is on voters' minds and how intensely they feel about particular issues. For instance, the Reno campaign used a set of Hickman-Brown research findings dated May 2001 to guide its efforts. It showed Florida voters as evenly split between Republicans and Democrats with some 25 percent identifying themselves as independents. There was about an even split between those who saw the country and the state as going in the "right direction" and those who felt Florida was on the "wrong track." Education was seen as the first or second most important issue. It was identified by 59 percent of the voters. The next most highly rated issues were crime at 21 percent and taxes at 19 percent.

The poll also asked about favorable and unfavorable ratings of a list of some dozen political figures. Jeb Bush, George W. Bush, Al Gore, and Janet Reno all had high unfavorable ratings. Reno's unfavorable ratings were actually slightly higher than her favorable. The Democrats competing with Reno in the primary were largely rated "Never Heard Of" or "Can't Rate." In matchups of each Democrat with incumbent Governor Jeb Bush, those responding to the poll showed Jeb a clear winner in every instance. Potential voters responding to the poll favored gun control by almost 10 percent, pro-choice by more than 10 percent, and 70 percent favored more for public education. Those responding also favored improving state services even if it did not mean taxes would be cut, and believed vouchers for private schooling took money away from public schools.

A *USA Today* poll also conducted a May survey in Florida. It showed Reno with high unfavorable ratings although lower than her favorable ratings. It did not consider the lengthy list of other potential Democratic nominees. Interestingly, the poll showed public education and crime as important issues, but the top issue in that poll was "Growth and over-development," a topic that had concerned only 10 percent of voters in the Hickman-Brown poll. There may have been a lot of dissatisfaction with Reno's decisions as attorney general, but almost 80 percent said her Parkinson's would have no effect on their vote, and 70 percent said they approved of the return of Elián to his father. Elián, then, was not a Florida issue. It was a Miami issue, but as such, would cost her dearly.

Some nine months later, in January 2002, a statewide poll by the Mellman Groups showed few changes. Both Jeb Bush and Janet Reno continued to have high unfavorable results; his were 34 percent, hers were 40 percent. Thirty-nine percent had never heard of McBride, and another 39 percent didn't know enough about him to have an opinion. When a series of questions were asked about Reno, over half saw her as a strong leader, straight talker, having integrity, and being tough on crime. The highest negative was the 42 percent who saw her as too liberal. In contrast, 47 percent found Bush too conservative and out of touch with Florida voters. However, he scored over 50 percent on most items. Indeed, overall, respondents preferred Bush by 2 to 6 percent.

The Mellman Groups poll had clearly been requested by the Reno camp, since it asked a series of questions about what Reno positions people liked, and what issues would get a voter to vote against Bush.[18] The expected issues included no recount in the Bush-Gore presidential election, education, cuts to Medicaid, and support for drilling in the Gulf of Mexico. Survey constructors asked respondents not only their party affiliation but also their age, level of schooling, Hispanic descent (9 percent), and if of Hispanic descent, from which country (only 32 percent were from Cuba), religion (22 percent Catholic; 21 percent Baptist/Southern Baptist), with half attending services at least a few times a month. Interestingly, 3 percent considered themselves upper class, 19 percent upper middle class, 50 percent middle class, 22 percent working class, but only 3 percent lower class. And—11 percent had family income under $20,000, and 23 percent had $20,000 to less than $40,000. Thus, one-third of families polled existed on less than $40,000 a year.[19]

By April, it was clear that education was the primary concern of voters. Florida was near the bottom of most statistics related to public education. As an incumbent, Jeb Bush needed to make an argument that under his leadership things were getting better. Months before the election, he began an expensive TV campaign to make that point. Ironically, he filmed his ad in a private Christian school! He used statements by four Teacher of the Year winners in his ads, but the largest teacher's union, the Florida Education Association, backed Democrat Bill McBride. Democrats noted that under Bush, spending per pupil had, indeed, increased—by a full $10.21 per student.

Fundraising was an all-important task, but there was a lot of other work to be done by volunteers. These included phone banks where volunteers could make fifteen to twenty personal calls an hour, and a recorded message made up to sixty. If necessary, individuals could be paid to make the calls. Another vital activity was precinct walks. A volunteer could average twenty homes an hour and would be provided a script that included an offer of a ride to the polls and an invitation to participate in the campaign. Volunteers were also given a list of DOS AND DON'TS, for example, don't walk on anyone's lawn, don't get bit by a dog, never put something in someone's mailbox (it's against the law), never answer a question if you are unsure of the right answer, and never phone during dinner (after 6:00 p.m.).

One enterprising supporter, Cathy L. Josey, thought ahead. In November 2001, she registered fifteen web addresses, for example, JANET4GOV. COM, WELOVEJANET.NET, JANETFORGOVERNOR.ORG. for a cost of $134.25. She wanted to donate any or all of the sites to the campaign.[20] And another supporter, Angela Davies, Manager of Waldenbooks Superstore on Kendall Drive, helped by providing space for a rally while expressing her dim view of negative and disruptive politicking. She also declared it "flauntingly hypocritical" to say "everyone gets a shot" in politics when Florida had a governor who was the son of one U.S. President and the brother of another.

While she was settling in for the campaign, out-of-office Reno continued to get hundreds of letters covering a wide range of topics. One came from Dana Bingham, the daughter of her former/first law partner. A second came from a member of the Justice Protective Service, who wrote that he had a special belt buckle with her name on it that he had been holding for six years, knowing her strict rules about receiving gifts, but now that she was out of office, he was sending it to her. Reno agreed "with pleasure" to a request that she tape a book, preferably *The Story of Johnny Appleseed*, for the Bookworm Project, which supplied tapes read by public figures to students at a school with mostly low-income students in Sarasota County, Florida. She agreed to an interview with a ninth-grade student from Westminster Christian School in Miami. The child had submitted a dozen questions, among them "Why do you want to be Governor" and "What is your happiest memory of your years in Washington?" A student from Shaker Heights High School in Cleveland described a project involving a display of photos of prominent individuals and the display of a favorite book. Reno's reply cited Doris Kearns Goodwin's *No Ordinary Time* about Franklin and Eleanor Roosevelt as being her favorite.

There was a lengthy letter typed on a thrift shop $6.95 typewriter from eighty-nine-year-old Rose Truesdale who enclosed a twenty-five dollar money order. Truesdale was sickened by the deals being cut by the Jeb Bush administration and by his brother, the president, who had swooped in on Air Force One as a quid pro quo for the Florida "fake" ballot count that put him in office. Commenting on a photo of "Dubya" picturing him seated on a bale of hay wearing pointy-toed boots while conducting a press conference, Truesdale noted that it reminded her of her kids' favorite TV show: *Howdy Doody!*

There were, of course, some less mainstream letters like the one from a woman from South Dakota who had published a book detailing the myriad cures she had discovered for her myriad afflictions—inconveniently the treatments took half a day every day. She noted that horseradish tea cures asthma, and that Hulda Clark's Parasite Zapper is so effective that the author hauls it with her everywhere. She no longer applies for jobs, though, because women who excel are likely to be poisoned or, alternatively, to be under the control of some pimp. Another woman typed four pages of religious cant. Reno answered: "I have very much appreciated your letters, and will do all I can to deserve your support. I share your concern for this great state." Another truly disturbing letter arrived in January 2002 from an inmate in Wabash Valley Correctional Facility who rejoiced at seeing Janet Reno's collapse on CNN.[21] She, he charged, murdered thirteen children in Waco and never expressed sympathy. Therefore, "The devil will have his way with you. But first the worms are gonna eat you. I will be praying for you, bitch. . . . Please rot in Hell for Eternity. Think about Ruby Ridge and Waco while you burn. Goodbye Bitch!"

McBride was a political novice but quickly learned to be an effective campaigner. One of his favorite quips was that a candidate should "Talk about God, talk about love, and talk about five minutes. And don't forget to ask for money."[22] He drew support: the Florida Democratic Party gave him $200,000 for his campaign; the 122,000 member Florida Education Association endorsed him, as did the Florida Building Trades Council; and the American Federation of Labor launched a Get Out the Vote campaign on his behalf.[23] McBride won the primary, but by less than 5,000 votes out of 1.3 million.[24] McBride went on to lose to incumbent Bush, 43 percent to 56 percent. When asked her plans following Bush's victory, Reno said, "I plan to learn how to play the piano more effectively than I can, I plan to perfect my 'Eskimo roll' [a kayaking move], visit the people that I have met along the way, and fight as hard as I can to make sure that Florida's voting process is one that people can be proud of."[25]

A lot of people shared in that sentiment. The Supreme Court's stay of a recount of Florida's votes in 2000 had made George W. Bush president of the United States, although the actual count remained uncertain. Florida was embarrassed. In May 2001, Governor Jeb Bush proclaimed that Florida's new election system would be "not only the envy of the nation, but the envy of the world."[26] The test came in the September primaries, and Florida flunked again. The state's $32 million invested in improving election processes had not averted a second fiasco in Broward and Dade counties, the two counties with the largest population. There were a lot of people focused on electoral reform and Reno remained concerned, but she was to go on to invest her personal energies in other efforts.[27]

One focus of her attention concerned the care of children. Florida had made national headlines over the grievous treatment of children under its care. Indeed, when Jeb Bush ran for governor in 1998, one issue that was central to his campaign was a call to reform Florida's Department of Children and Families (DCF). Once elected, Bush appointed Judge Kathleen Kearney to head DCF.[28] Further, the next year the Florida legislature passed new child protection legislation. A good idea, but what was probably an unintended consequence was an enormous increase in reports of child abuse and in children removed from what were deemed potentially abusive homes. In fact, in one year, the number of open child abuse investigations increased by a factor of five.[29]

When Bush was preparing for reelection in 2001, it was clear that the DCF and its new leader were continuing to fail Florida's children. The *Sun Sentinel* kept tabs on the issue noting that a federal magistrate recommended that a federal class action lawsuit against the state's foster care program proceed. A Broward Circuit Judge found DCF in contempt (May 12, 2001). The *Miami Herald* reported that abuse of foster children under state supervision had increased from 4 to 8 percent in the last year (August 16, 2001). And the *Florida Times-Union* (November 4, 2001) reported that one in eleven children in foster care were mistreated. By 2002, more scandalous data were published in the *Florida Times-Union* (February 21, 2002), and DCF became a campaign issue.

Two cases in particular shocked the public. One involved Rilya Wilson, a four-year-old, who had been placed in a foster home in 2000, but who had last been seen there in January 2001. Even though DCF workers were supposed to check on foster children once a month, it took more than a year for DCF to discover that Wilson had, in fact, disappeared.[30] That was in late April 2002. Within two weeks, Governor Bush had created a Blue Ribbon Panel on Child Protection that reported back in only three weeks that DCF was "underfunded, understaffed, underappreciated, and overworked." Bush did not warmly embrace his panel's findings and call for immediate action. Instead, he formed yet another study group to consider the panel's highest priority, the funding of a guardian ad litem for each foster child.

Then-gubernatorial-candidate Reno soon issued a call to enact many of the proposed reforms, emphasizing in a letter to Governor Bush the need to call a special session of the legislature to procure the funding needed to implement them. Bush may have hoped that the public would focus on other issues as the campaign heated up, but child abuse headlines surfaced again in July when two-year-old Alfredo Montez was beaten to death on the very day a DCF case worker had written a report stating she had visited him.

Reno did not entirely withdraw from politics, and she campaigned hard for John Kerry when he ran for U.S. President in 2004. At a talk in Saint Charles, Missouri, she recalled being ten years old and staying up all night waiting for the presidential election results. At 6:30 a.m., much to the shock of many, California gave the election to Missouri's Harry S. Truman. Reno then urged her audience not to give up, and to focus on the issues, while using dialogue that would bring along independents—and even some Republicans.[31] Issues Reno would continue to follow were public education, errors in the justice system (there had already been 151 exonerations based on DNA testing), and health issues.

Even after stepping off the campaign trail, Reno continued to receive fan letters. One fan, Mildred S. Weismann, sent a collection of her poems on a variety of topics, many of them political. An especially charming poem was titled "My Silent Friend." Only in the last line was it revealed that the "friend" was the piano that had been neglected, waiting to be played. The poem was inspired by Reno's voicing her plan to resume her piano-playing after she'd lost in her campaign for governor.

Reno was still sought out to give keynotes. For example, a November 3, 2005, address at Rice University's conference "Facing the Challenges of Increasing Diversity in the Legal Profession: Collaborating to Expand the Pipeline" and a February 15, 2008, address at Morning Star Renewal Center, where a Catholic nonprofit was sponsoring a seminar "My Faith in Practice: Resurrecting Our Moral Conscience" (a seminar that was certified for Continuing Legal Education). She also accepted a role as adviser to the American Constitution Society (ACS) designed to counter the conservative Federalist Society that had chapters at 150 law schools and 30,000 members. The ACS quickly formed chapters at eighty schools and claimed 6,000 members. Other supporters of ACS included Hillary Clinton, Ruth

Bader Ginsburg, and Rosemary Barkett. At a fundraiser for the group, Reno danced to ABBA's "Dancing Queen" with a variety of partners.

In 2003 Reno spoke to the fourth class at the Appalachian School of Law, whose dean, a professor, and a student had recently been murdered by an irate student over his failing grades. She urged the audience to focus on four roles: problem solver, peace maker, sword, and shield. That same year she presented an award to Deval Patrick at an Equal Justice Works event.[32] Patrick was by then General Counsel and Vice President of Coca-Cola, and the corporation had been implicated in a number of murders in Colombia. Thus, the event was picketed by the International Labor Rights Fund. Patrick contended that the Coca-Cola bottling plants had not worked with Colombia paramilitaries and averred that it would work with unions. But perhaps the project closest to Reno's heart was the Innocence Project. Her attention and concern arose from having been assigned to investigate James Richardson's 1968 case, which had then led to his exoneration in 1989.[33]

In 2003 Janet Reno's brother, Bob, diagnosed himself with Alzheimer's, and the family brought him to Miami. After brief periods in private nursing homes, which found him a difficult patient, he found comfort and care at the local Veteran's Administration hospital. He died on July 9, 2012, and his wake at the family home involved gospel singers, a good deal of wine, and a letter of condolence from President Barack Obama. In lieu of funeral flowers, the family asked that friends donate to the Obama presidential campaign "even if they are Republicans."

After raising four children with Jim, Maggy served as a commissioner in Martin County, Florida, for twenty years, acted as Janet's voice in an episode of *The Simpsons,* and remained dauntless both as an environmentalist and as a kayaker. Indeed, at age seventy, she joyfully navigated Class 4 rapids because "of the jubilant feeling of bouncing safely through chaos." In an interview Maggy noted, "I've spent my life trying to save the world. Kayaking reminds me of the awe and wonder that makes me care." Maggy Hurchalla spent several years fighting a Strategic Lawsuit Against Public Participation (SLAPP) intended to quash her environmental activism before her death on February 19, 2022.[34]

For Janet Reno, Parkinson's continued its insidious progress. Just as her mother had been cared for at home through a slow decline, so Reno was cared for by a set of devoted attendants. By 2007, Kareema Sabur, who had known Reno for a number of years, became her lead caregiver. The others who provided what became around-the-clock care included Dawn Cargill, Angela Pagon, Caridad Hung, Michael Edwards, Yvette Campbell, and Marjorie Smith. Daphne Webb was crucial during this time. Webb escorted Reno to Washington, DC, in a wheelchair for a ceremony honoring women World War II service members, which included Reno's aunt Winnie.[35] When Reno's health worsened, Webb was there to observe the hour and a half of warm attention Bill Clinton gave the partially alert Janet Reno when he came to visit her at Kendall, and also Eric Holder's smiling accusation that Reno hadn't told him what he was in for when he accepted his appointment as deputy attorney general.

Janet Wood Reno finally rested on November 7, 2016, at age seventy-eight.

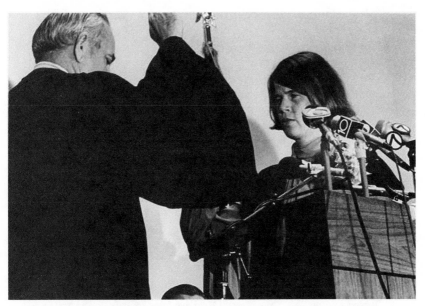

Janet Reno being sworn in as Florida's first woman state attorney, 1978. Florida Memory.

Janet and Jane outside the family home, c. 1980. Courtesy of Reno Family Archives.

Janet and Bobby L. Jones, director of Metro Public Safety Department, at the "Perspectives on Race, Crime and the Criminal Justice System" forum hosted by Miami-Dade Community College, 1981. Florida Memory.

Portrait of U.S. Attorney General Janet Reno, 1993, the same year that Reno was inducted into the Florida Women's Hall of Fame. Florida Memory.

Janet attending Pat Seitz's installation as the first woman president of the Florida Bar.
L-R: U.S. Attorney General Janet Reno, Patricia A. Seitz, and Chief Justice Rosemary Barkett.
Florida Memory.

Maggy and Janet, c. 2005. Courtesy of Reno Family Archives.

Bill Clinton visiting Janet at her home with caregiver Kareema Sabur, September 2014. Courtesy of Reno Family Archives.

Epilogue

News of Janet Reno's death circulated quickly.

Elián González was then a student of engineering in Cuba and engaged to be married. The Cuban Embassy called to send the message: "The family of Elián González would like to express their gratitude and love to Janet Reno for sending Elián home to his family."

Hundreds attended the December 11 memorial service held at the Kendall Campus of Miami-Dade College. The reach of Janet's life was reflected in the breadth of the participants. With her niece, Hunter Reno, presiding, the U.S. Border Patrol Color Guard began the ceremony by presenting the colors, then meticulously folded an American flag and presented it to the family. "The Battle Hymn of the Republic" was sung with a martial spirit that made one confident that the "the terrible swift sword" would indeed dispatch "the grapes of wrath" and that "his truth" would, indeed, march on.

Prayers and a reminiscence were offered by Rabbi Judith Siegal, who smiled and assured the audience that Reno wasn't actually Jewish; by Father Frank O'Laughlin of the Guatemalan Maya Center, whose work focused on immigrants and who rambled a bit, but who was clearly doing God's work and said that Janet Reno was too; and last, but by no means least, by Dr. Walter T. Richardson, Pastor Emeritus of Sweet Home Baptist Church. Richardson preached with such energy that many in the audience were soon clapping, although softly, and/or tapping their toes. Richardson described the Perrine Project in community policing, which brought such a change to that community that people were left "shaking." The pastor concluded by asking the audience to recite Psalm 23 with him.[1] Many of us were able to do so. Janet Reno had considered herself spiritual, though not conventionally religious and certainly not sectarian. Her spirit was well represented by the three who spoke—none of whom were "mainline" clergy.

Then a switch was made to Reno's Washington colleague Loretta Lynch, the current attorney general, and Bill Clinton under whom Reno had served, although certainly not always in just the way he might have preferred. Lynch set the tone by noting that it was wonderful to see old friends even if some were rather grayer and balder. In that way she established the fact that the Janet Reno stories were not only to be upbeat but also that laughing would be encouraged and permitted. Lynch recalled her first meeting with Reno while a very junior member in the DOJ's New York City office, and that Reno had shaken every hand in the office and encouraged each to be all they could be—a message well received by the young, Black woman who at that time did not see many like herself in the Department of Justice hierarchy.

Bill Clinton credited former Florida governor and senator Bob Graham with being the first to tell him "appoint Reno."[2] However, Clinton already knew about Janet Reno because he had visited his brother-in-law, Hugh Rodham, who was serving in Miami as a defense lawyer for those who could not afford an attorney; Hugh had recommended her also. Clinton observed with approval the drug courts Reno had created, and he told a story about one trial in which the prosecutor, judge, and defense lawyer befuddled the defendant by playing each other's roles. He emphasized what close observers knew—that Janet Reno believed her job included prevention, problem-solving, the saving of young people, and *never* punishing the innocent. Clinton said he admired the fact that "she never cut a corner" and never hesitated to acknowledge a mistake with humility. (Clinton specifically referenced Waco.) Bill Clinton closed his tribute by offering a lesson to the assembled: "Some of your decisions *will* be wrong. Admit it and move on."[3]

Sandy D'Alemberte, past president of the American Bar Association, president emeritus of Florida State University, and an early, continuing, and crucial mentor for Reno, noted that her championing of the Brady Bill was crucial and had resulted in a forty-seven-year low in illegal gun deaths. His summary of Janet Reno? "She was one of a kind—but she would not want to be."

Her sister, Maggy, got the last word. Maggy told a story about running away to Marco Island for twenty-four hours—with the family car—and of other exploring trips that could involve getting lost, perhaps sleeping out without proper equipment, or unexpectedly having to abandon a canoe and hike back to civilization without shoes. Their canoe trips and other adventures, Maggy said, were always a great success, although sometimes the success consisted primarily of having a good story to tell on themselves.

Among others, Maggy told a New York City story that involved a purse snatcher who they unsuccessfully pursued, and the offer by several other young men who looked rather like the snatcher who said, "Ma'am, can we walk you ladies home?" The night before Janet Reno was to be sworn in as attorney general, and the last time in a long time before she could move about without a security detail, she and Maggy took a long walk to each of the Washington memorials beginning with that of Abraham Lincoln, where they sang "The Battle Hymn of the Republic." Maggy closed her talk with the favorite Reno childhood family poem: "Wynken, Blynken, and Nod." The service itself closed with the hymns "Steal Away to Jesus" and "I Come to the Garden Alone" performed by Maryel Epps and the South Florida Ministers of Music.

NOTES

PROLOGUE

1. Miami is one of thirty-five cities in Miami-Dade County. When talking, writing, or reading about the area, one sometimes intends "Miami" to mean the county as a whole, and sometimes only the city that is the county seat. Other well-known cities in the county are Miami Beach, Coral Gables, and Hialeah.

2. Much of this history is drawn from Arva Parks's excellent books about Miami (see note on sources).

3. The railroad was extended to Key West in 1912, but it was destroyed by a hurricane in less than twenty-five years. Short life spans were, and arguably still are, typical of many Florida efforts.

4. The *Metropolis* became the *Miami News* in 1925, publishing until 1988. Founded in 1903, the *Miami Evening Record* became today's *Miami Herald* in 1910.

5. Residential areas, like the schools, were segregated, but many people in the Black community prospered. However, Black voting would not always be welcome, especially after the arrival of the Ku Klux Klan in 1921. In 1896, however, the votes of Black residents were essential to meet the total number of votes required for incorporation as a city.

6. The first bridge (wooden) from Miami to the beach was built in 1913. Coral Gables, "The City Beautiful," had strict zoning laws covering such things as the range of colors one could paint one's home. In addition, its Mediterranean architecture gave it distinction.

7. Stories abounded of buying land in the morning and selling at a huge profit in the afternoon. William Jennings Bryan was alleged to have earned $100,000 a year to promote the Coral Gables development.

8. In 1935 an even larger hurricane would strike the Florida Keys, taking more than four hundred lives.

9. Prohibition ended in 1933, but other illicit enterprises continued to flourish. Reporter Jane Wood Reno, Janet's mother, wrote that by 1940, gambling profits were $100 million a year, enabled by $1 million in bribes to police.

10. It is estimated that half of the Hispanics/Latinos are of Cuban heritage, thus, a bit under a third of the population.

CHAPTER 1. FAMILY

1. As a nineteen-year-old, Rasmussen had briefly worked as a lumberjack in the Northwest. Oral History, part 1, p. 7.

2. Henry emphasized to his children the importance of treating others well, remembering his early days in the United States when his language and clothes had made him an object of ridicule.

3. Between 1910 and 1960, three out of six Milwaukee mayors were members of the Socialist Party.

4. His coauthor was Wilson McGee, who described Reno as "an astonishing intellectual. He never could get enough to read and never felt he could learn all the things he wanted to know."

5. Located near Macon, the town today has a population of less than 150. Even after moving to Miami, the Woods would vacation at the family home in Sunnyside.

6. Wood was not a talker and was famous for one-page legal filings. When he lacked clients, he worked on and completed a life of Christ. Oral History, part 1, p. 6.

7. At first Jane found Miami dull. However, the drama of the hurricane changed her mind. This was especially because the family mistook the calm of the hurricane's eye for the end of the storm and were caught walking on the beach by the back of the storm. Oral History, part 1, p. 2.

8. Oral History, part 1, p. 3.

9. Her most thrilling interview was with Amelia Earhart, who was preparing for her ill-fated attempt to circumnavigate the globe. Earhart said she was doing it "just for fun." Jane soon adopted the phrase to explain many of her own actions. Oral History, part 1, p. 3.

10. The Avocado house has been replaced by a McMansion that faces Plaza Street, thus, 3600 no longer exists.

11. The area is now a part of South Miami, and the streets have been renumbered.

12. Oral History, part 1, p. 12.

13. The child, my tennis partner a half century later, was not allowed to go to the Renos' again.

14. The store-bought Palmolive soap at the grandparents' home was considered a treat.

15. *Janet Reno: Doing the Right Thing* is the title of a 1994 biography by Paul Anderson, published by Wiley.

16. Miami's grid of streets and avenues makes it easy to navigate—except where waterways interrupt, and except in Hialeah and in Coral Gables where developer George Merrick gave up the angular and gave names to his streets. Many streets have three names—a number, a name like Coral Way or Red Road, and the name of an individual—all crammed onto an overhead street sign.

17. The bathroom had no door until a woman friend took the initiative to install one. Later a breezeway connected the main house to an annex with two more bedrooms. The porch consumes 700 of the home's 1,707 square feet.

18. Maggy describes the family as living as though they were poor. While they had two cars, both were secondhand, and one had floorboards providing a clear view of the road below. For the Renos, life was never dull. One of Jane's more memorable exploits involved trapping eleven skunks then depositing them at the door of the police station to convey her disdain.

19. *Miami Daily News,* November 15, 1955. Front page story.

20. *Miami Herald,* September 26, 1965. Jane wrote a feature story detailing the solitary walk.

21. Janet was sensitized to the pain of segregation and also recognized that a young Black man and a young White man were treated quite differently in court proceedings. Oral History, part 1, pp. 6, 15, and 16.

22. See *Invitation to a Lynching* by reporter Gene Miller (New York: Doubleday, 1975).

CHAPTER 2. SCHOOL DAYS

1. Oral History, part 1, p. 18.

2. Many of my generation remember when we learned of Roosevelt's death. Just as the next generation remembers where they were when Martin Luther King Jr. and Jack Kennedy were killed. Each subsequent generation's tragedies are not forgotten.

3. Interview with Vera Porfiri, February 2, 2014.

4. Interview with Karen McCammon, December 14, 2015.

5. High school days are often described fondly. Just as often, people confide those times as miserable—Janet's opinion fell somewhere in between. She was clearly successful, but even intelligent and mature teenagers enjoy being "popular," and everyone knows exactly where they fall in that hierarchy.

6. Porfiri described Jane as pragmatic and action oriented. If there was a stump in her yard, she took it out—herself. Interview, February 2, 2014.

7. Porfiri interview, February 2, 2014.

8. The team won the state debate championship in Janet's junior and senior year. Coach Dickson persuaded her to drop chemistry and take a second year of speech saying, "You can sit in a lab for the rest of your life." Dickson left Miami because of his son's asthma, and Janet was not able to find him to thank him for years. Then, in the mid-1990s she got a letter in her attorney general's office with a phone number saying "You probably don't remember me." She was delighted and immediately invited him to visit her in Washington.

9. Porfiri noted that sister Maggy, in particular, knew how to "let you have it." Porfiri found brother Bob quieter and an excellent student. Mark she described as a good worker who reveled in the wilderness. Interview, February 2, 2014.

10. Reno had an uncle who had gone to Cornell as an undergrad and another who had gone to medical school there. Also, her high school principal's son had gone there. Oral History, part 1, p. 24.

11. Janet, describing herself as 6'1" and gawky, said high school was where she learned to be self-reliant. "The boys were my buddies, but I never dated." Another thing she learned was that if you were nice to people, they would reciprocate. And she was nice, and people were nice to her.

12. Sally, a single woman, was the daughter of Jane's sister, Daisy Wood.

CHAPTER 3. PREPARATION: CORNELL AND HARVARD, 1956–1963

1. The metropolitan area, however, has greatly expanded, and now encompasses a population of 100,000.

2. The land-grant schools include Agriculture and Life Science, Human Ecology (once Home Economics), Industrial and Labor Relations, and the graduate school of Veterinary Medicine. As a public institution it has a commitment to outreach and service to the state's

citizens. At the same time, the schools of Engineering, Hotel Administration, Architecture, Art and Planning, Arts and Sciences and the graduate schools of Law and Management are private schools.

3. Janet's yearbook pictures just under twelve thousand graduating seniors.

4. By her senior year women's dorms were offering cafeteria style dinner.

5. Beanies would be abolished the following year. Student riots during Reno's freshman year resulted in a new student government and a new faculty-student discipline system.

6. Discussing why students came to Cornell, the yearbook listed a number of possibilities, including to find a husband, but added "of course that's not why she came to college." Still the yearbook's class history, written by a man and a woman, referred to coming to campus, unpacking trunks, and hanging a *Playboy* calendar, and noted that "no senior men date senior women, and hardly anybody else does either." Even professors casually made jokes that now would be considered sexist.

7. Strangely, on special spring and fall weekends, women could sign out to stay overnight at a fraternity house—which at the time supplied chaperones.

8. She was wearing high black heels. The next day a fellow waitress said, "I saw you—You can wait tables or introduce a President, both with class." Oral History, part 1, p. 25.

9. Margaret Balfour, with whom she spent a year in Germany during high school. Her letter also included a variety of comments about family members: "I think my mother would make a first rate top sergeant"; Bob is a "senior statesman" in high school and surely going to be a lawyer; Maggy has no aspirations "other than to be brilliant and lazy."

10. Reno believed her freshman chemistry teacher was one of the best professors she ever had, and he was the inspiration for her to continue as a major. She believed the rigor and system of chemistry gave her a perspective she might not otherwise have acquired. Oral History, part 1, p. 28.

11. Perkins had been President Franklin Roosevelt's Secretary of Labor and the first woman to hold any cabinet position. Other faculty included Walter Berns who taught Constitutional Law, and Mario Anatti for Political Theory.

12. There was no mention of two very relevant items: sex and race.

13. Since she did not have the grade point for Phi Beta Kappa, and perhaps had only a C average, Reno must have had superb LSATs. She did not think she had a ghost of a chance and did not let her mother know about her application, applying to Harvard only after strong encouragement from her grandfather. Having low expectations for herself, she went to the movies the night before the all-important LSATs. Oral History, part 1, p. 29.

14. Women remained a novelty for some time. A report issued by the ABA in 2005 reported that women were 3 percent of the lawyer population in 1951. They increased to 8 percent by 1980 and to 27 percent by 2000. In 2000 they were overrepresented in government, legal aid and defender programs, and in judicial departments—but not as judges. "Researching Law," the American Bar Association, vol. 16, no. 1, Winter 2005.

15. Oral History, part 2, p. 3.

16. Anderson, 38. In contrast, Reno claimed not to feel discriminated against; see Oral History, part 2, p. 3.

17. The Nieman is a prestigious fellowship awarded to journalists.

18. She described herself as "so filled with wonderful times and people and new things, and places and people to know that for once in my life I am at a loss to write all about it and can only babble happily."

19. The day before, she had walked ten miles in a round trip to Boston. Another time she walked from Salem to Gloucester camping out near the ocean.

20. Her letters typically closed, "Love or Much Love, Me."

21. She was thinking about the English troops that had had such a walk just before the battle in Lexington.

22. Oral History, part 2, p. 4.

23. Oral History, part 2, p. 4.

24. *Gainesville Sun,* January 18, 1999, p. 1. See also the *Ledger,* February 2, 1999. She had earlier received a "Big Story" award when she persuaded a convicted robber to name a police officer as an inside man for a Miami gang.

25. "Calamity Jane: Is this any way for the prosecutor's mother to live?" *Miami Herald,* March 11, 1979.

26. Women had only been admitted to Harvard Law School for just over a decade. Reno's class had a grand total of fifteen women. In an address to the class, Reno urged more public service, which received faint applause. She also proposed a mandatory two-year public service requirement. That was soundly rejected. Maggy Hurchalla interview, October 26, 1993.

27. On a personal note, I remember having precisely the same feeling when I was told I could not even apply for a regular position in the University of Wisconsin Political Science Department where I was already teaching as a visitor. "No, you can't apply, you are a woman and will never be visible," said the Princeton graduate chairman.

28. Indeed, Chayes paved the way for this author to write a book about the integration of women at the U.S. Air Force Academy, *Bring Me Men and Women: Mandated Change at the U.S. Air Force Academy* (Berkeley: University of California Press, 1981).

29. One dinner was for Wendy Marcus of Nieman Marcus fame. She prepared lobster for the first time using a recipe provided by her neighbor, a minister's wife, who, Reno quipped, was a "wonderful conversationalist—actually she never says anything."

30. She noted one instance when men were smuggled in to East Boston as mourners in a funeral procession only to shape-shift into their real assignment—that of stuffing ballot boxes.

31. Letter, February 18, 1961.

32. Reno characteristically framed her thoughts in analogies. It is doubtful that anyone else could have dreamed up this one for torts. Another example was a description of filling out a financial statement for Harvard as again going "around the mulberry bush."

33. Letter, April 3, 1961.

CHAPTER 4. BUILDING A CAREER: MIAMI, 1963–1978

1. For an extended discussion of the status of South Florida Blacks during the period of large-scale Cuban immigration see Eric Tscheschlok, "Long Time Coming: Miami's Liberty City Riots of 1968," *Florida Historical Quarterly* 74 (Spring 1996): 440–60.

2. It was still somewhat unusual for women to try cases, and Janet was not given as much courtroom time as she would have liked. Oral History, part 2, p. 11.

3. Lewis's daughter, Pat, fondly remembered Janet teaching her how to dig for fishing worms—and, also, how to iron! Mother Jane taught Pat how to sew, and many weekends involved games of capture-the-flag and rambles through the woods, as well as attentive listening to adult political discussion and debate. A crucial theme was that one could (and should) try to make a difference. *The Star,* February 16, 1963.

4. Oral History, part 2, p. 8.

5. Miami's riot came late. There were many urban protests and riots beginning in the early 1960s. The Watts (Los Angeles) riot of 1965 may have been the first to fully capture national attention, but 1964 saw unrest in cities such as Philadelphia and Rochester, and the "long hot summer" of 1967 had at least fifteen. Miami's 1968 riot was one of perhaps ten that year and was relatively small.

6. It was a year of rare opportunity because the U.S. Supreme Court had declared in *Baker v. Carr* (369 U.S. 186, 1962) that districts for federal office must be based on population not geography. The "one man one vote" formula was applied to state legislatures soon thereafter in *Reynolds v. Sims* (377 U.S. 533, 1964). This meant that Miami suddenly had a set of new seats to fill.

7. Anderson, 53.

8. She also authored Florida's no fault divorce law.

9. Reno especially appreciated the help of circuit court judges Hugh Taylor and Guy Mc-Cord. Oral History, part 2, p. 15.

10. Remember, a constitutional amendment must be ratified by three-fourths of the states. It wasn't. And Florida would be one of the states that did not ratify it.

11. South Florida politics and government were riddled with corruption. It was said that one read the morning newspaper to see who had been indicted the day before and whether or not one knew them.

12. In 1972, Orr was elected mayor of Dade County. In the interval, he had worked as a prosecutor for the state attorney. Oral History, part 2, p. 18.

13. There were some items that needed expunging such as a fake driver's license, possession of baby alligators in a national park, and the turning off of the neon cross at the Sunset Presbyterian Church.

14. There were no children from Mark's first marriage (to Vera). His second marriage (to Donna) produced a son, Douglas, and a daughter, Hunter. At one point the partner of tennis star Martina Navratilova, Hunter had two children. Mark's third marriage (to Ann) yielded a daughter, Michelle, and a granddaughter, Piper.

15. Although the Vietnam War was raging, neither Mark nor Bob Reno were assigned there, although they both got veteran's benefits for serving in time of war.

16. Edited by Bill Moyers, *Newsday* was a liberal paper, and Bob Reno's columns were by no means typical of those found in most business sections.

17. The family believed him to be an alcoholic and possibly a drug user. Challa and Robert had one child, Meliha.

18. Hunter has described Jane as doing whatever she wanted to whenever she wanted to and as having a viper tongue, often directed at Janet, who was, nevertheless, steadfast in her devotion.

19. Douglas was pursuing a conventional career in mortgage banking when during a diving expedition his friend urged him to try out for the fire department. He did, was accepted, and felt happy in an occupation that is "of value." This note and the following are from an interview with Douglas on December 14, 2015.

20. During her state attorney campaign against deadbeat dads, in other words, those failing to pay owed child support, Janet found that Mark was one of them and paid his debt.

21. Mark was by then living on the Reno homestead, which was a continuing hub of activity presided over by "mule headed" Jane and featuring the consumption of "mucho" alcohol.

Douglas was clear that Jane was "impossible." He also revealed Janet's secret love of romance novels and expressed his view that Janet was so clear about integrity that "if she had been gay, she would not have been ashamed nor concealed it."

22. At 6'5" and with a glass eye, Gerstein dominated any room. He also managed to exercise de facto control of state funding. Being called to his office was said to cause a certain shaking in one's boots

23. Anderson, 64.

24. Oral History, part 2, p. 19.

25. State attorneys typically make a three-year commitment. Within five years, three-quarters of them have moved on. It is rather like a university postdoc—low salary, but important training and good preparation for a beginning professional.

26. The ABA encourages lawyers to provide fifty hours of pro bono (free) service a year to the poor and underserved.

27. Working with FPL, Reno said, taught her that one could work in a corporate environment and adhere to one's principles. Oral History, part 2, p. 21.

28. Greer first met Seitz when she and D'Alemberte were defending Richard Nixon's friend, Bebe Rebozo. They developed a friendship that led to marriage when they were two of a handful of single people on a 1980 People to People visit to China.

29. Smith's wife, Sara, was considered an important, though behind the scenes, player on women's behalf. Smith's "forward looking" also included doing work on behalf of Jimmy Carter and Cesar Chavez. When D'Alemberte, Smith, and Reno were in conversation, one could be sure they were planning ways to advance the common good and/or good government, which was in rather short supply in Miami at the time.

30. Seitz described the Renos as almost a pack, one in which Janet played the "Mom" who ensured serious and responsible behavior.

31. Reno's pithy remarks sometimes seemed off key. In 1993, when Pat was being sworn in as the first woman president of the Florida Bar by Florida Chief Justice Rosemary Barkett, Janet observed that Pat was "butt headed." Afterward, Pat's husband said, "I think to Janet that is a compliment."

32. Elly Canterbury interview, January 20, 2016.

33. There were some fifty applicants/nominees for the position. Janet actually wrote a letter of recommendation for another candidate.

34. Oral History, part 2, p. 27.

CHAPTER 5. MIAMI-DADE STATE ATTORNEY: TURBULENT
TIMES, 1978–1980

1. Purdy himself would be fired in May by Miami-Dade County Manager Merrett Stierheim.

2. After serving in the Senate from 1936 to 1951, Claude Pepper had taken some time off before returning to Washington as a member of the House of Representatives, where he served from 1963 to 1989.

3. Handwritten notes in file box 1879 to 1930a.

4. Her understanding that innocents could be convicted was exemplified by the case of James Richardson who served twenty-one years for the murder of his seven children. Reno was appointed by the governor to review the case and found that an injustice had been done. (The case is detailed in chapter 6.) Later, Reno described herself as haunted by the Luis Diaz

case. In 1980, her office convicted Diaz of rape, and he served twenty-five years before being exonerated by DNA testing in an appeal originated by the Miami office of Holland and Knight, the Florida Innocence Initiative, and the Innocence Project in which Reno played an important role. Oral History, part 3, pp. 2, 4, 10ff.

5. It was then common practice for prostitutes to plead guilty and be sentenced to time served, which could be a mere matter of hours. Reno's new policy was to try the cases and to be prepared for the possibility of up to a $500 fine and sixty days in jail. *Miami Herald,* June 9, 1978.

6. Anderson, 99–100.

7. Reno's approach was almost antithetical to that of Gerstein who 1) only saw people he wished to see, and 2) prosecuted the big cases himself, garnering a lot of press. Still, Reno was thoroughly covered by the press including more than a half dozen Spanish language media: *El Expreso, Replica, Diario Las Americas, El Miami Herald, Patria, La Nación, El Mataneer, La Verdad.*

8. Defendants could require trial within sixty days.

9. After the election Reno carefully refunded the $2,822 remaining in her campaign treasury.

10. Half of Reno's first hires were women.

11. Interview with Trudy Novicki, October 26, 2013.

12. Many young lawyers joined the state attorney's office to get experience. Those who stayed more than five years were, according to Yoss, the incompetent, the truly dedicated, and those who liked the work and could afford the relatively meager salary. Interview with George Yoss, no date.

13. When asked for "negatives" about Reno, Yoss could think only of her lack of delegation, a fact that led to efforts to take such an initiative. Yoss interview, no date.

14. They were eager for the experience but had no intention of staying much beyond the three year expected minimum. Interview with Samuel Rabin, no date.

15. Mariel, because that was the name of the port from which they exited. The Mariel refugees will be discussed in more detail later in the chapter.

16. The Country Walk child molestation case has been dissected many times; one of the most critical accounts is Russ Cheit's *The Witch-Hunt Narrative,* published in 2014.

17. Interview with Dan Casey, no date.

18. Interview with Shay Bilchik, June 20, 2016.

19. One observer described the change from Gerstein to Reno as being analogous to that of Kennedy to Johnson—high style to the unsophisticated but savvy and competent. Interview with Tom Peterson, April 9, 2014.

20. Interview with Ed Carhart, January 17, 2016.

21. The status of women was on the national agenda as well; the Susan B. Anthony dollar was issued the next year.

22. Unfortunately, only one recruit was able to pass the Florida bar. He eventually became a judge.

23. There have only been three state attorneys in Miami: Gerstein from 1958 to 1978, Reno from 1978 to 1993, and Rundle since 1993.

24. Bingo was legal if profits went to a charity. It was not supposed to be a business providing profit for the organizer. Charities, church groups, civic organizations, and senior citizens organizations were apparently receiving a fee for acting as official sponsors for large com-

mercial games. Reno and Metro Manager Merrett Stierheim surprised many of the bingo operators by enforcing the law, one which Reno had helped draft three years before. Among those arrested was a county commissioner, Neal Adams.

25. The *Miami Herald* on May 18, 1978, reported seventy cases "fumbled" because the chief juvenile prosecutor, Maria Korvick, had delegated the processing to a secretary. Note that the office handled as many as a thousand cases each month.

26. Even after she became U.S. attorney general, Reno took the time to fly to Miami to officiate at the wedding of Ellis's daughter.

27. Janet's sole criterion was that the haircut be "no work." Interview with Carol Ellis, March 19, 2014.

28. Much in this account comes from interviews with family members, from Anderson, 70ff., and *Miami Herald,* May 19, 1978.

29. In the first several years Reno spoke at a University of Miami conference on Family Violence; joined the Tiger Bay Club and became an honorary member of the Cuban ABA and of the Delta Kappa Gamma Society; received a Toastmaster's Communication and Leadership Award, the Annual Humanitarian Award from Florida Region Women's American ORT, the Outstanding Service Award from the Northeast Miami Improvement Association, and the St. Thomas More Award from the Miami Catholic Lawyers Guild; named Woman of the Year by the University of Miami chapter of Phi Delta Kappa, Citizen of the Year by the Grand Jury Association of Florida, and as one of the top women in public life by *Town and Country* magazine; gave a commencement speech at the University of Florida Law School; and served on the Board of Directors of Miami Dade United Way.

30. One constituent called her at home at 1:00 a.m. to listen to the crowing of his neighbor's roosters.

31. Peterson interview, April 9, 2014.

32. One of her assistant state attorneys had accumulated 116 parking tickets. He was potentially liable for $580 in fines, but a judge charged him only seventy-five dollars. When the story surfaced, Reno ordered him to pay the full fine. Soon thereafter he left for the public defender's office. Reno would not accept so much as a pizza as a gift. She expected similar behavior of her staff.

33. Peterson interview, April 9, 2014. When he arrived, the courthouse, built in 1961, had double everything: that is, Black and White restrooms and drinking fountains. While labels were removed by 1966, practice changed slowly. Note that some Miami schools were desegregated as early as 1959, but full integration took another decade, and not until 1975 were school boundaries established entitling all students to enroll in the school closest to their home.

34. Until establishing a juvenile justice system it would not have been unusual for a child who stole a pizza to be sent to adult court with a charge of robbery.

35. Peterson interview, April 9, 2014.

36. See Anderson, 87ff.

37. Dardis was understandably not happy that an error had blown the whole operation. He soon left the office, publicly criticized Reno as soft on public corruption, and endorsed her opponent in the next election. In 1972, Dardis had played a key role in linking the Watergate burglars to President Richard Nixon's reelection campaign through a check made out to Ken Dahlberg, a Minnesota businessman.

38. Chapman, Chair and CEO of Knight Ridder, Inc., a conglomerate that included the *Miami Herald.*

39. Marvin Dunn and Bruce Porter, *The Miami Riot of 1980: Crossing the Bounds*, 29–31.

40. They had a warrant, but it was for a different address.

41. "Report of Governor's Dade County Citizens Committee," October 30, 1980.

42. Dunn and Porter, 28–29.

43. In November, Reno also qualified with a revolver at the police gun range.

44. Miami Dade had a police force for the whole county. In addition, more than twenty municipalities had their own police force. This meant two different sets of officers had jurisdiction over a single geographic area.

45. Carhart was an interesting character. Brooklyn born, he attended high school and junior college in St. Petersburg, Florida. Abandoning Florida State University, he traveled to Mexico where he obtained a B.A. from the University of the Americas where courses were taught in English for the likes of Carhart. After obtaining a law degree from the University of Florida in 1964, he was recruited to the state attorney's staff by Gerstein, where he stayed for four years before going into private practice. He returned to work as executive assistant to Gerstein in 1973 and some thought he might succeed Gerstein when Gerstein retired in 1978. The governor, however, selected Reno. Carhart recalled an incident in which Reno and he got into a dispute in front of Gerstein and others, and Reno left the room slamming a metal door so hard it bent! Carhart interview, January 17, 2016.

46. The trial would not begin until April 1980.

47. Trillin, "U.S. Journal: Judging Johnny Jones," *New Yorker*, April 13, 1980, p. 78ff.

48. Barnes was tried separately and was sentenced to five years.

49. Note the time-lapse of almost five years

50. Quite separately, six months after the first conviction in October 1980, Jones was convicted of soliciting perjury and witness tampering in a case involving kickbacks from a consultant who had provided a $1.2 million reading program to the district. Jones received a two-year sentence that he served on a work-release program that permitted him to manage a restaurant, the Place at Palm Bay, but he had to spend nights in jail. His lawyer was Carhart.

51. Critics said the five officers should have been tried separately—and that giving immunity to one officer who had participated in the beating was an error. Among the critics was the losing candidate for Janet's job, Carhart. In retrospect, Carhart believed his team had not won, but that the state attorney lost through poor preparation. Adorno soon left to form a private practice, which would become the largest minority law firm in the country. But in 2010, Adorno was suspended over a fire service fee case in which he took a $2 million fee in a $7 million settlement of a class action lawsuit that included only seven plaintiffs who collectively had suffered less than $100,000 in damages. His highly successful law firm of Adorno and Yoss then imploded. Adorno would be disbarred but was later reinstated. See https://www.wsj.com/articles/BL-LB-39686.

52. Critics included U.S. Attorney General Benjamin Civiletti, Florida Governor Bob Graham, and Miami Mayor Maurice Ferré. Black leader H. T. Smith called Reno a racist, and in a *Miami Times* op-ed Garth Reeves wrote that Reno "is to the black community what Hitler was to the Jews."

53. Oral History, part 3, p. 4.

54. Oral History, part 3, p. 7.

55. Oral History, part 3, p. 6.

56. Oral History, part 3, p. 9.

57. "Report of Governor's Dade County Citizens Committee," October 30, 1980.

58. Ibid., 6.

59. The report found White unemployment was 26 percent, while that of Blacks was 44 percent.

60. Reno's 7 percent Black assistant state attorneys was a better rate than Florida was graduating Black lawyers: 2 percent. The report did note that 90 of 312 nonlawyer employees were Black.

61. Civil rights issues can also be found in "mundane" happenings. For example, once Reno had committed to hosting a Cornell dinner at a local country club. Shortly before the event she learned Jews were not allowed to be members. She pulled the dinner, and because the short notice meant other arrangements were difficult to make, the dinner was given at the Reno home on the famous screened porch. One of the serving staff for the event was her friend Lynn D'Alemberte. Ellis interview, March 19, 2014.

62. The story was that if a family was about to depart from Cuba by boat, officials required them to take another person of the official's choice. That was the way Cuba was able to send so many of its less desirable citizens, perhaps as many as ten thousand. Ultimately, about 2 percent of the refugees were declared unfit for permanent resident status.

63. Rundle's family had arrived in Miami in the first wave. She came to the state attorney's office as an intern in 1976, straight from obtaining her law degree in England. She then was assigned to the Organized Crime Bureau. When Peterson moved on, Rundle took his place as Reno's chief assistant.

64. One issue involved the taking of depositions. State cases made state witnesses available to the defense for depositions. The federal system did not. Also, Reno found that the FBI did not practice the same cooperation. That was something she would attend to when she became attorney general. Oral History, part 4, pp. 3–6.

65. "Career" criminals are those who have been convicted of three serious crimes.

66. That war would last eight years. At the time, most Americans had no idea that the United States was quietly assisting Iraq.

CHAPTER 6. MIAMI-DADE STATE ATTORNEY: BUILDING
COMMUNITY, 1981–1992

1. Hastings would later be impeached by the U.S. House of Representatives, convicted by the Senate, and removed from office. He promptly ran for and was elected to the House of Representatives.

2. One *Sentinel Star* article was headlined "Tough Woman in a Tough Town" (1981).

3. Anderson, 124ff.

4. According to the *Washington Times* (February 22, 1993) Reno charged forty law enforcement officials with major felonies.

5. See https://www.nytimes.com/1984/03/16/us/policeman-in-miami-is-aquitted-by-jury-in-slaying-of-black.html, accessed May 10, 2015

6. In a unanimous vote by the four commissioners present, the family was awarded $250,000 in cash. The city also bought an annuity for $210,000 that would pay Johnson's parents and siblings monthly benefits guaranteed to total $539,000. These were estimated to reach $847,000 over their lifetimes. The actual total cost to the city for the package would be nearly $460,000. It should be noted that the City Manager, Howard V. Garry, was Black. So was the assistant police chief, Clarence Dickson, who would become chief the next year.

7. As Reno noted in retirement, she had built support among Blacks by going to the community, by enforcing child support, by citing HUD to reform public housing—and by enforcing those rules. She also argued that "If you are soft spoken and polite while they are cursing you out, they think you are putting them off—but if you demand that they stop hollering and listen for a moment, they would realize I was not a robot." Reno acknowledged, though, that she had to guard against her temper in such encounters. Oral History, part 6, p. 17.

8. *Miami Herald,* October 25, 1984. Retrieved May 12, 2015.

9. Anderson, 97.

10. Thompson's charges were picked up on by others. After her nomination for attorney general, reporters raised the issue directly. Her response then? I am "an old maid who likes men."

11. Oral History, part 3, pp. 19–21.

12. The Joe Robbie Stadium has had a series of names. Its current name is Hard Rock Stadium, and it is in Miami Gardens although often listed as being in Miami.

13. See https://www.miamiherald.com/news/local/community/miami-dade/article4317878.html, accessed May 20, 2015. By the time of the acquittal in 1993, Reno was in Washington. In seeking racial balance, the trial was moved from Orlando to Tallahassee to ensure Black representation, but was moved back to Orlando to ensure Hispanic participation. The Miami jury had included three White, one Black, and one Hispanic juror. The Orlando jury included three White, two Hispanic, and one Black juror. Roy Black, a celebrity lawyer whose clients included William Kennedy Smith, Rush Limbaugh, and Peter Max, defended Lozano as he had Luis Alvarez.

14. See http://articles.latimes.com/1994-04-20/news/mn-48244_1_race-riot.html, accessed May 20, 2015.

15. See the *New York Times* for September 17, 1983.

16. See http://flashbackmiami.com/2014/09/10/miami-drug-wars/. accessed May 20, 2015.

17. *New York Times,* August 28, 1982.

18. This was the incident that brought about the creation of the Florida Drug Task Force led by Vice President George Bush.

19. Federal agents had been referring cases involving "only" a kilo of cocaine or a thousand pounds of marijuana to the state courts.

20. See https://harpers.org/archive/1982/01/the-informant/, accessed May 20, 2015.

21. Anderson, 90. Note that such traces could survive handling by a variety of individuals or even be acquired by nestling up to another bill in a cashier's drawer. For a quick overview of Miami's drug scene see "Flashback" in the *Miami Herald,* September 10, 2014.

22. See http://www.pbs.org/wgbh/pages/frontline/shows/drugs/archive/copsgobad.html.

23. In fact, Dade County was the "murder capital" of the country in 1984 with a rate of 23.7 murders per 100,000 population. Miami was only third among cities; its rate was 42.4. Number one was Gary, Indiana. See https://www.sun-sentinel.com/news/fl-xpm-1985-07-27-8501310244-story.html.

24. Anderson, 121ff. One of the attorneys assigned to help develop the Drug Court was Hugh Rodham, brother of Hillary Clinton, who introduced Clinton to Reno during the 1992 presidential campaign. A year earlier, Bill Clinton had visited the Drug Court when he was in Miami.

25. For background see https://news.google.com/newspapers?nid=1817&dat=19810809&id=ZzgdAAAAIBAJ&sjid=y6UEAAAAIBAJ&pg=6794,2334426&hl=en, accessed May 20, 2015. For more linking anti-Castro terrorists and the drug trade, see https://harpers.org/ar-

chive/1982/01/the-informant/, accessed May 18, 2015. This was an article by John Rothchild, "The Informant: Meet the biggest dealer in Miami's biggest industry," originally published in *Harper's*, January 1982.

26. In 1998, the provision was amended to allow individual counties to extend the waiting period to five days.

27. Anderson, 119–20, 157–58.

28. The tip apparently came from an American who had been "enslaved" by the family during an assignment in Saudi Araba.

29. See https://www.nytimes.com/1982/05/27/us/royal-saudi-family-in-miami-shows-it-has-a-gift-for-giving.html, accessed May 25, 2015.

30. In 2005, Conseco published a tell-all, *Juiced: Wild Times, Rampant 'Roids, Smash Hits and How Baseball Got Big*. New York: Harper Collins, 2005.

31. The Housing Department owned/managed some twelve thousand units.

32. Officially, the Miami Beach Architectural District, the area is also known as the Old Miami Beach Historical District. The district is architecturally coherent because the 1926 hurricane had obliterated the area; that meant that most of the rebuilding was accomplished in roughly a decade. For more details about preservation in Miami where preservation is about things less than a hundred years old, check out the activities of the Miami Design Preservation League.

33. See http://genius.com/Anquette-janet-reno-lyrics/, *Miami Herald*, November 30, 1988. The next year the piece would hit the list of the top ten national rap charts.

34. At the time of the trial the fine was thirty-seven dollars. In 2015 it was sixty dollars and three points. "Prosecuting for the sake of children," by Martin Dyckman, *Saint Petersburg Times*, May 12, 1991.

35. Anderson, 113–14.

36. This narrative is taken from a *nolle prosequi memorandum* concerning case number 3302-D prepared by Reno for the Circuit Court of the Twelfth Judicial Circuit in and for DeSoto County, Florida.

37. Charlie first said he couldn't remember who had told him about the poison only an hour previously. He then named Chris Robinson and Robert Jenkins, both of whom denied even speaking to Charlie. Adding to the mystery was a wine bottle with Smith's fingerprints found behind the shed that morning. Smith denied having been behind the shed.

38. After Richardson's release, former U.S. Attorney Robert Merkle issued a 260-page report calling for a second prosecution of Richardson. His report was paid for by the state, which was being sued by Richardson for damages. The defendants were the state, DeSoto County, State Attorney Frank Schaub, and Sheriff Cline. In 2014, Governor Rick Scott signed a bill designed to compensate Richardson for his ordeal. The sum was $1.2 million.

39. Joseph and Laurie Braga were neither psychologists nor psychiatrists. She had a degree in child development; his degree was in education. They created the National Foundation for Children and prepared a film "When Children Are Witnesses."

40. This is the only element of the many accusations that Ileana Flores did not deny. It may have been a custom from her homeland as a way to quiet an unsettled child.

41. The child's sample had been thrown away, so it could not be retested.

42. Much of the following comes from *New York Times*, March 3, 1993, accessed May 30, 2015.

43. See PBS interview with Flores http://www.pbs.org/wgbh/pages/frontline/shows/fuster/interviews/ileana.html, accessed May 31, 2015.

44. See http://www.ipt-forensics.com/journal/volume6/j6_4_2.htm, for the full transcript of Flores's 1994 sworn statement.

45. See footnote 6 of the transcript.

46. See http://www.pbs.org/wgbh/pages/frontline/shows/fuster/frank/summary.html, accessed May 31, 2015. See also http://www.pbs.org/wgbh/pages/frontline/shows/fuster/interviews/fuster.html.

47. In an interview in 2005, while the case was still under appeal, Reno acknowledged that there were critics of the conviction, but noted that the wife had testified against the husband, and that experts had worked with the children who were allowed to testify on closed-circuit TV. She reiterated her commitment to ensure that the innocent are not convicted, and cited two cases in which she helped to win the release of individuals who had been wrongly convicted. And, yes, she told the interviewer, you do stay awake at night wondering, "Have I wrongfully prosecuted somebody?" Oral History, part 3, p. 24. For a detailed rebuttal to the *Frontline* report see an account by the Brown University News Service by Professor Ross E. Cheit.

48. "George Snowden's Final Trial," updated October 28, 1998, accessed June 1, 2015.

49. See http://www.usmayors.org/bestpractices/usmayor01/BP_Miami_Dade.asp, accessed June 6, 2015. The teams should not be confused with Neighborhood Enhancement Teams (NET), which focus on community and police cooperation. The city of Madison, Wisconsin, pioneered NET teams under Mayor Paul Soglin.

50. See vol. 14, no. 3, March 1990, pp. 161ff.

51. Democrat Chiles faced a Republican legislature, so he appointed a lot of commissions. Another was a Commission on Government for the People. Janet, an appointee, commented that thirty-two of its thirty-seven members were White men—mostly fundraisers for Chiles.

52. Charles Fishman, "A few moments with Janet Reno, a big-city prosecutor who talks like a social worker," *Florida Magazine,* June 30, 1991.

53. The ABA's committee's report is at http://www.druglibrary.org/special/king/cjic.html, accessed June 7, 2015.

54. As early as 1986, Reno had become an advocate for developing programs for single mothers to enable them to return to work supported by childcare and health care. How did this issue get on a prosecutor's agenda? Via prosecutions for welfare fraud.

55. *ABA Journal,* April 1993.

56. During this period, Reno received accolade after accolade. Typically she would receive an award and give a talk. This kind of community engagement was typical of many elected officials. Reno did not restrict herself to the mighty. Among the awards were the following: Herbert Hoover Award from the American Judicature Society; Boss of the Year from the Miami Chapter of the Business Women's Association; the Certificate of Honor from Soroptimist International; a Merit Diploma from the Interamerican Chamber of Commerce, Miami Chapter; Distinguished Service Award, from Florida Council on Crime and Delinquency; Adopted Favorite Daughter by Municipio Caimito del Guayabal; Coral Gables High School Hall of Fame; the YWCA's Women Who Make a Difference Award; an award from the South Florida Perinatal Network; a Commendation from the United States Postal Service; the Hannah G. Solomon Award of the Greater Miami Section of the National Council of Jewish Women; the Florida Bar Association's Medal of Honor; and Miami Dade Community College's Women of Strength and Vision Award.

CHAPTER 7. ATTORNEY GENERAL, 1993–2001: CONDUCTING THE NATION'S BUSINESS

1. The second would be a Black woman, Loretta Lynch. She was preceded by Eric Holder, also Black, and by a Hispanic, Alberto Gonzalez. The first three were Democrats; Gonzalez was a Republican. No woman has served as Secretary of Defense. Janet Yellen has served as Secretary of the Treasury. Madeleine Albright, Condoleezza Rice, and Hillary Clinton have served as Secretaries of State. So has Colin Powell. The very day Reno was sworn in, the *Los Angeles Times* reported that the National Rifle Association's Director of Federal Affairs was fired for spreading rumors during the confirmation process that Reno had been stopped, but not charged, on suspicion of drunk driving.

2. There is no record of a male nominee having been queried about the immigration status of his personal employees.

3. It was Ellis and Janet McAliley who would take Reno on a Bal Harbour shopping trip to get attractive "large and tall" clothes for her swearing in.

4. Anderson, 127

5. Oral History, part 4, p. 19ff.

6. Every detail of her records was queried. One payment turned out to be tuition Janet was paying for a young Black girl. She was not the only person Reno provided financial support.

7. Hubbell only lasted one year in Washington. He resigned and returned to Little Rock to face legal problems dating back to his law practice in the Rose Law Firm, where he had practiced with Hillary. Convicted of one charge of wire fraud and one of tax fraud, he was given a twenty-one-month sentence. Later Special Counsel Kenneth Starr would actually indict Hubbell on three different occasions. The only result was a plea bargain related to a charge of conflict of interest and probation. Hubbell has since written his autobiography and several mysteries.

8. Pedrosa ran against her for state attorney in 1984. Even Jack Thompson, her 1988 challenger, was contacted. He took it upon himself to go public with his old accusations but failed to derail her nomination.

9. Anderson, 143.

10. Republican Senator Orrin Hatch specifically denounced the "scurrilous" rumors that had been circulating at Reno's confirmation hearing.

11. And she did. Prosecutors secured a sentence of eighteen years for one Idaho man's illegal use of toxic chemicals and collected more than $3 billion from electric utility companies for violation of the Clean Air Act and Clean Water Act.

12. As things developed, Clinton probably wished Reno were political—and grateful to him for her appointment.

13. This next section draws heavily on Oral History, part 5, p. 1ff.

14. Like Reno, Gorelick was a Harvard Law graduate. Upon graduation she came to a Washington law firm where she sat out the Republican presidencies. She was, though, very much an insider, and when Clinton won the White House, she was appointed General Counsel for the Department of Defense. A year later, she would become deputy attorney general. During her time at the Pentagon, the department had had to wrestle with gays in the military and women in combat. Gorelick's boss John Deutch said "three chiefs cried" when she left— two who would miss her help, one in relief. Gorelick's thirteen months there, he said, had shown her to be "glamorous, competent, and disputatious." Reno said, "I hope I never have to cross her." She was sworn in by Ruth Bader Ginsburg. Box of speeches, April 13, 1994.

15. Few negatives had arisen, although Miami's *New Times* carried a story critical of her lack of support for Black Americans and another lengthy story critical of the Country Walk prosecutions.

16. Shortly after the hearings, Neil Kinkopf, a legal adviser, prepared a memo for Reno listing every promise she had made during the confirmation hearings. These included promises related to antitrust such as mergers in the defense industry, criminal law (including a number of promises related to gun control and enforcement of drug laws), and immigration. The list was four pages long and continued Reno's practice of having a lengthy list of "to dos." Reno was confirmed on a Friday. On Saturday, Washington was hit by "the Storm of the Century." Offices were closed on Monday, but Reno walked to work where she was tutored on the internet and encryption. She was also told that applications for electronic surveillance were not handled in a timely fashion. She took care of that promptly and told the National Security Agency contact to call her directly if there were further problems. Soon, the U.S. Attorney for the Southern District of New York came to get approval to arrest the "blind sheikh," Omar Abdel-Rahman, for his role in the bombing of the World Trade Center. That was the occasion for Reno's beginning her practice of bringing together all the relevant people when an important decision was to be made. This would include people from different agencies who could have quite different views. The meetings went as long as necessary. Oral History, part 5, p. 1.

17. Interview with Daphne Webb, no date.

18. See chapter 8. Events that took place between the time Clinton took office and Reno took up her duties included an attack on CIA headquarters in which two were killed, and a bombing at the World Trade Center in which six died. Also, Congress slashed the budget of the Office of National Drug Control Policy and reduced its staff from 112 to 25; at the same time it made its director a member of the National Security Council.

19. Chris McAliley interview, January 16, 1916. Chris was a graduate of Coral Gables High, Tufts, and New York University Law School. She returned to Miami following a boyfriend who was to begin a residency there but broke up with him and was able to get a clerkship with Stanley Markus in the U.S. (not state) state attorney's office.

20. Neal McAliley was less connected to Miami. He worked at the Department of Justice in Washington for four years, then continued to work for DOJ in its Miami office. Neal once asked Reno about the Elián incident, as the events had broken the unity and invincibility of Cuban leader Jorge Mas Canosa. Reno's only regret she shared: "I should have gone in earlier."

21. Neal did remember early days with Reno as Black Beard, an act that she repeated at her sixtieth birthday party! There were also once a month parties at the Ranch where she played games with the kids—something no other adult present did.

22. Many of the women had first met during President Jimmy Carter's administration. They did other things during the Republican years but reunited when Clinton assumed the presidency.

23. Nina J. Eastout and Ronald J. Ostrow, "Ms. Reno Objects: Can the Popular A.G. Muster the Political Savvy to Sell Her 'Tough Love' Vision of Justice?," *Los Angeles Times*, October 31, 1993.

24. In an Academy of Pediatrics address (October 10, 1999), Reno noted that in the United States thirteen kids die of gunshot wounds each day and that in one five-year period Toronto had one hundred gun homicides a year, while Chicago had three thousand!

25. Her temper was described as the size of Biscayne Bay, and one was always wary of a neck "double veiner."

26. This was almost exactly ten times the number of employees she managed as state attorney. Even without interviews, Reno became a hot topic. She made *Esquire's* list of "Women We Love" and *Glamour's* "Ten Women of the Year." The *New Yorker* offered "The Janet Reno Collection"—paper dolls with unstylish clothes. One cartoon depicted her as Clint Eastwood and another as Rambo.

27. Oral History, part 5, p. 8ff.

28. The others were Shay Bilchik, Ray Havens, Marshall Service, Richard Scruggs, and Kevin Di Gregory. John Edward Smith and Samuel Dubbin helped prep her for the congressional hearings. Dubbin would later come to work at the Department of Justice. Bilchik would become Administrator of the Office of Juvenile Justice and Delinquency Prevention. When Republicans took over in Washington, Bilchik became CEO of the Child Welfare League of America. In 2007, he moved to Georgetown University to lead the Center for Juvenile Justice.

29. She was the daughter of Ewart Guinier, one of two Blacks admitted to Harvard College in 1929. Although he did not finish at Harvard, he received degrees from CCNY, Columbia, and from NYU Law School. A trade unionist for much of his career, he returned to Harvard in 1969 as Chair of the Afro-American Studies Department, now known as the African and African American Studies Department

30. Awkwardly, she announced, thus upstaging the White House announcement.

31. *Miami Herald,* January 28, 1994. One story had it that she had asked for a report on minimum sentences and jail/prison overcrowding, which had not appeared ten months later. Moreover, Reno was capable of even dressing down Heymann in front of the rest of the staff.

32. Ronald J. Ostrow, "Reno's Top Deputy Resigns Over Differences in 'Style': Shake-up— Philip Heymann says they couldn't function as a team. Separately, another assistant quits," *Los Angeles Times,* January 28, 1994. Bilchik saw the problem as one in which Reno expected Heymann to efficiently run the office—to be an administrator—a skill Bilchik thought he did not have albeit he was quite brilliant. Bilchik interview, June 20, 2016.

33. The conduit from DOJ was Clinton insider Webster Hubbell. Apparently there was not a specific liaison in the White House.

34. Interview with Jamie Gorelick, April 13, 2016.

35. After J. Edgar Hoover's thirty-seven-year reign, a law limiting the position to a ten-year term was passed. Also, the FBI Director could only be removed by the president. The idea was to grant a certain independence but also to prevent undue power accruing to the position.

36. Anderson, 243.

37. His efforts to enlist women and minorities as agents were not appreciated by what was a well-developed agent culture.

38. Actually he *was* an Eagle Scout, as was his son and two grandsons.

39. Reno did not discuss the allegations with Sessions, even as they worked together on things like the Waco siege. Her decision was based on the report.

40. One embarrassment involved Lula Rodriguez who had come from Miami to work with Reno. Rodriguez took a vacation to visit her sister, who was married to Raul Martinez, then running for mayor of Hialeah. Two years before, he had been convicted on six counts including conspiracy, extortion, and racketeering and had been sentenced to ten years. While that case was on appeal, Martinez again ran for mayor and won by under 300 votes. More than 400 votes were absentee ballots suspicious enough that a state judge ruled a special election must be held. (Martinez won.) Lula had been in Miami election weekend, and her name was listed as a witness on thirteen of the absentee ballots. All this was in accord with Hialeah's "normal"

politics, but Reno felt she could not have Lula in her office. She subsequently found a position in the United States Information Agency's International Visitor's Program.

41. Oral History, part 2, p. 2. Once, when Reno was giving a speech at the American Law Institute, she noticed her old Harvard dean Erwin Griswold in the audience. She publicly thanked him for serving as a mentor and said she hoped her career demonstrated that she had done right by her Harvard education.

42. This reaction, however, would never have happened after Reno's Elián decision. People would cross the street, if they saw her coming; ties were severed with numerous and close friends including a once devoted personal assistant.

43. Interview with Douglas Reno, December 14, 2015.

44. Her priorities were usually more extensive. For instance, a handwritten attorney general's "must-do" list contained thirty items. She also maintained a "getback" list, one from September, 21, 1999 contained 244 items—some originating in 1994. Organized by topics the "guru" for each and most recent disposition were all noted.

45. See https://www.ojp.gov/ncjrs/virtual-library/abstractsviolent-crime-control-and-law-enforcement-act-1994.

46. The Division of Juvenile Justice and Delinquency Prevention had been in existence since 1974.

47. See http://www.ojjdp.gov/pubs/gun_violence/173950.pdf, accessed July 19, 1915; see p. 3.

48. Oral History, January 31, 2008, p. 3.

49. The CDC's expertise on drug abuse and sales was quite pertinent.

50. The TVA case was one of some forty prosecutions.

51. Press conference, November 3, 1999.

52. Anderson, 278.

53. *U.S. News* reported in the June 7, 1993, issue a poll showing Reno's approval rating at 67 percent versus Clinton's 41 percent.

54. Reno was fifty-seven at the time of her Parkinson's diagnosis.

55. These figures were cited in a number of letters. Note that 1995 was the year in which President Clinton established a Presidential Council on HIV and in which National HIV Testing Day was begun.

56. Korbut held the position under the Bush presidency but Reno retained him.

57. The Division of National Security would be added in 2006. While top officials changed with the administration, some divisions had large numbers of career officials. The Civil Rights, Antitrust, and Environment and Natural Resources divisions were more responsive to the political climate than others, but Reno, herself, was almost uniquely apolitical. She had been preceded by Edwin Meese III, John D. Ashcroft (who covered the breast of a statue in the briefing room so as not to offend TV viewers), and Alberto Gonzalez, who tried to politicize even DOJ hiring. Reno's "clean" and serious reputation gave a boost to and energized the long-serving professionals on her staff.

58. Three items concerned the Department of Justice: money laundering, terrorism, and illegal drugs. The second Summit of the Americas was held in Santiago, Chile, in 1998. Reno and three other cabinet members were part of a high-level team that accompanied President Clinton and his wife, Hillary, to the meetings.

59. American Airlines had merged with US Airways, Delta with Northwest, and United with Continental.

60. The airlines were Vanguard, which ceased operations in 2000; Western Pacific, which

went bankrupt in 1998; and Sun Jet International, which reorganized as Southeast in 1998 but which went out of business in 2004.

61. See http://www.justice.gov/atr/case-document/memorandum-and-order#_1_48. Later analysis found some predation. See the paper by Connan Snider, "Predatory Incentives and Predation Policy: The American Airlines Case," http://www.econ.ucla.edu/people/papers/ Snider/Snider508.pdf.

62. Gates wrote a number of books himself. His father also wrote about him, and there is a children's book about him too. The only biography currently available at the time of writing this book was Michael Beacraft's *Bill Gates: A Biography* (Santa Barbara: ABC-CLIO, 2014). See also, the brief bio at https://www.biography.com/business-figure/bill-gates.

63. See https://www.tech-insider.org/windows/research/1994/07.html.

64. Like Carnegie and Rockefeller, Gates with his then-wife Melinda created a philanthropic foundation. It was launched in 2000 with $28 billion. Its divisions are Global Development, Global Health, Global Policy and Advocacy, and the U.S. Division, which focuses on education and, in the state of Washington, vulnerable children and families.

65. The question as to how a feature differed from a product remained ambiguous. Contractual bundling was not allowed, but technological bundling was. Again, issues involved were protection for innovation, for competition, and for the consumer.

66. See https://scholar.google.com/scholar_case?case=489010973099333247&hl=en&as_ sdt=6&as_vis=1&oi=scholarr. See also http://www.stern.nyu.edu/networks/Microsoft_Anti-trust.final.pdf.

67. One reason for so many reversals of judicial decisions was surely because the industry and technology were new. They didn't fit past categories/models. Lawyers were engaged in research and novelty just as the techies were. Issues would continue. One issue involved/involves requests by law enforcement officials for information about customer data. Other issues involve U.S. National Security Orders and dealing with other nations' different rules. Reno was the first attorney general to grapple with the law and the new technology, but decades later, some issues are unresolved and others are emerging. For a report from 2014 see http://blogs.microsoft.com/on-the-issues/2014/09/26/microsoft-updates-reports-government-access-data-calls-additional-reforms/.

68. See http://www.justice.gov/atr/case-document/review-final-judgments-united-states-and-new-york-group.

69. See http://articles.sun-sentinel.com/1993-03-12/news/9301140864_1_reno-priority-abortion-clinics-janet-reno, accessed August 1, 2015. On May 14, Reno would give testimony on the issue before the Senate Labor and Human Resources Committee, *Washington Post,* May 13, 1993.

70. Griffin's defense was that he had been brainwashed by activist John Burt, who was ordered to testify at the trial by the judge.

71. A few of German or Italian descent were interned; also, Japanese in eastern states were not sent to camps.

72. In 2017, at the time of this book's writing, 80 percent of these visas go to Chinese applicants.

73. Cubans had a special status. Basically, any who could make it to shore could claim permanent residency. This contrasts dramatically with the experience of their Haitian neighbors. INS has been quick to repatriate Haitians without papers; Haitians have even been apprehended at sea and returned to Haiti.

74. More than 1 million were apprehended and turned back at the border. The Center for Immigration Studies provides up-to-date data, http://www.cis.org/ImmigrationStatistics1993.

75. This, of course, was a prelude to the devastating collapse of the Twin Towers that came on September 11, 2001. (A total of 2,763 people were killed in the crashes, fires, and subsequent collapses.)

76. Operation Gatekeeper had begun in 1994 but had been ramped up since then.

77. According to the Immigration Policy Institute, the Border Patrol budget in 1993 was $363 million, and by 2000 it was $1,095 million, and by 2012 $3,531 million.

78. Asylum could be based on race, religion, nationality, political opinion, or social group, and a fear of persecution or torture. One case involved Fauziya Kassindja, a young woman from Togo who successfully argued that if she were returned to Togo she would be tortured—by being subjected to genital mutilation.

79. Some estimated that more than half of "unauthorized" immigrants have lived in the United States for more than a decade.

80. See http://articles.latimes.com/1997-05-09/news/mn-57116_1_central-american and http://www.nytimes.com/1997/07/11/us/reno-acts-to-suspend-deportations.html.

81. Anderson, 283. It may require the same of other countries as well.

82. This was a post–Civil War amendment particularly focused on former slaves.

83. See https://publichealthlawcenter.org/sites/default/files/resources/master-settlement-agreement.pdf.

84. The National Infrastructure Protection Center was later transferred to Homeland Security and eventually disbanded.

85. P-8 referred to the G-7 plus Russia. The G-7 nations—Canada, France, Germany, Italy, Japan, the United Kingdom, and the United States—included the largest western economies. The group addressed a large number of common concerns. Reno's address was delivered on January 21, 1997.

86. Not long after his government service, Charney joined Microsoft where he became Vice President of Trustworthy Computing.

87. The issue of the government's right and capacity to crack encrypted messages is alive and well today. By 1999, Reno was arguing the importance of government having that capacity in a July 17, 1999, address to the National District Attorneys Association. She saw analogies to wiretapping and search warrants. An administration bill relating to encryption that year did not pass.

88. Reno noted the problems associated both with the volume of transcripts and with grasping the meaning and implications of conversations conducted, for instance, in Indonesia's Bahasa.

89. Oral History, January 31, 2008, p. 10.

90. McVeigh was the first federal prisoner to receive a death sentence in almost forty years.

91. Talk by Janet Reno to the National Banker's Association, May 20, 1996.

92. In 2012, Weed and Seed would be replaced by the Byrne Criminal Justice Innovation Program also focused on local revitalization and redevelopment.

93. A reduction of 23 percent in the three prior years.

CHAPTER 8. ATTORNEY GENERAL, 1993–2001: THREE DRAMAS

1. According to material prepared for congressional testimony by Reno dated October 25, 1999, the Bureau of Alcohol, Tobacco, Firearms and Explosives (ATF) had been told by a for-

mer member of the group that Koresh had fathered at least fifteen children and that he used serious physical abuse in disciplining members including children and even infants.

2. This is the opening of the *Tribune-Herald* article dated February 27, 1993, which was the first in a series:

> If you are a Branch Davidian, *Christ lives* on a threadbare piece of land 10 miles east of here called *Mount Carmel*. He has dimples, claims a ninth-grade education, married his legal wife when she was 14, enjoys a beer now and then, plays a mean guitar, reportedly packs a 9mm Glock and keeps an arsenal of military assault rifles, and willingly admits that he is a sinner without equal.

3. All remembered too well the 1978 mass suicide ordered by cult leader Jim Jones in Jonestown, Guyana, in which 918 members died, including 276 children.

4. Overall, the FBI would report that it spoke with fifty-four individuals for a total of more than two hundred hours.

5. The Arkansas group, called the Covenant, the Sword, and the Arm of the Lord, was an anti-Semitic, White supremacist, apocalyptic group.

6. A brief history prepared by the Christian Research Institute appears at https://www.equip.org/articles/the-branch-davidians/. The DOJ issued its own report dated October 8, 1993, which can be obtained from the Government Printing Office (see ISBN 0-16-042973). Further, Loren Johns prepared a research bibliography on Waco, last updated in 2004, that included forty-three books and articles, twelve government reports, seventeen websites, and sixteen video recordings: http://ljohns.ambs.edu/waco.html, last accessed June 20, 2015.

7. The FBI had at one point successfully planted an agent inside the compound acting as a Branch Davidian. He had installed microphones that picked up some conversations. Among them was talk that suggested gasoline had been deliberately poured in a number of locations.

8. By 1996, the Republicans were in charge and a new house report was critical of the choices made. See Report 104–749 dated August 2, 1996, "Investigation into the Activities of Federal Law Enforcement Agencies toward the Branch Davidians."

9. The ATF is in the U.S. Department of the Treasury.

10. The Reagan administration secretly sold weapons to Iran, which was supposed to be under an embargo. It then used the money to fund Contras opposed to Castro—even though Congress had specifically prohibited such funding.

11. The administration of H. W. Bush's son, George W. Bush, who followed Clinton, would again feature a host of scandals.

12. Impeachment is like an indictment and requires a majority vote in the House of Representatives. A trial is then held in the Senate where a two-thirds majority vote is required to remove an official from office. The first president to be impeached was Andrew Johnson for violating an act of Congress by trying to remove the Secretary of War. The Senate failed to convict him by a single vote in 1868. The next president to face impeachment was Richard Nixon for the Watergate cover-up. He resigned before action by the house in 1974. The third president to be impeached was Donald Trump, who was also the first president to be impeached two times.

13. Note that this is not the same as the Office of Special Counsel, which considers the rights and responsibilities of federal employees. Further, the attorney general can appoint an independent counsel to pursue a particular case.

14. Ironically, the first person to be investigated would be his Attorney General Meese.

15. When the act again expired in 1999, many believed it should not be renewed—that it was an overreach. Among those who testified against its renewal was Kenneth Starr.

16. About this time Starr switched his allegiance from the Democratic to the Republican Party.

17. It was rumored that Starr would get an appointment to the Supreme Court, but some in the attorney general's office believed he was not conservative enough; the appointment went to David Souter instead.

18. A second member of the Rose Law Firm who went to Washington was Webb Hubbell who became number three in the DOJ. He would be the subject of indictment by Kenneth Starr. The third was William H. Kennedy III who served only two years and was untouched by scandal.

19. *Washington Post,* July 1, 1994, accessed July 21, 2015.

20. Previously the attorney general also had that responsibility.

21. After his seven-year stint as independent counsel, Starr resumed the practice of law and served as a visiting professor at New York, Chapman, and George Mason universities. In 2004, he returned to California as Dean of the Law School at Pepperdine University. In 2010, he went home to Texas as president and chancellor of Baylor, a Christian university, in Waco. Ironically, he was caught up in a scandal related to the football team and forced out of office. One summary of the events, "Untangling Whitewater" by Dan Froomkin, can be found at https://www.washingtonpost.com/wp-srv/politics/special/whitewater/whitewater. htm, accessed July 26, 2015. A second informative source is http://www.historyplace.com/ unitedstates/impeachments/clinton.html, last accessed July 26, 2015.

22. *New York Times,* October 11, 1997, accessed July 20, 2015.

23. See https://www.internetlivestats.com/internet-users/#trend. Six years later, there would be 413 million users. Accessed July 20, 2015.

24. Hillary Clinton eventually had to testify about the matter before a Grand Jury.

25. In 1994, Hale pled guilty to two felony counts for defrauding the Small Business Administration.

26. Clinton's friend Vernon Jordan had counseled Hubbell about Whitewater. Because Jordan had also counseled Lewinsky, Starr requested permission to investigate Lewinsky, which Reno granted. Thus did a narrow investigation about a suicide and a local real estate/banking fraud expand and become about intimate relations of the president of the United States.

27. Aides admitted that the voice was Clinton's but argued that the tapes had been doctored. The tapes have never been tested to prove or disprove that charge. Years later, in a deposition in another case, that of Paula Jones, Clinton admitted to relations with Flowers, although in his even later autobiography he said it was "only once."

28. The suit was preceded by an article in the conservative *American Spectator* in which a Clinton bodyguard was reported as saying Clinton had met with "Paula" in a hotel room. Also, earlier that year, Jones had attended a meeting of conservative political activists in Washington, DC.

29. Ultimately, this lie had no impact on the Jones case, but it would have serious consequences—impeachment.

30. In August, Clinton would go on national TV to admit that he had had "inappropriate relations" with Lewinsky.

31. Elián's father, Juan Miguel González-Quintana, was represented by Gregory B. Craig of Williams and Connolly LLP.

32. At a press conference on February 3, 2000, Reno was questioned about a report that one of the grandmothers said on Cuban TV that in an effort to make Elián more comfortable, she joked with him by biting his tongue and pulling down the zipper on his pants. Reno said she had no knowledge of that. However, such treatment of a child by a caregiver had loomed large in the Country Walk child abuse case that Reno had prosecuted some years earlier.

33. Raquel Rodriguez was the second grandmother.

34. Coffey's letter concluded: "We appeal to you as individuals who are wielding the entirety of the power of the United States government, a power that could crush the fragile psyche of a little boy who has already suffered beyond human description."

35. The team was composed of Paulina Kernberg M.D., of New York Hospital, Jerry M. Weiner M.D., of George Washington University Medical School, and Lourdes Rigual-Lynch Ph.D., of Montefiore Medical Center.

36. "Here" was the forty-eight-year-old home at 2319 NW 2nd Street.

37. Lott was Majority Leader of the Senate, which was considering legislation to make Elián González a naturalized citizen or, alternatively, give him and "certain relatives" permanent resident status. Reno's assistant attorney general, Robert Raben, wrote a five-page letter to Lott opposing both proposals citing the "primacy" of parents' right to make decisions regarding their children. The letter outlined the current law on naturalization and noted that generally no provisions exist to use it for honorary or political purposes—and certainly naturalization would not be bestowed on one who did not request it!

38. See *Miami Herald,* April 30, 2000, for a detailed account of last-minute efforts to find a way to an agreement that would honor the decision to give Elián's father legal and actual custody of Elián.

39. Judicial Watch filed an amicus curiae brief charging the raid on the 22nd had used "excessive and unreasonable force," violated twenty-three rights, and involved an "apparent deal with the Castro regime."

40. Plans had been carefully crafted some time before and generally followed procedures similar to those involved in the rescue of hostages. They included the use of gas, shouting, and intimidation and a quick release of the hostage. The raid capturing Elián was over in less than three minutes.

41. It should be noted that for all the public uproar, Reno received many letters of support and praise. Some suggested that even in Miami a majority of the population supported Elián's return. If so, it wasn't publicly evident.

42. Janet Reno to Sister Jeanne O'Laughlin, letter dated July 14, 2000.

CHAPTER 9. HOME AGAIN

1. Others were not so sure Reno should run for governor. On January 14, 2002, the *Baltimore Sun.*

2. McBride's wife, Alex Sink, would herself become a candidate for governor in 2010. While Sink got 48 percent of the vote, Republican Rick Scott got 49 percent. There were two other well-regarded candidates in the race, Daryl Jones and Debbie Wasserman Schulz—both then serving in the Florida legislature.

3. *Miami Herald,* July 22, 2002, p. 1B.

4. The thinking, illustrated by a letter to Reno from George C. Bedell, was that even if she won the Democratic primary, her negatives meant she could not beat incumbent Jeb

Bush—so it was better to go with a new face. Bedell noted the parallel to Roy Collins, who had similarly returned home to run for Senate, barely won the Democratic primary, but then was walloped by a Republican. Like Reno, his long experience in politics included a variety of negatives.

5. American Mohamed "Mo" Elleithee, the son of Egyptian immigrants, was an experienced campaign manager. He would be central to Hillary Clinton's 2008 campaign, and in 2015 he became Director of Georgetown's Institute of Politics and Public Service.

6. The *Miami Herald*'s Peter Wallsten reported on the down-home style of Reno's campaign in a column on November 18, 2001. Wallsten noted her attire—a bright orange camp shirt, khaki pants, white leather sneakers, and a Panama straw hat—and that she pumped her own gas at a Chevron station. He noted, too, the CDs nestled between the two bucket seats—country music from the 1960s and 1970s. The truck's bed was covered by a camper top making it ideal for transporting a kayak and camping gear, but also for sleeping, which saved a motel bill and enabled Reno to sleep while someone else drove to the next destination. Wallsten described Reno's arrival at midnight at a truck stop on Florida's turnpike near Pahokee, where she stood in line at a Burger King to order a coffee and a strawberry shake. That was followed by an early morning four-mile walk with hikers from the Florida Trails Association. Reno's campaign regularly featured the story about her home's survival of Hurricane Andrew, a survival based on the fact that her mother had built it right; other stories include traveling and kayaking throughout Florida. Polls showed the incumbent Bush with a 34 percent lead; still many Democrats enthusiastically supported Reno. In Republican Marion County, she drew 250 to a dinner one night and 200 to a breakfast the next morning. Others noted that the songs most played in the red truck were those featuring Johnny Cash and Hank Williams.

7. Even Governor Jeb Bush was concerned and conceived an A+ Plan, which involved vouchers for children in low-performing schools, money directed toward high-performing schools, and more testing and reporting of school ratings.

8. Restoration of voting rights after a felon has served his or her time was a theme at events with a Black audience.

9. Polls also showed Reno losing to incumbent Bush 54 percent to 39 percent

10. Sheen had some sixty arrests for civil disobedience in protests related to nuclear power, defense power, and U.S. training of Latin American troops at the School of the Americas. In fact, when Reno was attorney general, her office prosecuted him for protesting the Strategic Defense Initiative. Sheen got two years' probation.

11. There were twenty-four Miami-Dade County Democratic clubs. Only five of the twenty-four club presidents signed a letter supporting her decision on Elián.

12. Gore de-emphasized his Clinton connection, and he lost the presidency after the Florida recount had been stopped by the U.S. Supreme Court.

13. *Guardian,* August 11, 2001. Accessed at www.theguardian.com/world/2002/aug12/gender.un1 on May 10, 2015.

14. Much of the preparatory summer work was done by Patricia Lauck, Hugh Westbrook, and Carole Shields.

15. Early supporters included Myron Marlin, Frank Greer, Lisa Versaci, Robert Raben, and John Hogan.

16. At a meeting of the National Parkinson's Foundation, Reno discussed her condition in a straightforward way—and with some humor, too. *Miami Herald,* October 11, 2001.

17. Florida had recently passed a law banning adoption by gay couples.

18. Political scientists note that people mostly vote against rather than for.

19. Nineteen percent fell in the $40,000 to less than $60,000 income range; 10 percent in the $60,000 to less than $80,000, 5 percent in the $80,000 to less than $100,000, and 8 percent over $100,000. (Twenty-four percent did not answer the question.)

20. Working with the campaign, Susan S. Vodicka had already reserved a half dozen including renoredtruck.com. Further, Josh D'Alemberte had purchased thirteen websites. His preferred was votejanet.com. Again, the reason for such purchases was to prevent an opponent from purchasing them and then using them against Reno. A less attractive offer came from Donald Bowman in Columbus, Ohio, who had purchased a site and offered it for $3,500 and two tickets to her inaugural ceremonies and ball.

21. Reno had collapsed while giving a talk in New York. She emphasized that it was due to heat and a failure to eat and not to her Parkinson's. She also remarked that President George Bush had recently fainted after an encounter with a pretzel while watching TV. "At least I don't have a bruise on my cheek," she commented.

22. See https://groups.google.com/forum/#!topic/alt.true-crime/VEpho3WixzI, accessed September 11, 2015.

23. The Florida chapter of the International Union of Painters and Allied Trades did endorse Reno, but the big AFL-CIO endorsement would go to McBride.

24. Black American Daryl Jones came in third with about 15 percent of the vote. Jones was well qualified. A graduate of the USAF Academy where he majored in math and was a boxing champion, he served as an F-14 pilot before returning to Miami and entering the University of Miami Law School, from which he graduated cum laude. He served in the Florida legislature from 1990 to 2002 before running for governor. Pundits are unclear about how his candidacy affected those of Reno and McBride, both of whom had sought support from Black voters. Another issue not widely discussed was Reno's Parkinson's disease. By then her hands shook noticeably.

25. See http://articles.sun-sentinel.com/2002-09-18/news/0209180175_1_bill-mcbride-primary-vote-voting-problems, accessed September 11, 2015.

26. *Election Reform Since November 2001: What's Changed, What Hasn't and Why* (Washington, DC: Election Reform Project 2002).

27. While the emphasis then may have been on voting machinery, issues such as registration requirements and certification continued to be debated. After her run for governor, Reno became very involved in a variety of projects. A continuing interest was the welfare of children, and Florida's children were clearly in need of some support. Some of Florida's national rankings included 34th in teen birth rates, 37th in percentage of low birthweight babies, 39th in 4th grade students who scored below basic reading level, 41st in teen high school dropouts, and 42nd in families with children headed by a single parent.

28. The previous governor, Democrat Lawton Chiles, had appointed Kearney to serve on a Child Abuse Task Force. All informed on the issue recognized that DCF was failing the children it was intended to serve.

29. John Kennedy, "Abuse Hotline Rings Off the Hook; Since the Slaying of Kayla McKean Shocked Central Florida, Calls Have Strained the Child-Protection Service," *Orlando Sentinel Tribune*, November 25, 1999.

30. It took more than a decade for the child's guardian to be convicted of kidnapping and child abuse. The guardian would avoid a conviction for murder, although the jury had voted to convict her 11–1.

31. See http://www.stltoday.com/stltoday/emaf.nsf/Popup?ReadForm&db=stltoday%5Cn ews%5Columnists.

32. Formerly known as the National Association for Public Interest Law.

33. See earlier discussion of the Richardson case in chapter 6 and also note 4 on page 67.

34. SLAPP is a lawsuit intended to intimidate and silence critics by burdening them with legal expenses. Plaintiffs do not necessarily expect to win. Their purpose is to squelch criticism and opposition.

35. Going through security, Reno had grapes confiscated, which she'd carried as a snack. Daphne protested, saying, "This is the former attorney general." Reno's response was that she was an American citizen and could accept no privilege.

EPILOGUE

1. Psalm 23 may be the best known of the Psalms. Some have called it the Shepherd's Prayer; many will remember that it begins: "The Lord is my shepherd, I shall not want."

2. It should be remembered that years before, then-governor Bob Graham had not been happy about the way Reno had handled the 1980 riots in Miami.

3. There might be some who think Clinton had adopted that mantra a bit late in life.

Note on Sources

I knew Janet Reno, and when she returned to Miami after her stint as attorney general, I took her to lunch and urged her to write her autobiography. She began the task by organizing her years of papers into cardboard boxes—enough to fill a large shed in her backyard. After her death, friends of Janet's urged me to take up the flag. I did so with trepidation. It was a new kind of project for me—not at all like the political theory I taught and wrote about at Florida International University. I began by spending a year systematically going through those boxes in the shed. Materials ranged from a box with Christmas cards received one year to boxes of drafts for important decisions she made as attorney general. Reno's papers have since been donated to the University of Miami, but they are in storage and have not been made available to the public. Reno also spent some time taping accounts of some portions of her life. I have had access to print copies of those tapes as well.

South Florida newspapers such as the *Miami Herald* and *Miami New Times* provided additional information on the Wood/Reno family, and Janet Reno's professional life was covered extensively across other major national media such as the *Washington Post, Wall Street Journal, Los Angeles Times,* and PBS *Frontline.*

A crucial source was the American Bar Association's Women Trailblazers in the Law Project, a major initiative to capture, preserve, and share oral histories of women lawyers' experiences. Oral History of Janet Reno, ABA Senior Lawyers Division, Women Trailblazers in the Law, Six Parts, 2005–2008. See https://www.americanbar.org/groups/senior_lawyers/women_trailblazers_project_listing/janet_reno/.

Several published books provided excellent information and are recommended reading: Paul Anderson, *Janet Reno: Doing the Right Thing* (Hoboken, NJ: John Wiley, 1994); Marvin Dunn and Bruce Potter, *The Miami Riot of 1980: Crossing the Bounds* (Lexington, MA: Lexington Books, 1984); Arva Moore Parks, *Miami, The Magic City* (Continental Heritage Press, 1981); Arva Moore Parks and Carolyn Klepser, *Miami Then and Now* (Miami: Centennial Press, 1992). More recently, George Hurchalla published *The Extraordinary Life of Jane Wood Reno: Miami's Trailblazing Journalist* (Gainesville: University Press of Florida, 2020).

Interviews with Reno's family and friends provided many details and insights: Maggy Hurchalla, October 26, 1993; Trudy Novicki, October 26, 2013; Carol Ellis, March 19, 2014; Thomas K. Peterson, April 9, 2014; Vera Porfiri, February 2, 2014; Karen McCammon, December 14, 2015; Douglas Reno, December 14, 2015; Chris McAliley, January 16, 2016; Jamie Gorelick, April 13, 2016; Shay Bilchik, June 20, 2016; Edward Carhart, January 17, 2016; Elly Canterbury, January 20, 2016. Dates were not recorded for the following additional interviews: Dan Casey, Neal McAliley, Samuel Rabin, Daphne Webb, George Yoss.

INDEX

Balfour, Marshall, 6
Bal Harbour, FL, 137, 175n3
Ball, Lucille, x
Baltimore, MD, 65
Bangor, ME, 13, 32
Baptists, 146
Barkett, Rosemary, 151, 155, 167n31
Barnes, Solomon, 64, 170n48
Barr, William P., 97, 98, 120
Barron, Dempsey, 42
Barry University, 69, 133
Batar, Paul, 26
Batista, Fulgencio, x, 38
"Battle Hymn of the Republic, The," 157, 159
Battle of Lexington, 25, 165n21
Baylor University, 182n21
Bay of Pigs, 26, 38
Becraft, Michael, 179n62
Bedell, George C., 183n4
Beethoven, Ludwig van, 25
Begun, Joseph, 69
Behavioral Science Research Corporation, 67
Bell, Griffin, 96
Bennett, Robert S., 130
Bergman, Marilyn, 87
Berkeley Law School, 93
Berlin, Germany, 14
Berns, Walter, 164n11
"Best We Could, The" (Jane Wood Reno), 6
Biden, Joe, 89, 94
Bilchik, Shay, 56, 103, 177n28, 177n32
Bill Gates: A Biography (Becraft), 179n62
Biltmore Hotel, ix
Bingham, Dana, 147
Bingo, 168n24
Biscayne Bay, ix
Black, Roy, 172n13
Blacks: as assistant state attorneys, 67; Bahamians, viii; Caribbean, viii; and Cubans, 38; in Dade County, xi; and Janet Reno, 65, 67; and law enforcement, 62, 64, 66–67, 70, 71, 72, 140; police shooting and killing of, 2, 63, 70, 71, 72, 140; and riots, 2; and segregation, ix; and unemployment, 171n59; and unions, 38; and voting, viii, 161n5, 184n8
Blackwell, Walker, and Gray, 40
Blair, Diane Divers, 89
Blake, William, 32
Block, Irwin J., 66
Bloomingdales, 52
Blue Ribbon Panel on Child Protection, 149
Bob Moore's Welding Shop, 54–55
Bond Plumbing Supply, 64
Bookworm Project, The, 147

Boston, MA: corruption in, 24; cultural and tourist attractions in, 25, 30, 32; Irish Catholics in, 29; Janet Reno in, 25, 30, 165n19; recruiting of Black attorneys in, 56; and weather, 31
Boston Athenaeum, 30
Boston Museum of Fine Arts, 32
Boston Symphony, 25, 30
Botts, Derrick, 26
Bowman, Donald, 185n20
Boxer, Barbara, 108
Brady, James, 99
Brady Handgun Violence Prevention Act, 99, 103, 158
Braga, Joseph, 82, 173n39
Braga, Laurie, 82, 173n39
Branch Davidians: and child abuse, 124, 180n1; Congressional hearings on, 104, 125–26; David Koresh as leader of, 123, 124, 125, 180n1; FBI agent posing as, 181n7; history of, 123; news series on, 181n2; and polygamy, 124; scholarship on, 181n6; settlements of, 123–24, 181n2; and siege near Waco, TX, 2, 92, 98, 106, 117, 123, 124–25, 126, 158; and weapons, 124, 181n2
Brandeis, Louis, 23
Braswell, Ron, 61
Brazil, 108
Bring Me Men and Women: Mandated Change at the U.S. Air Force Academy (Stiehm), 165n28
Britton, John, 112
Bronstein, Sanford, 47
Brooklyn, NY, 170n45
Brooklyn Dodgers, 18
Brooklyn Eagle, 5
Brooks, Jack, 106
Brothers Karamazov, The (Dostoevsky), 8
Broward County, FL, 148–49
Brown, Ernest, 26
Brown, Ronald, 102, 128
Brown and Williamson, 115
Browner, Carol, 103
Brown University, 128
Brown v. Board of Education, 12, 14–15, 16
Bryan, William Jennings, 161n7
Bunning, Jim, 135
Burger, Warren, 128
Burke, James, 66
Burt, John, 179n70
Burton, Dan, 126
Bush, George H. W.: as father of George W. Bush, 181n11; as father of Jeb Bush, 62; as president, 69, 98, 127, 128; as vice president, 62, 172n18
Bush, George W.: and 2000 presidential election, 136, 145, 147, 148; as brother of Jeb Bush, 147; and Elián González case, 136; as president, 139,

Sixty Minutes interview on Gennifer Flowers allegations, 130; and Vince Foster, 128; and Webb Hubbell, 89, 96, 175n7; and Whitewater, 129–30, 182n24

Clinton, William J.: and 1985 Arkansas siege, 125; and 1992 presidential campaign, 172n24; on accepting mistakes, 186n3; and Al Gore, 184n12; approval rating for, 178n53; as Arkansas attorney general, 129; as Arkansas governor, 129, 130; and boot camp for juvenile offenders, 94; and Branch Davidians, 125; and Diane Divers Blair, 89; and Drew S. Days III appointment, 118; and Elián González case, 136; female appointments by, 87; firing of William S. Sessions by, 98; fundraising by, 119, 120; and Gennifer Flowers, 130, 182n27; and immigration legislation, 114; impeachment of, 123, 126, 130, 182n29; and increase in numbers of police officers, 94; and Independent Counsel Act, 127; investigations of cabinet members of, 127–28; and Janet Reno, 1, 2, 86, 87–88, 89, 90, 94, 101, 152, *156*, 158, 172n24, 175n12; and Lani Guinier nomination, 95; legal problems of, 2–3; and Miami Drug Court, 172n24; and Monica Lewinsky, 130–31, 182n29, 182n30; pardons by, 128; and Patricia Seitz, 49; and Paula Jones, 130, 131, 182n27, 182n28, 182n29; and Presidential Council on HIV, 178n55; resignation of, from US Supreme Court bar, 131; revocation of law license for, 131; and second Summit of the Americas, 178n58; and TV violence, 120; and Whitewater, 127, 129, 130

Clooney, Rosemary, x

CNN, 148

Coalition for Juvenile Justice, 120

Coalition to Protect Citizen's Rights, 74

Coca-Cola, 151

Coconut Grove, FL, 6, 7

Coconut Grove Elementary School, 16

Coco Plum Women's Club, 15

Coffey, Diaz and O'Naghten, 133

Coffey, Kendall, 133, 183n34

Collins, Roy, 183n4

Colombia, 151

Colorado, 18, 133

Columbia Law School, 59

Columbia University, 56, 177n29

Columbus, OH, 185n20

Commission on Government for the People, 174n51

Commission on Racial and Ethnic Diversity in the Profession, 86

Commission on the Status of Women, 26

Communists, 14

"Community Attitudes and Riot Participation in the Miami Riots of 1980 . . ." (Ladner), 67

Comprehensive Employment Training Act (CETA), 57

Computer industry, 179n65, 179n67

Concord, MA, 32

Connecticut, 26, 111

Conseco, Joe, 76, 173n30

Continental Airlines, 178n59

Continuing legal education, 150

Conyers, John, 126

Coral Gables, FL: Alan Greer in, 47; establishment and development of, viii, 162n16; as part of Miami-Dade County, FL, 161n1; real estate in, 161n7; recreational facilities in, 9; Reno family in, 10; Wood grandparents in, 10; zoning laws in, 161n6

Coral Gables High School: academic ranking of, 15; activities at, 15, 16, 17, 163n8; Black students at, 16; Bob Reno at, 13; Chris McAliley at, 176n19; classes taught at, 17; Hall of Fame of, 174n56; Hunter Reno at, 43; Janet Reno at, 7, 13, 14–15, 16–18, 21, 163n5, 163n8, 163n11; leadership of, 15; Lisa Reno at, 7; Maggy Reno at, 13; Mark Reno at, 13; as new facility, 13, 15; number of faculty at, 15; number of students at, 15, 16

Coral Gables Lions Auxiliary, 15

Cornell Hotel School, 22, 163n2 (chap. 3)

Cornell Law School, 23, 163n2 (chap. 3)

Cornell University: Benton F. Rogers at, 18; characteristics of, while Janet Reno attended, 20, 21–22, 164n3, 164n4, 164n5, 164n6, 164n7; coed education at, 20; establishment of, 20; faculty of, 164n11; Harry S. Truman at, 22; Janet Reno at, 2, 20, 21–23, 164n8, 164n10, 164n12; location of, 20; minority students at, 20–21; Reno family connections to, 163n10; schools at, 163n2 (chap. 3); student population at, 20

Council for Prosecution of Organized Crime, 57

Council for Tobacco Research, 116

Country Walk molestation case, 55, 81–82, 173n40, 173n41, 174n47, 176n15, 183n32

Covenant, the Sword, and the Arm of the Lord, The, 181n5

Coverdell, Paul, 135

Craig, Gregory B., 137, 182n31

Craig, Larry, 135

C-SPAN, 92

Cuba: Al Webb in, 44; and Bay of Pigs invasion, 26, 38; and Cuban Missile Crisis, 26; Fidel Castro as leader of, 26, 38; Jackie Gleason in, 44; and migration, 131, 146, 168n15, 171n62; return of Elián González to, 3

Dudley, Robbie, 32
Duke University School of Law, 128
Dunn, Marvin, 64
Duval County, FL, 80

Earhart, Amelia, 162n9
Eastern Europeans and countries, 112, 140
Eastwood, Clint, 177n26
Edwards, Michael, 152
Eig, Spencer, 132
Einstein, Albert, 109
Eisenhower, Dwight D., 14
El Expreso, 168n7
Elk, TX, 123
Elleithee, Mohamed "Mo," 142, 184n5
Ellis, Carol, 57–58, 64, 87, 169n26, 175n3
El Mataneer, 168n7
El Miami Herald, 168n7
El Salvadorans, 114
Environment: federal programs and agencies
   related to, 96, 103, 106, 107, 127, 178n57; Janet
   Reno and, 52, 90, 103–4, 143, 175n11, 178n50;
   legislation related to, 103, 175n11; Maggy Reno
   and, 151
Epps, Maryel, 159
Equal Justice Works/National Association for
   Public Interest Law, 151, 186n32
Equal Rights Amendment (ERA), 41, 69
Espy, Michael, 128
Esquire, 177n26
Essen, Richard, 17
Estefan, Gloria, 137
Ethics in Government Act, 127
Everglades, ix, x, 39, 45, 48, 92
Executive Office of the President, 48–49

Face the Nation, 136
"Facing History and Ourselves," 141
Fagan, Lemuel T., 79
Fair Housing Act, 118
Faison, Ruby, 79
Falcon, Augusto "Willy," 62
Fascell, Dante, 5
Faust (Gounod), 14
Federalist Society, 150
Feinstein, Diane, 108
Feminism, 49, 77
Ferguson, Danny, 130
Ferré, Maurice, 170n52
Fijnje, Bobby, 83
Fishman, Janet, 85
Fiske, Robert, 128, 129
Flagler, Henry, viii
Flores, Ileana, 81, 82–83, 173n40

Florida: and 2000 presidential election, 144,
   145, 184n12; 2002 gubernatorial election in,
   141–47; and abortion, 145; and adoption by
   gay couples, 184n17; birth weights in, 185n27;
   Black law school graduates in, 171n60; civil
   rights in, 118; class in, 146; crime in, 144;
   Cubans in, 146; Democrats in, 144; divorce
   law in, 166n8; education in, 142, 144, 145, 146,
   184n7, 185n27; election system in, 148–49,
   185n27; and Elián González case, 132, 145;
   and Equal Rights Amendment, 69, 166n10;
   government corruption in, 166n11; guns and
   gun control in, 74–75, 145, 173n26; health care
   in, 146; Hispanics in, 146; history of, vii–viii;
   income in, 146, 185n19; Janet Reno's fame
   in, 93; judicial system in, 41, 51; lottery in,
   69; and offshore drilling, 146; protection of
   children in, 149; railroad in, 161n3; religion
   in, 146; Republicans in, 144; and segregation,
   42; single-parent households in, 185n27; state
   attorneys in, 167n25; taxes in, 144, 145; teen
   birthrates in, 185n27; and *US v. Microsoft,* 111;
   weather in, 161n3
Florida Bar Association, 12, 29, 47, 48, 155,
   174n56
Florida Bar Journal, 83, 86
Florida Building Trades Council, 148
Florida Bureau of Law Enforcement, 81
Florida Comptroller, 42
Florida Council on Crime and Delinquency,
   174n56
Florida Democratic Party, 148
Florida Department of Children and Families
   (DCF), 144, 149, 150, 185n28
Florida Department of Law Enforcement, 74
Florida Drug Task Force, 172n18
Florida Education Association, 146, 148
Florida Highway Patrol, 8, 39, 62. *See also* Police
Florida Innocence Initiative, 167n4
Florida International University, xi, 64
Florida Keys, 161n8
Florida legislature: and budget for Miami-Dade
   state attorney's office, 72; and child protec-
   tion legislation, 149; Daryl Jones in, 183n2,
   185n24; Debbie Wasserman Schulz in, 183n2;
   Dempsey Barron in, 42; and Equal Rights
   Amendment, 41; Gerald Lewis in, 40; and
   gun control, 74; House of Representatives of,
   40, 41, 42; Republican dominance of, 174n51;
   Sandy D'Alemberte in, 41; Senate of, 40, 41,
   42
Florida Magazine, 85
Florida National Guard, 39
Florida Power and Light (FPL), 39, 47, 167n27

Griswold, Erwin, 24, 178n41
Guatemalan Maya Center, 157
Guatemalans, 114
Guggenheim Museum, 26
Guinier, Ewart, 177n29
Guinier, Lani, 95, 177n29
Gulf of Mexico, 146
Gunn, David, 112
Guns and gun control: in Florida, 74–75, 145, 173n26; Janet Reno and, 74, 99, 100, 103, 108, 158, 170n43, 176n16, 176n24; legislation on, 99, 100, 102, 103, 158, 176n16; and survivalist culture, 117; Terry Nichols and, 117; Timothy McVeigh and, 117; and violence, 103, 176n24; and waiting periods, 99, 173n26

Haddam, Anwar, 121
Hagel, Chuck, 133
Haitians, 179n73
Hale, David, 129, 182n25
Hale, Lorraine, 101
Hamdi, Yaser Esam, 121
Hardin, Robert, 60
Harding University, 128
Hard Rock Stadium, 172n12
Harper's magazine, 72, 172n25
Harvard Law School: acceptance of Janet Reno by, 23; establishment of, 26; Jamie Gorelick at, 175n14; Janet Reno at, 1, 2, 24–27, 28, 93, 164n16, 164n18, 165n26, 165n32, 175n14; Philip Heymann at, 96; as rival of Cornell Law School, 23; women at, 24, 28, 165n26
Harvard Law School Association, 26–27
Harvard University, 24, 93, 109, 164n17, 177n29
Hastert, Dennis, 133
Hastings, Alcee, 69, 171n1
Hatch, Orrin, 101, 110, 119, 135, 175n10
Havana, Cuba, 132
Havens, Ray, 177n28
Hawaii, 105
Hayes, Gordon, 78, 79
Headley, Walter, 40
Health care: in Florida, 146; Janet Reno and, 76, 140, 142, 143, 150, 174n54; and Medicaid, 115
Heath, Randy, 63, 66
Heaven's Gate, 120
Hector and Faircloth, 24–25
Helms, Jesse, 92, 135
Herman, Alexis, 128
Heymann, Philip, 96, 100, 177n31, 177n32
Hiaasen, Carl, 119
Hialeah, FL, viii, 63, 161n1, 162n16, 177n40
Hialeah Park Race Track, xi
Hickman-Brown research, 144, 145

Higginbotham, A. Leon, 86
Hill, Paul Jennings, 112
Hiroshima, Japan, 14
Hispanics/Latinos, xi, 115, 118, 146, 161n10. *See also* Cubans
HIV, 106, 178n55
Hogan, John: background of, 56; and Janet Reno, 52, 56, 72, 88, 95, 184n15; at Miami-Dade state attorney's office, 52, 55, 56, 72; and private practice, 95; at US Department of Justice, 95
Holder, Eric, 96, 137, 152, 175n1
Holistic Animal Center, 105
Holland and Knight, 95, 142, 167n4
Hollywood, CA, 120
Hollywood Women's Caucus, 87
Hoover, J. Edgar, 177n35
Hopwood v. Texas, 117
"Horace the Peacock Is His Name" (Winslow), 18
Horne, Leroy, 11
Houseman, A. E., 28
Houtoff, Florence, 123
Houtoff, Victor, 123
Howard Hughes Medical Research Institute, 23
Howard University, 56
Howdy Doody, 147
Howe, Mark DeWolfe, 24
Howell, Vernon. *See* Koresh, David
Huang, John, 119
Hubbell, Webster Lee "Webb": as Arkansas chief justice, 89; and Arkansas Ethics Commission, 89; as author, 175n7; and Hillary Clinton, 89, 96, 175n7; and Janet Reno, 89, 96; at Rose Law, 89, 96, 175n7, 182n18; at US Department of Justice, 89, 96, 175n7, 177n33, 182n18; and Whitewater, 129–30, 175n7, 182n18, 182n26
Hubble telescope, 69
Hulda Clark's Parasite Zapper, 148
Hung, Caridad, 152
Hungary, 108
Hurchalla, Jim, 27, 151. *See also* Reno, Margaret Sloan
Hurricanes: Andrew, 69, 140, 184n6; destruction of railroad by, 161n8; in Miami, ix, x, 5, 69, 140, 184n6; Reno family and, 5, 27
Hurston, Zora Neale, 32
Hussein, Saddam, 95
Hyde, Henry, 119

IBM, 110
"I Come to the Garden Alone," 159
Illegal Immigration Reform and Immigration Responsibility Act, 114

Illinois, 133

Immigration and naturalization: and 1993 World Trade Center bombing, 113; and asylum, 180n78; and birth of children in US, 114–15; Chinese and, 179n72; Cubans and, x-xi, 55, 67–68, 113, 168n15, 171n62, 179n73; Haitians and, 179n73; history of, 112–13, 179n71; illegal, 104, 180n74, 180n79; Janet Reno and, 101, 104, 112, 113, 114–15, 176n16; legislation on, 114; and Operation Gatekeeper, 113, 180n76; origins of, 112, 113, 114; US Congress and, 112; volume of, 113, 114

Immigration Policy Institute, 180n77

Immokalee, FL, 39

Impeachment (definition), 181n12

Independent Counsel Reauthorization Act, 128, 182n15

Independent counsels, 182n20. *See also* Starr, Kenneth

Indiana, 126

Indian Creek Island, 75

Indonesia, 180n88

"Informant, The: Meet the biggest deal in Miami's biggest industry" (Rothchild), 172n25

InfraGuard, 116

Innocence Project, 81, 151, 167n4

Interamerican Chamber of Commerce, 174n56

International Jurists Association-American Barr Association Commission on Juvenile Justice Standards, 46

International Labor Rights Fund, 151

International Law Enforcement Academy, 108

International Union of Painters and Allied Trades, 185n23

Internet, 129, 182n23

Internet Crimes Against Children Task Forces, 116

Internet Explorer, 110

Internet Fraud Initiative, 116

Iowa, 111

Iran, 68, 69, 171n66, 181n10

Iran-Contra, 127, 181n10

Iran-Iraq war, 69, 171n66

Iraq and Iraqis, 68, 69, 121, 171n66

Italians and Italian Americans, 179n71

Italy, 108, 180n85

Ithaca, NY, 20, 31, 163n1 (chap. 3)

ITT, 47

Jackson, Andrew, viii

Jackson Health system, 66

Jackson Memorial Hospital, 6, 144

Jacksonville, FL, 18, 80

"Janet Reno" (Anquette), 77, 173n33

"Janet Reno Dance Party" (fundraiser), 143

Janet Reno: Doing the Right Thing (Anderson), 162n15

"Janet Reno's Dance Party" (*Saturday Night Live* skit), 139

Japan, 180n85

Japanese and Japanese Americans, 112, 179n71

Jenkins, Robert, 173n37

Jews, viii, 112, 171n61

Joe Robbie Stadium, 71, 172n12

Joe's Stone Crab Restaurant, 101

John, Elton, 143

Johnson, Andrew, 181n12

Johnson, Lyndon B., 2, 96, 168n19

Johnson, Neville, Jr., 70, 171n6

Jones, Bobby L., *154*

Jones, Daryl, 183n2, 185n24

Jones, Jim, 181n3

Jones, Johnny, 64, 170n49, 170n50

Jones, Loren, 181n6

Jones, Paula, 130, 131, 182n27, 182n28, 182n29

Jones, Willie T., 62, 66

Jonestown, Guyana, 181n3

Jordan, Vernon, 182n26

Josey, Cathy L., 146

Judicial Watch, 183n39

Juiced: Wild Times, Rampant {ap}Roids, Smash Hits and How Baseball Got Big (Conseco), 173n30

Justice Protective Service, 147

Juvenile justice: American Bar Association and, 46; Bill Clinton and, 94; coalition for, 120; commission on, 46; International Jurists Association and, 46; Janet Reno and, 59, 83, 84–85, 91, 94, 102, 119, 120, 158, 169n25, 180n93; in Miami, FL, 59, 169n34; task force on, 85; US Department of Justice and, 103, *107*, 177n28, 178n46

Juvenile Justice Gallery of Honor, 85

Kafka, Franz, 28

Kagan, Gerald, 74

Kansas, 111

Kansas City, MO, 118

Kansas State University, 47

Kassindja, Fauziya, 180n78

Kauffman, Roger, 29

Kaufman, Irving, 46

Kearney, Katherine, 149, 185n28

Kearns, Doris, 147

Kefauver, Estes, x, 11

Kendall, FL, 14, 58, 157

Kennedy, John F.: assassination of, 163n2 (chap. 2); and brother Robert F. Kennedy, 2, 91; Janet

McBride, William: 2002 Florida gubernatorial campaign of, 141–42, 143, 145, 146, 148, 185n23, 185n24; background of, 142; and private practice, 142; wife of, 183n2

McCaffrey, Barry, 49

McCammon, Karen, 15–16

McCarthy, Edward, 72

McCarthy, Joe (author), 29

McCarthy, Joseph (US senator), 12

McCarty, Daniel T., 14

McCord, Guy, 166n9

McDougal, James, 129

McDougal, Susan, 129

McDuffie, Arthur, 63, 72

McDuffie trial, 63, 64, 65, 66, 170n46, 170n51

McEnroe, John, 109

McGee, Wilson, 162n4

McGovern, George, 42

McMartin preschool, 81

McVeigh, Timothy, 117, 180n90

Meadows, William, 66

Media: and Janet Reno, 60, 70, 87, 94, 98–101, 144, 168n7, 171n2, 171n4, 176n15, 177n26, 177n32; and violent crime, 120–21

Meditations (Descartes), 28

Meese, Edwin, III, 2, 85, 90, 127, 178n57, 181n14

Meet the Press, 137

Meissner, Doris, 103, 104, 132, 136

Mellman Group, 145

Memoirs (Truman), 28

Mendez, Jacqueline, 137–38

Menendez, Robert, 135

Merkle, Robert, 173n38

Merrick, George, 162n16

Metro-Dade Police Department, 63. *See also* Police

Metropolis, viii, 161n4

Metropolitan Dade County police, 53. *See also* Police

Metro Public Safety Department, 154

Mexico, 108, 113, 114, 170n45

Mexico City, Mexico, 108

Miami, FL: in 1950s–1960s, 15–16; 1968 Liberty City riots in, 39–40, 70, 166n5; 1980 Liberty City riots in, 2, 40, 64–67, 186n2; 1989 Liberty City riots in, 2, 71; and 2002 Florida gubernatorial election, 138; abortion clinics in, 49; and agricultural crime, 75; Alan Greer in, 47; art and culture in, xi; attempted assassination of Franklin D. Roosevelt in, ix; and Bay of Pigs invasion, 26; Black voters in, 161n5; bridge to beach from, 161n6; Chris McAliley in, 176n19; and class, 67; Country Walk suburb of, 81;

County Commission of, 63; crime in, 102; and Cuban Missile Crisis, 26; Cubans in, 38, 69, 132, 161n10; Dan Casey in, 55; Democrats in, 41; descriptions of, vii; drugs and drug crime in, 61–62, 72–74, 172n21, 172n24, 172n25; economy of, ix, 5, 72; electoral seats in, 166n6; and Elián González case, 3, 131, 133, 136, 138, 139, 145, 183n36, 183n41; first tourist hotel in, viii; flooding in, 10; football stadium in, 71, 172n12; guns in, 74; historic preservation in, 173n32; history of, vii–xi, 161n2; Hugh Rodham in, 158; hurricanes in, ix, x, 5, 69, 162n7; and immigration, 55, 67–68, 113, 171n62; incorporation of, 161n5; Janet Reno as native of, 132; Janet Reno on, 52, 101–2; justice system in, 59; juvenile justice system in, 59, 169n34; law firms in, 24–25, 95; layout of, 162n16; Neal McAliley in, 176n20; Neighborhood Resource Teams in, 83; as part of Miami-Dade County, 161n1; Patricia Seitz in, 48; police in, 71–73, 170n44, 171n6; population of, viii–ix, x, 67; as port of entry, 61; and race, ix, 16, 38, 59, 61, 62–63, 64–67, 70, 71, 161n5, 169n33, 171n6, 171n59; and railroad, viii; Reno family's move to, 4; schools in, 16, 161n5; sections of, viii, 83, 137; summers in, 9; Summit of the Americas meeting in, 108; Thomas Peterson in, 59, 169n33; tourist attractions in, xi; Turki bin Abdulaziz in, 75; unemployment in, 171n59; US attorney's office in, 93; US District Court in, 122; and wealth, xi, 67, 85; Wood family in, 162n5

Miami Beach, FL, viii, 1, 39, 76–77, 161n1, 173n32

Miami Book Fair, xi

Miami Catholic Lawyers Guild, 169n29

Miami Citizens against Crime, 62

Miami-Dade College, 157

Miami Dade Community College, xi, 154, 174n56

Miami-Dade County, FL, 38, 53, 134, 161n1, 168n8, 184n11

Miami-Dade state attorney's office: Black attorneys in, 168n22; increased size of, xi; Katherine Fernandez Rundle in, 57, 68, 171n63; number of employees in, 177n26; Organized Crime Bureau of, 171n63; short tenures in, 167n 25, 168n12, 168n14; as starting job for attorneys, 167n25, 168n12; Thomas K. Peterson in, 171n63. *See also* Reno, Janet, career of, 1963–1978: at Miami-Dade state attorney's office; Reno, Janet, career of, 1978–1992 (Miami-Dade state attorney)

Miami Dade United Way, 169n29

Miami Daily News, 11, 27

Miami Evening Record, 161n4

Miami Gardens, FL, 172n12

Miami Herald: and 1951 Pulitzer Prize for Public Service, 5; 1984 endorsement of Janet Reno's opponent by, 70; 1988 endorsement of Janet Reno by, 71; on abuse of foster children, 149; on "bungled" juvenile cases, 169n25; on David Gunn murder, 112; Doris Reno at, 7; and Elián González case, 135; Frances Webb at, 44; on fundraising at the White House, 119; Henry Reno at, ix, 2, 4–5, 6, 11; Janet Reno's gap year account published in, 14; on Janet Reno's US attorney general nomination, 90; Jane Wood Reno at, 6, 9; lawsuit against, 50; Martha Musgrove at, 70; as part of Knight Ridder, 169n38; Peter Wallsten at, 184n6; predecessor of, 161n4; "Reno: Year One" published in, 60; and report on 1980 Liberty City riots, 67; on Richard Gerstein, 49–50; Robert Reno (grandfather) at, 4; Robert Reno (grandson) at, 43; testing of $20 bills for cocaine traces by, 72

Miami International Airport, 72

Miami Juvenile Justice Center, 59

Miami Law School. *See* University of Miami Law School

Miami Method, 82, 83

Miami News, 5, 161n4

Miami Police Benevolent Association, 8

Miami Police Department, 8. *See also* Police

Miami Public Safety Department, 23

Miami River, vii

Miami Times, 170n52

Miami Vice, 62

Michigan, 126

Microsoft, 109, 110, 179n65, 180n86

Midler, Ernie, 11

Midsummer Night's Dream, A (Shakespeare), 25

Milwaukee, WI, 4, 162n3

Minneapolis, MN, 65

Minnesota, 111

Miranda v. Arizona, 51, 85

Missouri, 45, 150

Mitchell, John, 90

Molina, Marta, 135

Money laundering, 178n58

Montefiore Medical Center, 183n35

Montez, Alfredo, 150

Montgomery bus boycott, 15

Morales, Ricardo, 73–74

Morgan, J. P., ix

Morning Star Renewal Center, 150

Morrill Land-Grant schools, 20, 163n2 (chap. 3)

Mortar Board, 21

Mosley-Braun, Carol, 95

Mothers Against Repression, 137

Motor voting, 100, 118

Mount Carmel Center Ranch, 123–24

Mount Washington, 32

Moyers, Bill, 166n16

Municipio Caimito del Guayabal, 174n56

Musgrove, Martha, 70

"My Silent Friend" (Weismann), 150

NAACP, 42, 66, 95, 118

Naples, FL, 64

National Association for Public Interest Law/ Equal Justice Works, 186n32

National Association of Drug Court Professionals, 141

National Council of Churches, 132, 135

National Council of Jewish Women, 174n56

National District Attorneys Association, 180n87

National Forensic League, 17

National Foundation for Children, 173n39

National Geographic, 77

National HIV Test Day, 178n55

National Honor Society, 17

National Infrastructure Protection Center, 116, 180n84

National Missing Children's Day, 141

National Newspaper Association Governmental Affairs Conference, 99

National Parkinson's Foundation, 184n16

National Press Club, 100, 140

National Register of Historic Places, 77

National Rifle Association (NRA), 74, 90, 175n1

National Security Council, 176n18

Native Americans, viii, 11, 27, 118

NATO, 14

Navratilova, Martina, 166n14

NBC, 96

Nebraska, 121

Neelius, Richard, 79

Neighborhood Enhancement Teams (NETs), 174n49

Neighborhood Resource Teams (NRTs), 83, 174n49

Neiman Fellows, 24–25

Neiman-Marcus, 52

Netscape, 110

Neurology, 105

Newark, NJ, 65

New Bedford, MA, 32

"New Colossus, The" (Lazarus), 112–13

Newcombe, Don, 18

"New Light" (Koresh), 124

New Orleans, LA, 43

Newsday, 43, 166n16

New Times, 176n15

New York, NY: 1993 World Trade Center bomb-
ing in, 98, 113, 176n18, 180n75; 2001 World
Trade Center attack in, 121, 180n75; Bob Reno
(grandson) in, 43; bomb plots in, 98; churches
in, 27; corruption in, 24; Guggenheim
Museum in, 26; Janet Reno in, 26, 30, *36*, 159;
Maggy Reno in, *36*, 159; riots in, 65; Thomas
Peterson in, 59
New Yorker, 64, 177n26
New York Hospital, 183n35
New York State, 135, 136
New York Times: on crime prevention programs,
59; crossword puzzle in, 101; daily Department
of Justice summary of, 97; and Elián González
case, 137; first front-page color photo in, 87; on
Janet Reno as US attorney general, 100–101;
on press conference announcing Philip Hey-
mann's departure, 96
New York University, 56, 182n21
New York University Law School, 176n19
New Zealand, 88
Nicaraguans, 114
Nichiren Shōshū, 105
Nichols, Terry, 117
Nigeria, 43
9/11, 121, 180n75
Nixon, Richard: and 1960 presidential election,
28; and 1968 presidential election, 42; and
Bebe Rebozo, 5, 167n28; and John Mitchell,
90; resignation of, 181n12; and Watergate, 127,
169n37, 181n12
"No Electronic Theft" Act, 116
No Ordinary Time (Goodwin), 147
Normandy, France, 14
North American Free Trade Agreement
(NAFTA), 108, 114
Northeast Miami Improvement Association,
169n29
Northwest Airlines, 178n59
Novicki, Trudy, 53, 91
"Nuclear Physics: The Career of the Future"
(Janet Reno), 17–18
Nussbaum, Bernie, 88

Obama, Barack, 151
Ocala, FL, 5
O'Connor, Sandra Day, 69
Odense, Denmark, 4
Office of Independent Counsel, 127
Office of National Drug Control Policy, 48,176n18
Office of Special Counsel, 181n13
Office of Special Prosecutor, 127
Ohio, 4
Okefenokee Swamp, 40

Oklahoma City bombing, 3, 117, 180n90
O'Laughlin, Frank, 157
O'Laughlin, Jeanne, 133, 134, 138
Omaha, NE, 65
Operation Rescue, 49
Operation Tick-Talks, 73–74
Oracle, 110
Orange Bowl, ix
Organization of American States, 108
Organized Crime/Drug Enforcement confer-
ence, 99
Orlando, FL, 71, 172n13
Orlando Sentinel, 144
Orr, John, 42, 166n12
Orseck, Phyllis, 66
Oscars, 143
Our Miss Brooks, 10

P-8 Group, 180n85
P-8 Group on Transnational Organized Crime,
116
Padilla, Joseph, 121–22
Pagon, Angela, 152
Palm Beach, FL, viii
Panama City, FL, 142
Panetta, Leon E., 104
Parachute Club, 21
Parkinson's Disease, 104–6, 143, 178n55
Parks, Arva, 161n2
Parks, Rosa, 15
Patria, 168n7
Patrick, Deval L., 118, 151
Patton, George S., 109
Payton, John, 95
PBS, 131
Pearson, Michael, 134
Pedrosa, Jose, 136, 175n8
Pell grants, 102
Penelas, Alex, 134
Pennsylvania, 55
Pensacola, FL, 112, 142
People to People, 167n28
Pepper, Claude, 14, 41, 51, 167n2
Pepperdine University, 182n21
Pereira, Sergio, 52
Perkins, Frances, 22, 23, 164n11
Perry, FL, 142
Persia, 88
Peterson, Thomas K., 53, 56, 59, 171n63
Pew Foundation, 113, 114
Phi Beta Kappa, 21, 164n13
Phi Kappa Phi, 21
Philadelphia, PA, 65, 166n5
Philip Morris International, 115

life during, 60; and social programs, 76, 86, 94, 174n54; and Spanish lessons, 58; staff of, 57, 103, 171n63; state recognition of, 85; swearing in as, *153*; tenure of, 2, 168n23; and testimony before Senate Judiciary Committee, 89; and tough law enforcement, 52, 53, 83, 86; and truth, 76; and Turki bin Abdulaziz case, 75, 173n28; and underfunding for criminal justice system, 86; and US Attorney's office, 68; and victim advocacy, 54, 75; on wealth in Miami, 85; and welfare fraud, 174n54; on workday length, 84, 85

Reno, Janet, career of, 1993–2001 (US attorney general): and 1993 World Trade Center bombing, 98; and abortion clinics, 100, 111–12, 179n69; and American Disabilities Act, 100; announcement of top staff by, 96, 177n30; and antitrust cases, 108–9, 110–11, 176n16; and applications for electronic surveillance, 176n16; approval rating for, 126; and Bill Clinton impeachment, 106, 123, 126, 127; as boss and agency administrator, 93, 94, 95, 96–97, 106, 158, 177n26, 177n31; and Branch Davidians siege, 2, 92, 98, 104, 106, 117, 123, 124, 125–26, 148, 158, 177n39; and career Department of Justice employees, 100, 178n57; and civil rights, 90, 92, 117–18, 119; consultations by, on important decisions, 176n16; and crime prevention, 91, 102, 119, 158; and criminal law, 176n16; and criticism, 104; criticisms of, 101; and cybercrime and cybersecurity, 116–17, 180n87; and DEA, 101; and death penalty, 99; on defendants' access to representation, 99; definition of her role by, 2, 90–91, 94, 98, 127, 178n57; and Department of Justice-Senate Judiciary Committee interaction, 102; and domestic violence, 104; and drugs and drug crimes, 100, 102–3, 108, 120, 176n16, 180n92; and education, 102; and Elián González case, 3, 106, 123, 132, 134, 135, 136, 138, 176n20, 178n42, 183n32, 183n41; and environment, 90, 92, 103–4, 175n11, 178n50; and ethics report on William S. Sessions, 98; and FBI, 101, 171n64; first day as attorney general, 176n16; and fundraising on government property, 119; and gay persons, 113; on government disclosure, 99–100; and gun control, 99, 100, 103, 108, 158, 176n16; and gun violence, 176n24; and immigration and naturalization, 101, 104, 112, 113, 114–15, 176n16; and Independent Counsel Act, 127; influence of mother's memory on, 97; international activities of, 100, 108, 140; and Jamie Gorelick, 97; and juvenile crime and juvenile justice, 91, 94, 119, 120, 158, 180n93;

lateness of appointment of, 92; on length of court proceedings, 99; and media, 87, 94, 98–101, 176n15, 177n26, 177n32; as newcomer to Washington, DC, 92–93; nomination and confirmation of, 1, 87–92, 105, 158, 175n1, 175n6, 175n8, 175n10, 176n15, 176n16, 177n28; and nondiscrimination in lending, 100; and nonviolent criminals, 90; and Oklahoma City bombing, 117; and Paula Jones investigation, 131; photos of, *154–55*; political judgment of, 94; popularity of, 94, 178n42, 178n53; and pornography, 119; and prevention of discrimination against employees, 101; and prosecution of Martin Sheen, 184n10; and protection of children, 53, 92, 96, 97, 103, 116, 120, 132, 158; and protection of innocent persons, 53, 158, 174n47; and public speaking, 98–100, 101–2, 113, 114, 117, 119, 120, 137, 176n24, 178n41, 180n85, 180n87; and punishment, 94; and redemption, 94; and rehabilitation, 102; and relationship between federal, state, and local governments, 91, 99, 100, 102, 171n64; and relationship with Bill Clinton and White House, 2, 100, 101, 119, 175n12; and relationship with other cabinet members, 94, 100; resources available to, 103; and Senate testimony, 101; and sentencing, 119; social activities during, 93, 94, 176n21; and social programs, 94, 119, 120; staff of, 95–97, 100, 103, 116, 118, 175n14, 177n28, 177n31, 177n32, 177n33, 177n40, 178n56; and stress, 93; swearing in of, 159; and technology, 179n67; and terrorism, 108, 117, 180n88; and tobacco, 115; and tough law enforcement, 53, 90, 102; underestimating of, 93; and US attorneys, 106, 176n16; and US-born children of immigrants, 114–15; vigilance of, against favoritism, 98; and Vince Foster's death, 128; and violent crime, 102, 120–21; and Virginia Military Institute, 100; and voter registration, 100; and Washington, DC, leadership, 93–94; and White House Easter Egg Hunt, 97; and Whitewater investigations, 128, 182n26; and William Sessions, 177n39; work habits of, 178n44; and women, 92, 100, 103

Reno, Janet, career of, 2001–2016: and 9/11, 144; and 2004 presidential election, 150; and access to justice system, 140; and airline security, 144; and American Constitution Society, 150, 151; and belief in importance of family, 140; and belief in putting people first, 140; and benefits for senior citizens, 142, 143; and Black community's distrust of law enforcement, 140; and Bookworm Project, 147; and ceremony honoring women WWII service members, 152,

Watergate, 85, 99, 127, 169n37, 181n12
Waters, Maxine, 133, 135
Watts riot, 166n5. *See also* Race
Weaver, James, 81
Weaver, Randy, 117
Webb, Al, 44
Webb, Ann, 44
Webb, Danny, 44, 45
Webb, Daphne, 44, 45, 88, 92, 152, 186n35
Webb, Frances, 44
Weed and Seed program, 120, 180n92
Weekly News, 144
Weinberger, Casper, 75
Weiner, Jerry M., 183n35
Weismann, Mildred, 150
Welch, Raquel, 44
Welch, Robert, 12
Westbrook, Hugh, 184n14
Western Pacific airlines, 178n60
Westminster Christian School, 147
West Palm Beach, FL, 43
West Virginia, 55
West Wing, The, 143
Wharton School, 139
"When Children are Witnesses" (Braga), 173n39
Whipp, Gene, 105
White, Mary Jo, 106
White Anglo Saxon Protestants (WASPs), 112
Whitewater, 3, 127, 128, 129–30, 182n26
Wichita, KS, 112
Wiley publishing company, 162n15
Williams, Hank, 184n6
Williams, Tennessee, 44
Williams and Connolly LLP, 182n31
Wilson, Rilya, 149, 185n30
Wind in the Willows, The (Grahame), 9, 10
Windows operating system, 110, 111
Winslow, Sally Wood, 18, 45, 163n12
Withee, WI, 4
Wizard of Oz, The (Baum), 30
WJTV, x
Wolfe, Thomas, 25
Women: on American Bar Association Commission on Juvenile Justice Standards, 46; in armed forces, 29, 175n14; as attorneys, 137,

164n14, 165n2; as cabinet members, 164n11, 175n1; commission on status of, 26; at Cornell University, 20, 21, 164n6, 164n7; discrimination against, 2, 28, 38, 165n27; and domestic violence, 77; as FBI agents, 177n37; on floor of Florida legislature, 38; and Florida Bar, 12, 47, 48, *155*, 167n31; at Harvard Law School, 24, 27, 28, 29, 165n26; John Edward Smith's promotion of, 48; at Miami-Dade state attorney's office, 56, 168n10; network of, in Washington, DC, 94, 176n22; Richard Gerstein's promotion of, 50; Sandy D'Alemberte's promotion of, 48; status of, 168n21; and Susan B. Anthony dollar, 168n21; at US Air Force Academy, 165n28; at US Department of Justice, 103, 158; on US Supreme Court, 25; at Virginia Military Institute, 100
Women Airforce Service Pilots (WASPs), 17
Women's Self-Governing Association, 22
Women Who Make a Difference Award, 174n56
Wong, Kim Loy, 141
Wood, Daisy Sloan Hunter, 5, 10, 163n12
Wood, George (son), 13, 32
Wood, George W., Jr. (father), 5, 10, 162n6
Wood, Kimba, 87
Wood, Roy, 13, 14
Wood, Winifred, 17, 152
Wood family, 162n5
World Ministerial Conference on Organized Crime, 108
World Trade Center, 98, 113, 121, 176n18, 180n75
Wright, Frank Lloyd, 26
Wright, Susan Webber, 130, 131
"Wynken, Blynken, and Nod," 87, 159

Xena, Warrior Princess, 142

Yale Law School, 87, 95, 118
"Yankee Doodle Dandy," 77
Yearling, The (Rawlings), 47
Yoss, George, 54, 56, 168n12, 168n13
Young Republicans, 21
YWCA, 174n56

Zedillo, Ernesto, 108

JUDITH HICKS STIEHM is professor emerita of political science and former provost and academic vice president at Florida International University. Among her many books are *It's Our Military Too! Women and the US Military* and *Champions for Peace: Women Winners of the Nobel Prize for Peace.* Stiehm is the recipient of the Frank J. Goodnow Award from the American Political Science Association for distinguished service to the profession.